LATE-NIGHT IN WASHINGTON

Political Humor and the American Presidency

Stephen J. Farnsworth, S. Robert Lichter, and Farah Latif

NEW YORK AND LONDON

Designed cover image: Getty/CBS Photo Archive

First published 2024
by Routledge
605 Third Avenue, New York, NY 10158

and by Routledge
4 Park Square, Milton Park, Abingdon, Oxon, OX14 4RN

Routledge is an imprint of the Taylor & Francis Group, an informa business

© 2024 Stephen J. Farnsworth, S. Robert Lichter, and Farah Latif

The right of Stephen J. Farnsworth, S. Robert Lichter, and Farah Latif to be identified as authors of this work has been asserted in accordance with sections 77 and 78 of the Copyright, Designs and Patents Act 1988.

All rights reserved. No part of this book may be reprinted or reproduced or utilised in any form or by any electronic, mechanical, or other means, now known or hereafter invented, including photocopying and recording, or in any information storage or retrieval system, without permission in writing from the publishers.

Trademark notice: Product or corporate names may be trademarks or registered trademarks, and are used only for identification and explanation without intent to infringe.

ISBN: 978-1-032-25416-6 (hbk)
ISBN: 978-1-032-25415-9 (pbk)
ISBN: 978-1-003-28304-1 (ebk)

DOI: 10.4324/9781003283041

Typeset in Sabon
by Newgen Publishing UK

"Farnsworth, Lichter, and Latif provide a first-rate assessment of the influence that late-night television hosts and their political jokes have on the portrayal of American presidents, especially during the Donald Trump and Joe Biden administrations. Scholars of the American presidency and the media, along with anyone who cares about the state of American politics in contemporary times, will find this book a pleasure to read and that it will greatly enhance their knowledge about the role of the media on our chief executives."

Adam Warber, *Clemson University*

"Farnsworth, Lichter, and Latif have given us the definitive volume on political humor and the American presidency. Arguing that humor is an important societal coping mechanism, they document historical inflection points providing rich examples along the way. The book is a lively read that offers an alternative frame for examining political discourse. The detailed analyses of the Trump and Biden presidential eras provide compelling empirical verification of the pervasiveness and significance of political humor. Scholars will appreciate the volume's academic rigor and students will be drawn in by the richness of the illustrative evidence."

Diana Owen, *Georgetown University*

"As the 2024 presidential campaign gears up, longtime coauthors Farnsworth and Lichter (joined here by Latif) continue their groundbreaking work on presidential humor with *Late-Night in Washington*. Their latest book, a lively and compelling successor to 2020's *Late Night with Trump*, updates their findings through the post-Trump presidency. *Late-Night in Washington* is a must-read for anyone interested in the intersection between presidential politics and popular culture."

Jeffrey Crouch, *American University*

LATE-NIGHT IN WASHINGTON

This book traces the trajectory of late-night political humor, which has long been a staple of entertainment television and is now a prominent part of social media political discourse, especially when it comes to the presidency. From Richard Nixon on *Laugh-In* to Donald Trump's avatar on *Saturday Night Live*, this book takes the next step and considers how late-night comedy treats Joe Biden, the new American president who strives to restore a civil public tone but offers far less comedy fodder than his predecessor. Employing content analysis, public opinion surveys, and a variety of other quantitative and qualitative research, the authors look beyond the day-to-day memes and mimes of late-night comics and show how political humor may evolve. For students and scholars of politics and the media, this book will appeal to the general public and political pundits as well.

Stephen J. Farnsworth is Professor of Political Science at the University of Mary Washington, where he directs the university's Center for Leadership and Media Studies.

S. Robert Lichter is Professor of Communication at George Mason University, where he directs the Center for Media and Public Affairs.

Farah Latif is a fellow at the Center for Media and Public Affairs (CMPA) and an instructor at George Mason University whose research has included political gaslighting and developing a personal reputation scale.

CONTENTS

About the Authors	*ix*
About the Contributors	*x*
Acknowledgments	*xii*

1 The Importance of Political Humor   1

2 Political Humor and the Rise of Donald Trump the Politician   36
Coauthored with Noah Gardner, Jeremy Engel, Deanne Canieso, and Shaelyn Patzer

3 Political Humor and the 2020 Presidential Campaign   75
Coauthored with Kate Seltzer and Sally Burkley

4 Late-Night Political Humor and the Two Presidents of Early 2021   106
Coauthored with Sally Burkley

5 The Challenge of Creating Conservative Comedy   131

viii Contents

6 Political Consequences of Late-Night Humor:
Learning about Politics via Political Comedy 158

7 The (Near) Future of Political Humor 184

Bibliography 207
Index 234

ABOUT THE AUTHORS

Stephen J. Farnsworth is Professor of Political Science at the University of Mary Washington, where he directs the university's Center for Leadership and Media Studies.

S. Robert Lichter is Professor of Communication at George Mason University, where he directs the Center for Media and Public Affairs.

Farah Latif is a fellow at the Center for Media and Public Affairs (CMPA) and an instructor at George Mason University whose research has included political gaslighting and developing a personal reputation scale.

CONTRIBUTORS

Sally Burkley is a 2022 graduate of the University of Mary Washington, where she received the Colgate Darden Award as the top-ranked student in her graduating class. She was a double major in Political Science and Communication. She is now attending William and Mary Law School.

Deanne Canieso has more than 15 years' experience in project management, advocacy, and strategic communications. Her research interest lies in the study of emotional contagion in mass media and in the computer-mediated context. She earned her PhD in Communication at George Mason University in 2021.

Jeremy Engel is a 2020 graduate of the University of Mary Washington, where he majored in Political Science. He is currently a policy fellow with the Maryland Association of Counties and has worked as a paralegal. He plans to attend law school in the coming years.

Noah Gardner is a 2018 graduate of the University of Mary Washington, where he majored in Political Science. He is currently a senior research specialist with Gartner, a research and consulting firm.

Shaelyn Patzer is a doctoral candidate at George Mason University's Department of Communication. She earned her MA from Johns Hopkins University and her bachelor's degree from the University of Pennsylvania.

Kate Seltzer is a 2021 graduate of the University of Mary Washington, where she was a double major in Political Science and Communication and served as editor in chief of the university's student newspaper. She earned her master's degree in Journalism at the University of Maryland in 2022 and is now the Howard Center for Investigative Reporting Fellow for Connecticut Public Media.

ACKNOWLEDGMENTS

This project is the result of support generously offered from many sources. The first debt is to those who have made their surveys available to scholars, including the public opinion and news consumption surveys produced by the Pew Research Center. We are also very grateful for our previous research collaborations and many political conversations with Diana Owen, Stuart Soroka, Sergei A. Samoilenko, Jim Lengle, Roland Schatz, and Jody Baumgartner. These scholars have done much to shape our thoughts about presidential portrayals in news and entertainment mass media over the years. We also thank the anonymous reviewers of this book, and other scholars who have offered suggestions regarding our previous collaboration on political humor: *Late Night with Trump: Political Humor and the American Presidency*, also published by Routledge.

Special thanks are due to our research assistants, Sally Burkley, Deanne Canieso, Jeremy Engel, Noah Gardner, Shaelyn Patzer, and Kate Seltzer, who join us as coauthors of some of the individual chapters of this work. We also thank Hilyatuz (Lia) Zakiyyah, Cassandra Atkinson, Emily Hemphill, Aisha Shafi, and Joshua Wartel for research and editing assistance.

Thanks to political science and political communication colleagues who commented on various research papers over the last several years that are the building blocks of this book. Our arguments here were refined in light of the generous advice and gentle critiques offered at research panels at the meetings of the American Political Science Association (2017, 2019, 2022), the APSA Pre-conferences on Political Communication (2016, 2018, 2021), the Southern Political Science Association (2021), the Northeastern Political Science Association (2018), the Eastern Communication

Association (2023), the Southwestern Social Science Association (2019), the Virginia Association of Communication Arts and Sciences (2018), the CARP Conference on Character Assassination (2017, 2019, 2021), and the White House Historical Association Conference on The White House and Popular Culture at the Library of Congress (2022).

Thanks as well to Leanne Hinves, Jennifer Knerr, and Sandrine Pricilla and their teams for guiding our political humor projects as well as the prompt and professional treatment of our book manuscripts.

We thank George Mason University and the University of Mary Washington, in particular the university's sabbatical and Waple Fellowship programs, which provided financial support for this project. Thanks are also due to Mason's Center for Media and Public Affairs and to Mary Washington's Center for Leadership and Media Studies, which also provided financial support for this project.

Thanks to Routledge for allowing us to use here some of the tables and arguments from our previous book on political humor, *Late Night with Trump: Political Humor and the American Presidency*. Thanks to Lexington Books for allowing us to use here some of the tables and arguments from our chapter, "Partisan Trends in Late Night Humor," in *Still good for a laugh? Political humor in a changing media landscape* (Jody Baumgartner and Amy Becker, eds.).

All conclusions in this work, as well as any errors and omissions, are our responsibility.

Stephen J. Farnsworth
S. Robert Lichter
Farah Latif

1

THE IMPORTANCE OF POLITICAL HUMOR

Political humor has long been a staple of late-night television. Large parts of the media audience turn to the post-prime-time comics for entertainment and even for an alternative source of news (Baym 2005). As far back as Senator John F. Kennedy's unprecedented appearance on *The Tonight Show* during the 1960 presidential election campaign, presidents and presidential candidates have sought to humanize their image and bolster their public standing by appearing on late-night talk shows (Gould 1968; Lichter et al. 2015). They have done so to respond to satirical attacks, and to minimize future attacks, as the hosts increased the amount of political material incorporated into their stand-up routines. The candidates have even redirected their campaign approaches in response to comedic barbs, such as when Al Gore tried to loosen up after being mocked as too stiff and overbearing in a *Saturday Night Live* skit about the first 2000 presidential debate (Jones 2010).

While a variety of presidents, presidential candidates, and other political figures have faced the skewers of late-night comics in recent decades, Donald Trump stands head-and-shoulders above the rest in terms of the amount of ridicule directed his way, first as a presidential candidate, then as president, and still later as a former president (Farnsworth and Lichter 2020; Farnsworth et al. 2022). Of course, Trump consistently makes a bad situation for himself on late-night comedy even worse. By attacking the late-night comics who ridicule him on Twitter and other social media outlets, Trump drew – and draws -- even more attention to their attacks and may even encourage more of them (Brice-Sadler 2018; Farnsworth and Lichter 2020).

DOI: 10.4324/9781003283041-1

2 The Importance of Political Humor

Partly owing to Trump's outsized personality and frequently outrageous pronouncements, the late-night hosts had an unprecedented amount of material to work with during the combative 2016 presidential campaign and then during Trump's time in the White House – and even beyond (Farnsworth and Lichter 2020; Farnsworth et al. 2017, 2018, 2021, 2022; Lichter et al. 2016). The growing aggressiveness of late-night comedians also takes place in a media environment that expands the attention they receive. Market forces encourage the comics to do so when traditional news outlets connect with smaller and more partisan audiences, when growing numbers of news consumers want their media diet to be highly entertaining, and as the boundaries between news and satire have become increasingly blurred by journalists, news consumers, and politicians alike (Farnsworth and Lichter 2020).

This blurring of media roles can reach absurd lengths. During his heyday as host of *The Daily Show* on Comedy Central, survey respondents identified Jon Stewart as one of the most admired journalists in America, tying with real-life network news anchors Tom Brokaw and Dan Rather in public admiration (Baumgartner and Morris 2011). CBS reportedly even considered Stewart as a possible replacement anchor for the *CBS Evening News* (Eggerton 2005).

In this book, we use mainly content analysis, supplemented with public opinion data, to study the rise and importance of political humor in recent years. The Center for Media and Public Affairs (CMPA) at George Mason University coded the jokes on late-night programs that focus on the president and his administration, identifying the source, target, and topic of every humorous political comment during the opening monologues of the leading late-night shows during recent presidential elections and presidencies. We apply this content analysis approach across recent elections to four leading late-night comedy programs offering commentary at least four nights a week: *The Daily Show* on Comedy Central, *The Late Show* on CBS, *The Tonight Show* on NBC, and *Jimmy Kimmel Live* on ABC. For the later part of 2021, we examine the content of *Gutfeld!* – a new Fox News late-night comedy show that premiered as a nightly program in April 2021. *Gutfeld!* already has become far more popular and successful than previous conservative attempts at late-night humor (Roig-Franzia 2022). The CMPA has coded late-night comedy monologues for decades, and therefore we can employ data from previous eras of presidential humor to provide a broader context for understanding the late-night humorists' treatment of Presidents Trump and Biden.

But not all political humor comes in nightly doses. In this project we also employ more qualitatively oriented discussions of some of the most prominent once-a-week humorists during recent years: *Full Frontal* on TBS with Samantha Bee, *Last Week Tonight* on HBO with John Oliver, and of course *Saturday Night Live* on NBC. While far from a complete list of the late-night programs we could examine, the comics selected provide a mix of broadcast and cable outlets and program formats.

Humor as Catharsis (and Coping with Politics)

Humor has always been with us. Jokes provide a way to lighten the frustrations of the day as well as to address the challenges of collective human existence. As long as there have been human collectives, there have been public desires to poke fun at their leaders. The Egyptians, the Greeks, and the Romans of antiquity all provided ways of mocking authorities to ease the burdens of daily survival (Berger 1997; Combs and Nimmo 1996). "There is, in human beings, it would seem, a need to laugh at ourselves and this need takes many different forms – from plays and poems to cartoons, comic strips, and jokes," notes Arthur Asa Berger (2011: 237).

Humor is a key coping mechanism for a world run by others, people who claim or at least presume to be one's betters. Jokes and mockery seem to be common responses to the sometimes-unpleasant realities of the moment, whatever they might be. Even where the expression of critical humor could be dangerous, it has continued to occur in some fashion. Bitter political humor circulated underground in totalitarian societies like the Soviet Union, even as it thrived in freer societies (Combs and Nimmo 1996). Several years ago, the U.S. Central Intelligence Agency released some Soviet-era political jokes demonstrating the universality of humor, even of the politically risky sort: "A man was jailed 15 years for calling Joseph Stalin a fathead. One year for sedition, 14 years for revealing a state secret" (quoted in Hopper 2018).

While humor appears to be something close to a universal human desire (or perhaps even a universal personal need), expressing satire could be dangerous if conducted out in the open in less-free times and places. Earlier Greek comedy, like that of Aristophanes, delighted in ridiculing the powerful, something permitted openly during the days of Greek self-rule. Later, the military successes of Alexander the Great led to more centralized governmental control and the rise of a new set of leaders who took a dim view of political satire. As a result, subsequent generations of Greek writers focused their humor on domestic, not political, matters.

> There's comedy tonight so long as it doesn't threaten the imperial powers that be. Early in the history of civilization, it became very clear to those in authority that political comedy was dangerous, something that needed to be suppressed or displaced.
>
> *(Combs and Nimmo 1996: 5)*

4 The Importance of Political Humor

The development of modern political institutions and increasing public literacy created a fertile environment for political satire and comedy. During the Renaissance, Machiavelli wrote plays that mocked the political authorities he examined in a more serious vein in works like *The Prince*. With apparent glee, Dante consigned many political leaders of his era to Hell in his *Divine Comedy*. In England, Shakespeare mocked political figures for vanity and poor judgment in his plays (though of course he provided flattering portrayals of some other leaders). More than a century after that, Jonathan Swift wrote with venom about the British government's failure to deal with the deadly famines in Ireland, satirically asserting that the Irish could prevent starvation by eating their children.

On this side of the Atlantic, the distant British monarchy and the restive nature of the colonials created a vibrant culture of political humor comparable to that found in Europe and one that intensified after independence. The mocking gibes of Ben Franklin during the colonial era later gave way to the bitter humor of Mark Twain and H.L. Mencken in a subversive tradition that has existed throughout America's history (Combs and Nimmo 1996).

U.S. political humor has often focused on the virility or presumed lack thereof of politicians and leading figures in political discourse. Two centuries ago, humorists attacked President James Madison along these lines for his allegedly inept leadership during the War of 1812 – some commentators mocked their commander-in-chief as Mrs. Madison's husband. Decades later another generation of humorists attacked Mark Twain for his vigorous opposition to U.S. policies in the Spanish–American war, belittling him by calling him an "aunt" (Winter 2011).

Like the jesters or "fools" of European royal courts, who had some license to "speak truth to power" at the royal court via a sharp comment, today's late-night humorists occupy a space of "play" that protects them, at least to a degree. That space enables them to say taboo things that may be too critical or too controversial to be expressed safely by mainstream political actors without severe consequences (Gilbert 2004). The absurdity of the extreme exaggerations, in other words, provides a level of "comedic insulation" that minimizes the repercussions against humorists. They can always claim they were only kidding if the authorities (or the audience) view the joke as going too far (Palmer 1988).

Societies may relish the opportunity to cut their political leaders down to size, or at least enjoy others doing so in an entertaining way. A joke, even a sharp one, is a humorous way to try to reduce the arrogance and perhaps the creeping authoritarianism that is a potential risk in centralized, powerful modern governments, even ones possessing democratic institutions and sentiments. In fact, the more arrogant the leader, the larger the target that leader represents.

But political humor is more than a defense against political figures who think too highly of themselves. Comedy also contains at its core an expression of optimism: the conviction that the future can be brighter than the past.

> A comic perspective fearlessly diagnoses the ridiculousness of politics, including but not endorsing the harm or pain; it is irreverent, even subversive, but not doctrinaire, since doctrine is just another part of the political comedy ... Comedy offers a hopeful and larger view of things: beyond every winter chill is a fertile new spring, where death is carried away and there are new human tangles for our comic pleasure.
>
> *(Combs and Nimmo 1996: 12)*

Indeed, in times of great suffering, like the aftermath of the horrific terrorist attacks of 2001, many Americans found comfort in the revival of humor following a period of deep mourning. When *Saturday Night Live* returned to the air few weeks later, the program began with a solemn tribute to New York City's emergency responders, followed by permission to resume the jokes provided by none other than New York City Mayor Rudy Giuliani, the heroic face of America's largest city in the weeks after the Twin Towers fell.

> Viewers who tuned in on September 29 to the first show that aired after the attacks found New York City mayor Rudolph Giuliani opening the night surrounded by city firefighters and police officers. After an earnest discussion of the attacks and the nature of heroism, followed by a musical performance by Paul Simon, *SNL*'s executive producer Lorne Michaels joined Giuliani on stage, and the mayor affirmed the significance of *SNL* to New York City as "one of our great New York City institutions." After an awkward pause, Michaels asked Giuliani, "Can we be funny?" The audience laughed anxiously, perhaps in anticipation of a restored play frame. Giuliani responded to Michael's question with one of his own: "Why start now?" Seemingly relieved, the live audience laughed again, harder, at the political comedian and the comedic politician.
>
> *(Greene and Gournelos 2011: xii)*

If comedy sometimes seems to involve a construction that starts with pain followed by time, the horrific deaths of 9/11 followed by the jokes of later

6 The Importance of Political Humor

that month reminded a shell-shocked country that the period of mourning would not last forever and normality would soon return to the traumatized nation.

The second U.S.-led Iraq War, which began less than two years after the 2001 terrorist attacks, helped make what was old new again for political humor. Theaters revived traditional stories of political satire, including *Lysistrata* and *Hair*, during the Iraq war years, even though they harkened back to earlier conflicts, like the Peloponnesian War of antiquity or the more recent war in Vietnam (Winter 2011). On the April 23, 2003, edition of *The Daily Show*, host Jon Stewart channeled the 1964 Cold War parody film *Dr. Strangelove*, explicitly comparing Deputy Defense Secretary Paul Wolfowitz, a hawkish foreign policy voice, to the ex-Nazi rocket scientist played by Peter Sellers. Stewart remarked Wolfowitz was "a wheelchair away from Dr. Strangelove" (quoted in Winter 2011: 170).

The relative powerlessness of most comedians offers some further insulation from retaliation, at least apart from periods of intense crisis. Comics' positions outside the power structure can make them less threatening and therefore more able to offer biting social criticism (Gilbert 2004). It is not as if comedians have votes in Congress, after all.

Consider, for example, Stephen Colbert's commentary about President George W. Bush at the 2006 White House Correspondents Dinner in Washington. Colbert spoke, not as himself, but as his cable news character, a parody of a Fox News conservative commentator.

> I stand by this man [President Bush]. I stand by this man because he stands for things. Not only does he stand for things, he stands on things. Things like aircraft carriers and rubble and recently flooded city squares. And that sends a strong message: that no matter what happens to America, she will always rebound – with the most powerfully staged photo ops in the world.
>
> *(Colbert, quoted in Greene 2011: 119)*

Such a stinging rebuke would have seemed out of place immediately after 9/11 or during the combat phase of the Iraq War. By the time of this performance, however, Bush's approval ratings had fallen far below their peak. The Bush Administration's mishandling of the aftermath of Hurricane Katrina in 2005 and the rising resistance to the continuing U.S.-led occupation of Iraq had sapped the president's approval ratings and made him a less risky target for Colbert to mock (Farnsworth 2009, 2018). Even so, several Washington politicians and journalists condemned Colbert's remarks as too harsh for the setting. The pushback to the comedian, whose jokes that night attacked both presidential misjudgments and excessive journalistic deference to authority, offered another reminder (if we need one) that official Washington sometimes finds it tough to appreciate jokes made at its own expense. The fact that Washington reporters and politicians cannot abide jokes aimed at them makes the barbs all the funnier to those who live beyond the Washington Beltway.

As the Colbert example demonstrates, comics sometimes may have a lot of latitude when it comes to making jokes, but at other times they do not. Contemporary political humor is aggressive, and modern comics enjoy some the level of insulation against reprisal, to be sure. Even so, some critics observe that late-night comedians, whose programs air on for-profit broadcast and cable networks, must be somewhat cautious, given the risk of offending advertisers or raising the blood pressure of nervous corporate executives (Greene and Gournelos 2011). Comedy is a business, after all.

Cancelling a show over controversial political content is not an idle threat. Throughout the history of television, there have been such incidents of popular show cancellation by business executives worried about a public backlash. A famous example was the *Smothers Brothers Comedy Hour*, which offered countercultural messages and critical comments regarding government policies in the Vietnam War. The highly rated show battled network executives and censors during its contentious two seasons on CBS in the late 1960s, until the network brass decided the program was not worth the trouble and shut it down (Bodroghkozy 1997).

The risk of cancellation for political reasons was not limited to the more cautious era of 1960s' entertainment television. Several decades later, Phil Donahue lost his talk show on MSNBC because he opposed the second Iraq War after 9/11 (Carter 2003). In mid-2002, ABC cancelled *Politically Incorrect*, a late-night talk show hosted by Bill Maher, after the host frustrated advertisers and the White House with his white-hot comments regarding the early U.S. military responses to the 2001 terrorist attacks (Carter 2003).

> Living up to his show's title, Mr. Maher took issue with characterizations of the hijackers as cowards, arguing that "we have been the cowards, lobbing cruise missiles from 2,000 miles away." ABC's desire to bolster its late-night ratings and profits was also at the heart of its ultimately unsuccessful effort to woo David Letterman away from CBS two months ago.
>
> *(Carter 2003)*

Maher did eventually return to television, with a show called *Real Time*, which premiered on HBO roughly a year after his cancellation on ABC

8 The Importance of Political Humor

(Gurney 2011). Because HBO is a subscription-based cable channel with a smaller audience than the broadcast networks, it is willing to offer more controversial content than the networks, which expect larger audiences and few if any controversies from their on-air hosts. These different financial metrics for different entertainment outlets are issues we will consider further when we examine another controversial HBO program, *Last Week Tonight*.

Such programming cancellations serve as reminders that for-profit media outlets are in the business of satisfying viewers, also known as customers. Television talk show hosts and comedians do not have a First Amendment right to have their programs broadcast on someone else's network, and these examples suggest that the level of criticism of government officials must remain within a range that allows the show to continue to attract a substantial audience.

Three Forms of Humor

There are many different kinds of jokes, of course. In fact, humor often takes the form of one or more of three broad categories: incongruity, superiority, and catharsis. Incongruity involves the connection between two seemingly unrelated matters or frames of interpretation that fit together once placed side-by-side. Superiority-oriented humor involves laughing at people or places seen as inferior to oneself. Catharsis humor involves the release of tension in a stressful environment, such as laughing at a faux pas (Davis 1993; Greene and Gournelos 2011; Martin 2007).

Incongruity humor – the distinction between what people expect and what is revealed – is probably the most common type of humor. "Jokes offer a good example of incongruity. The punch line of the joke is funny, incongruity theorists argue, because it offers an unexpected but acceptable resolution of the events described in a joke" (Berger 2011: 235).

Superiority humor has a long history. Aristotle observed that humorists can make men already "worse than average" look still worse, and Hobbes noted in *The Leviathan* that laughter sometimes comes from recognizing that another person is inferior to oneself (Berger 2011).

Catharsis humor may involve masked aggression, or the satisfaction of an instinct in the face of an obstacle (Berger 2011). According to Freud (2003[original 1905]), this type of humor can involve responses to lustful or hostile feelings or some other aspect of human sexuality.

This includes the significant amount of political humor that raises masculinity questions, as in dialogue voiced by *Dr. Strangelove* characters about retaining "precious bodily fluids" and the sexual demands expected of male nuclear war survivors living in female-filled bunkers following a nuclear missile exchange (More recently, this humor manifests itself in jokes about the disconnect between the macho bluster and hawkish policies of Donald Trump and George W. Bush as presidents and how they behaved as young men, when both found ways to avoid military service in Southeast Asia during the Vietnam War).

> We make humorous responses to tragedies because doing so has some kind of a therapeutic value for us, collectively speaking, even if the humorous texts are repugnant. It strikes me that using riddles to deal with tragedies is, psychoanalytically speaking, a kind of regression – to a period in our childhood when we were innocent and where the countless tragedies of the world did not mean anything to us … "Sick humor" cycles that circulate after every tragedy and possibly help us to deal with the anxiety we face, ultimately, about our own deaths. Making light of 9/11 or other tragedies doesn't make them disappear but does seem to help us get on with our daily lives.
>
> *(Berger 2011: 237–238)*

Political Humor in a Contentious America

The rise of late-night television talk shows as forums for political discourse roughly parallels a number of other trends in politics and political news. First, politics has become more divisive and partisan in recent decades, as the previous ability of political parties to serve as "big tents" for a variety of views gave way to more ideologically aligned and doctrinaire partisan organizations (Bond and Fleisher 2000). With the virtual disappearance of conservative Democrats and liberal Republicans, Democrats have come to represent the party of liberalism and Republicans the party of conservatism (Mann and Ornstein 2012). Voters have grown increasingly polarized during recent decades as well (Campbell 2016).

As political debate in the U.S. moved toward more ideologically defined political parties, political discourse involving politicians broadened to include heretofore-ignored factors of that conversation. This era was marked by an increasing emphasis on private behavior and personal character, particularly when linked to sexual behavior (Sabato 1993). These factors became political wild cards, employed for maximum impact during election campaigns (Sabato et al. 2000).

The news media communicated these changes to the public even as journalism itself was changing in its composition, its norms, and its attention paid to behavior previously considered off-limits for news stories. Increasingly, this produced coverage of personal scandals that journalists were often ambivalent about reporting, and which contributed to a long

10 The Importance of Political Humor

decline in public respect for both journalists and politicians (Cappella and Jamieson 1997; Patterson 1994, 2013). It did not help that those purveyors of infotainment joined the mix, and did so with even less regard for privacy or decorum. Inevitably, old-fashioned journalists and the new breed of cable and social media ringmasters were painted with the same broad brush of public disapproval (Sanford 1999; Pew Research Center 2016a, 2016b, 2017).

This course of events and the broad cultural changes it brought were reflected in the normalizing of personal ridicule as a tool of political debate, public spectacle, and a means of discrediting opponents. Accusations of personal misbehavior, gaffes in which a garbled or inappropriate statement proved embarrassing, and even personal characteristics such as unattractive physical traits, lack of dexterity, or less than stylish dress and grooming all became grist for the political mill (Sabato 1993; Wayne 2000). In addition, political campaign ads became more negative, partly through the incorporation of personally embarrassing material (Geer 2006).

Meanwhile, both political parties began ramping up opposition research, which was intended to keep the stream of criticism flowing. Simultaneously, the widespread use of digital mobile devices made it possible for partisan voters to document statements and behavior on the campaign trail that once would have gone unnoticed or attracted only brief attention (Chadwick 2013; Stromer-Galley 2014). As a result, journalists began competing with entertainment venues for this embarrassing material. Mainstream journalists seeking "clickbait" content sometimes even referenced the late-night comics in their news reports to attract and retain audiences increasingly looking beyond traditional media for information.

Tina Fey's imitation of Sarah Palin, the Republican 2008 vice presidential nominee, on *Saturday Night Live* represents a great example of the synergy between traditional news and entertainment media. In the wake of Palin's stumbling interview with Katie Couric of CBS News shortly after being selected as John McCain's running mate, Fey offered an over-the-top imitation of the Alaska governor that included both quotations from Palin's own public utterances and fictional comments that moved further toward the realm of absurdity and incoherence. That mocking became a key part of news reports on Palin, who was frequently portrayed during the campaign as ill-informed about policy and a poor choice for vice president (Greene and Gournelos 2011).

The Pivotal Politics of the 1980s and 1990s

The widening reach of both political journalism and political partisanship was exemplified by three events clustered together in the late 1980s: The destruction of Senator Gary Hart's 1988 presidential campaign, the failure of Judge Robert Bork's 1987 nomination to the Supreme Court, and the nomination of Dan Quayle as the Republican Party's vice presidential candidate in 1988.

The first example demonstrated how much milder political scandals of the past were compared to the current era. By mid-1987, Hart was the front-runner for the 1988 Democratic presidential nomination. Given his strong but ultimately unsuccessful 1984 nomination campaign, Hart was well ahead of his potential 1988 campaign rivals when rumors of his "womanizing" and an anonymous tip led the *Miami Herald* to stake out his Washington, DC, townhouse. The paper's reporters documented an affair that the married Hart was having with a young woman named Donna Rice.

Hart denied the charges at first, but a picture appeared in the tabloid *National Enquirer* (and was reprinted in newspapers around the country) of Rice sitting in Hart's lap. Hart was wearing a t-shirt bearing the name of the yacht "Monkey Business." From that moment, he was followed by a scrum of reporters pressing him about his marital infidelity, a situation political scientist Larry Sabato (1993) popularized as a media "feeding frenzy."

Hart soon withdrew from the 1988 race, bitter that he had endured a new standard of what was newsworthy. And he was right – numerous presidents, most notably John F. Kennedy, had carried on sexual affairs while in the White House, without any notice by the press at the time. But the floodgates had opened into a new era in which the personal had become political. In the years after Hart's fall, Sabato, Stencel, and Lichter (2000) cataloged dozens of cases in which political careers had been ruined by media investigations into private behavior, including cases of adultery that had occurred decades earlier. They concluded that many of these served no larger public purpose than titillating audiences. And titillate they did, as late-night hosts followed suit, turning their comedic attention increasingly to matters of human weakness among the nation's political leadership.

Although Hart's political collapse happened before late-night comedy became heavily political, *The Tonight Show* host Johnny Carson helped shape public preferences about Hart (Shales 1987a). As *Washington Post* television critic Tom Shales noted at the time, Carson made negative news coverage even worse for these candidates via his late-night audience:

> It was over for Gary Hart when Gary Hart became a nightly fixture in the Carson monologue. The roar of the crowd was heard in the land, but not the kind of roar politicians like ... "It's hard to be funnier than what's happening, sometimes," says Carson.
>
> *(Shales 1987a)*

12 The Importance of Political Humor

Public discussion of marital infidelity was enough to sink a campaign in the 1980s, as Gary Hart learned in the run-up to the 1988 presidential election. Four years later, Bill Clinton demonstrated that marital misconduct soon ceased to be politically fatal to presidential candidates. By 2016, Donald Trump demonstrated a successful presidential candidate could brag of his serial marital infidelity and still win the votes of a large majority of Christian conservative voters. As demonstrated in the pages that follow, brutal takedowns of Trump as a candidate and as president did little to undermine the intensity of the support he received from his followers.

Around the same time that the Hart sex scandal was unfolding, an increasingly partisan political environment emerged in the wake of President Reagan's nomination of conservative judge Robert Bork to fill a vacancy on the Supreme Court. Fearful that Bork's decisions on the bench would help validate Reagan's conservative policies, liberal activist groups decided to broaden the nomination process into a national referendum on Bork's previous decisions and his general judicial philosophy. On the floor of the Senate, Ted Kennedy (D-Mass.) predicted that Bork's confirmation would lead to the return of back-alley abortions, segregated lunch counters, and midnight raids by rogue police. A flood of mailings and political ads echoed these themes, including a TV spot narrated by actor Gregory Peck, which charged Bork with having "a strange idea of what justice is." (URL: www. youtube.com/watch?v=NpFe10lkF3Y).

The subsequent wave of bad press doomed Bork's chances for success, and the Senate rejected his court nomination on a 58–42 vote, the widest margin ever (O'Brien 1988). This was the first time in memory that a Supreme Court nomination failed because of the application of no holds barred partisan politics, and the success of the anti-Bork forces inaugurated a new era of partisanship in the confirmations of presidential nominees (Shales 1987b). But the scandal offered opportunities for the late-night comics to mock the judge. Johnny Carson, for example, offered this assessment during the Bork nomination process: "Bork isn't having a very good week. I saw him at a bar this afternoon sharing a margarita with Valerie Harper" (Shales 1987b). Harper, a well-known television star of that era, was famously fired from her own television series when she demanded a pay raise and greater control over the program (Shales 1987b).

While he did not have a verb named after him (as Bork did), Judge Douglas Ginsburg, Reagan's subsequent nominee for that same Supreme Court vacancy, faced the same fate. Ginsburg withdrew his nomination after press accounts emerged that he had occasionally smoked marijuana as a Harvard Law School professor in the 1970s (O'Brien 1988). This disclosure led to some late-night comedy mockery, but nothing compared to the mockery that Bork and Hart endured.

Still more abuse was on its way. The following year, George H.W. Bush's surprise choice for Vice Presidential candidate, Indiana Senator Dan Quayle (R-IN), was widely panned by political reporters as a callow youth who was in over his head in national politics. After initial rumors of scandal in his past proved baseless, journalists settled for treating him as a figure of fun. His stammering replies to their questions and his apparent lack of gravitas turned him into the court jester of the first Bush administration (Leibovich 2001). Thus, allegations of stupidity joined those of sexual misconduct as fair game for critics, be they on late-night TV or elsewhere, in the wake of Hart's and Quayle's appearances on the national stage.

By this time, media critics had begun to characterize political journalists as "character cops" who had arrogated to themselves the task of determining whether personal qualities and behavior disqualified politicians from high office (Sabato 1993). The factors behind this development included new technologies, heightened competition, alternative media sources, and the increasing use of cutthroat campaign practices such as opposition research and attack ads (Geer 2006; Patterson 1994, 2013). Of course, Gary Hart's personal behavior gave those journalists considerable material as early as the 1980s (Shales 1987a).

Any remaining reluctance of journalists to take on the character cop role disappeared following the appearance of presidential candidate Bill Clinton on the national political scene in 1992. Clinton appeared while trailing a string of potential scandals behind him, including public charges of adultery from former girlfriend Gennifer Flowers, questions about how he avoided military service during the Vietnam War, and charges that he had smoked marijuana in his youth (Leibovich 2001). Voters selected Clinton despite this list of demerits, which only grew longer after the new president arrived at the White House. Clinton's two terms in office featured a seemingly endless stream of scandal allegations, mostly dealing with sex but occasionally with the financial dealings of Bill and Hillary Clinton, as in the so-called Whitewater affair (Isikoff 2000). Hillary Clinton captured the raging partisanship of the period with her assertion that "a vast right-wing conspiracy" was behind the many scandal charges. All this famously culminated in the President's 1998 admission, after months of denials, of an affair with Monica Lewinsky, a young White House intern (Campbell 2000).

For the late-night comics, the Bill Clinton presidency was like eight years of Christmas every day, and it triggered new scandals directed as Republicans, as the subsequent efforts to drive Clinton from office backfired on the Republican majority in Congress. Amid charges of hypocrisy, journalists began to delve into the past peccadilloes of party leaders. *Hustler* publisher Larry Flynt joined the fray with a million dollar "bounty" on scandalous revelations about GOP lawmakers. The most prominent victim

14 The Importance of Political Humor

of this backlash – and of Clinton's aggressive efforts to spin the story in the direction of a partisan GOP witch-hunt – was Rep. Bob Livingston (R-LA), who was in line to be House Speaker in 1998 but was driven from office after revelations of a past affair emerged (Farnsworth and Lichter 2006).

Considering these tawdry developments that affected both Democrats and Republicans, it is not surprising that scholars reported increases in negativity expressed by politicians, particularly during political campaigns, and in the coverage that political journalists gave to these events (Cappella and Jamieson 1997; Geer 2006; Patterson 1994). Nor was it surprising that the public's approval ratings of both partisan camps reached new lows (Mann and Ornstein 2012), even as each side blamed the other for the parlous state of political discourse (Sabato et al. 2000). While analysts may disagree on where the fault lies, the decade from the late 1980s to the late 1990s clearly saw the rise of a political culture of personal ridicule, endured – and indulged in – by politicians, journalists, and late-night comics alike. And if anything, those patterns of political attacks have only become more common in the decades that followed.

The Evolving Norms and Changing Hosts of Political Humor

A parallel development to the changing political news landscape of this era was the simultaneous expansion of political humor on late-night television talk shows. In their early decades, talk shows and variety programs had mostly steered clear of political material as more trouble than it was worth. This reflected the show business adage attributed to Broadway playwright George S. Kaufman that "satire is what closes on Saturday night" (quoted in Elliot 2014). The exception to this rule was NBC's *Saturday Night Live*, which began airing in 1975. The show's sketch comedy occasionally focused on political topics, most frequently in a faux newscast called "Weekend Update."

Foreshadowing the future tone of late-night humor, however, comedian Chevy Chase found stardom by parodying President Gerald Ford's stumble when disembarking from Air Force One. Chase opened many shows by turning Ford's fall into a pratfall, knocking over or bumping into various objects, such as the presidential desk (Liebovich 2001). Unlike subsequent presidential imitators, Chase did not attempt to sound like or look like the president he was portraying, relying instead on Chase's own over-the-top stumbling, physical comedy. Ironically, what became the popular image of Ford as a clumsy oaf belied the reality of Ford's athletic past – he was a Collegiate All-Star on a University of Michigan football team that twice went undefeated and won national titles.

While *SNL* regularly offered presidential impersonators and parodies of presidential debates during those years, these were mostly individual sketches on weekly shows here and there, a far cry from the regular drumbeat of political material that would be featured nightly in the monologues of late-night talk show hosts in the years that followed.

The Carson Era

The genre of late-night talk became institutionalized under the direction of Johnny Carson. His *The Tonight Show* on NBC dominated the ratings competition from 1962 until his retirement three decades later in 1992. Operating in an environment with little competition, Carson aimed for the great middle of the national audience, with monologues and guests that were for the most part comforting and inoffensive. As prominent film director Billy Wilder put it, "He's the cream of middle-class elegance ... He has captivated the American bourgeoisie without ever offending the highbrows, and he has never said anything that wasn't liberal or progressive" (quoted in Tynan 1978).

Carson included political material in his monologues, but usually in a way that would not offend most viewers. This meant making fun of politicians who were embroiled in scandals and those who committed gaffes, and then moving on. His apparent centrism and relatively light touch when it came to politics left it to his various competitors to tap into the underserved audience for more contentious or ideological material. These competitors included Merv Griffin and Dick Cavett, who brought in political material and controversial guests on the Vietnam War. His rivals, though, were always a sidelight to Carson and the relatively gentle humor he brought to political comedy. Carson lasted far longer on the air than did his more combative competitors.

As *Washington Post* television critic Tom Shales wrote in a story reviewing Carson's first quarter century as a late-night host:

> [Carson] balks and scoffs at intense interpretation of the monologue and its effect on public careers. "I never analyze it," he says. "I never analyze the show. Analyzing it would be a wasted exercise. I just go out and do it. Like George Burns said, 'If it gets a laugh, it's funny.'"
>
> Jack Paar's *Tonight Show*, which preceded Carson's, was as hot as Carson's is cool, a teapot for innumerable tempests. Once his monologue is over, Carson is not interested in topical guests or, really, in the latest controversies.
>
> *(Shales 1987a)*

16 The Importance of Political Humor

Then along came Dan Quayle, whose rise to national prominence brought journalists and late-night comics together in making fun of George H.W. Bush's vice president. To drive home their image of Quayle as an unprepared half-wit, journalists began to refer to TV talk show punch lines to illustrate their points. Thus, Quayle became the first nominee for national office in memory whom the press defined as a national joke (Farnsworth and Lichter 2006). Of course, Quayle did not help make his case for seriousness when he criticized *Murphy Brown*, a fictional TV character on a popular sitcom, for contributing to the moral decline of Americans by having a child on the show out of wedlock (Liebovich 2001).

When he retired in May 1992, Johnny Carson used his final monologue to thank Quayle for the comedic material, including the spat with a fictional TV character.

> But the events of this last week have helped me make a decision. I am going to join the cast of *Murphy Brown* and become a surrogate father to that kid. During the run on the show there have been seven United States Presidents, and thankfully for comedy there have been eight Vice Presidents of the United States. Now I know I have made some jokes at the expense of Dan Quayle, but I really want to thank him tonight for making my final week so fruitful.
>
> *(quoted in Weinraub 1992)*

The politicians were noticing as well. Bush campaign manager Lee Atwater remarked that he monitored audience responses to *The Tonight Show* monologues to see how politicians were playing in Peoria (Lichter, Baumgartner, and Morris 2015: 207). Atwater's efforts were an early indication that humor was becoming a key part of the political milieu. Much of that evolution was thanks to Dan Quayle. A study of jokes on *The Tonight Show* and *The Late Show* from Inauguration Day in January 1989 through September 1991 found that Vice President Quayle topped all other political figures as the target of 417 jokes; President George H.W. Bush finished a distant second with 331 (*Media Monitor* 1991: 6).

The hapless vice president sought the presidency for himself years later, but his campaign quickly fizzled. Quayle simply could not emerge from being under the cloud of spending so much time as a key target of Carson's political humor.

The Leno-Letterman Years

Carson may have enjoyed launching barbs at Quayle, Hart, and other political figures, but his approach was mild compared to what would come next. The modern era of politicized monologues can probably be dated from 1992, when Jay Leno replaced Johnny Carson as host of *The Tonight Show* on NBC. The competition to succeed Carson was one of the most intense in the history of late-night television. The unhappy loser was David Letterman, who had long followed Carson's on NBC's *Late Night*. Letterman then moved to CBS to host *The Late Show* to compete directly with Leno. Both men stayed in these posts for over two decades (apart from a brief effort by Leno in 2009–2010 to switch to a prime-time show). Throughout their runs, the two hosts dominated late-night talk show ratings against a changing cast of competitors, until Leno retired in 2014 and Letterman followed in 2015.

Together, they set the tone for late-night humor, despite competition at various times from Conan O'Brien, Arsenio Hall, Bill Maher, and others. The great exception to the conventional late-night format, discussed in detail later, was the satirical "fake news" format developed by Jon Stewart on Comedy Central (Warner 2007).

Leno was the closest match of his generation to Carson, relying on old-fashioned zingers and one-liners that would get a laugh in Middle America but not necessarily among urban hipsters. Even so, Leno did the most to redirect the central themes of his routines toward politics. In 1993, the year when Leno and Letterman went head-to-head for the first time, Leno provided nearly twice as much political material as his rival, by a margin of 1,535 to 883 jokes (Lichter, Baumgartner, and Morris 2015). Leno's humor was relatively low key, and he was less likely than his rivals to be accused of partisanship.

Eventually, Republican politicians and conservative commentators began to adopt Leno as their favorite late-night comedian. In fact, a *Breitbart* reporter labeled him "the last fair, balanced late night host" (Toto 2014). The politics of Hollywood being what they are, Leno found it necessary to protest publicly that he was in fact a dyed-in-the-wool liberal – a Michael Moore fan whose joke writers include no Republicans. Specifically, Leno said, "I'm not conservative. I've never voted that way in my life" (Franzen 2009). Compared to some of the current highly political late-night entrants, from Stephen Colbert and to John Oliver and Bill Maher, it's easy to see why conservatives would have longed for more of the old-fashioned middle of the road humor popularized by Johnny Carson and Jay Leno.

By contrast, David Letterman was widely regarded as apolitical until late in his tenure. The transformation appears to have occurred in the wake of the tumultuous 2008 presidential election (Carter 2009). During that campaign, Republican nominee Sen. John McCain made the mistake of cancelling his *The Late Show* appearance at the last minute. An outraged Letterman fought back through his monologues, with a profusion of ridicule

18 The Importance of Political Humor

that eventually brought the abashed candidate back on the show, where he delivered an abject apology, admitting to his inquisitor, "I screwed up." This incident produced Letterman's famous pronouncement, "the road to the White House runs right through me!" That may be hyperbole, but the exchange certainly illustrates the changing balance of power between politicians and comedians (Lichter, Baumgartner, and Morris 2015).

Letterman's highly visible feuds with McCain and other politicians may have contributed to the politicization of Letterman's monologues as his career progressed (Carter 2009). That observation is supported by the CMPA data showing that Letterman's political joke totals jumped from 1,208 in 2007 to 3,187 in 2008 and 3,206 in 2009. By 2013, Letterman was using his "Stooge of the Night" routine to wage war against the Republican-majority Congress for its opposition to gun control. The segments showed images of senators opposing tougher background checks in gun purchases with superimposed graphics showing how much money they had received from pro-gun groups.

The Daily Show **Rises**

During this period of Leno versus Letterman, the only major change in the late-night landscape came in 1999 on the cable network Comedy Central, where Jon Stewart turned *The Daily Show* into a satirical "fake news" program. Stewart's success eventually led to spin off shows by cast members. Unlike the traditional stand-up comedians on most television talk shows, who relied heavily on one-liners, the Comedy Central comedians engaged in satire and were taken more seriously as popular commentators on politics and the news media. Stewart gained a strong following and was rated in national surveys as one of the most trusted and admired journalists in America (Baumgartner and Morris 2011; Garber 2009; Pew Research Center 2007).

Thus, even as Leno and Letterman were dominating late-night comedy on the broadcast network stage, the action was moving to the cable network Comedy Central. Put simply, Stewart brought satire to nightly late-night talk. In addition, the show focused more narrowly on the world of politics and public affairs than any other television talk show. The nightly skewering of politicians and the journalists who covered them found a strong audience among younger viewers, in sharp contrast to the graying audience for Leno and Letterman on NBC and CBS, respectively.

The redirection of *The Daily Show* and its new host benefited early on from some lucky timing. A continuing feature satirized the foibles of the candidates and the campaign news throughout the 2000 elections under the rubric "Indecision 2000." As it happened, the 2000 presidential election featured the greatest indecision in modern American politics, helping to build an audience for the show right up until the determination of who was going to be president was made, not by the voters but by the Supreme Court, on December 12, 2000.

Stewart also became personally involved in occasional political causes. For example, he helped push through the Senate a bill to provide health care for 9/11 emergency responders, by bludgeoning recalcitrant senators with a barrage of jokes, and by inviting some of the workers onto his show. More generally, as noted above, Stewart was widely regarded as a valued social and political critic and even by some as a legitimate journalist. His work was a major factor in getting politicians and the public alike to recognize late-night humor as a valuable source of information about politics. Thus, partly through Stewart's innovations and influence, political humorists have become increasingly important sources of political criticism, even going so far as becoming shapers of news content and public opinion.

Political Humor's Public Roles

Many of these humorists serve at least two critical public functions: first, they comment upon and reveal potential failings or hypocrisies of American society, especially those perpetrated by individuals in positions of political and/or economic power; second, and less overtly, they function as supplemental gatekeepers and framers in the agenda-setting work of the media (Gurney 2011: 3).

In 2005, *The Daily Show* produced a highly successful spin-off called *The Colbert Report*. Stephen Colbert, previously a contributor to *The Daily Show*, adopted the persona of a loud-mouthed right-wing pundit, at least partly modeled on such Fox News personalities as Bill O'Reilly and Glenn Beck. Colbert became involved in real-world national politics by attempting to run a parody presidential campaign (running as both a Democrat and a Republican) and later by forming a super-PAC, which raised over a million dollars. Some of the money was used to air spoof campaign ads. Colbert also teamed up with Stewart to stage a "Rally to Restore Sanity and/or Fear," which drew over 200,000 people to the National Mall in Washington, DC, for the avowed cause of mobilizing reason and moderation against partisanship and extremism. Colbert also testified before a Congressional subcommittee on the plight of migrant workers.

Journalists wrote about the actions and jokes of Stewart and Colbert as the two Comedy Central stars increasingly became public figures. But that doesn't mean the journalists always liked what they heard from the humorists, particularly when reporters themselves became the targets of

20 The Importance of Political Humor

the jokes, rather than elected officials. At one point in Stephen Colbert's remarks at the 2006 White House Correspondents dinner, he faulted reporters for not being more aggressive in challenging the George W. Bush administration over its handling of Iraq and Katrina, among other issues (Carr 2007).

> Listen, let's review the rules. Here's how it works. The president makes decisions. He's the decider. The press secretary announces those decisions, and you people of the press type those decisions down. Make, announce, type. Just put 'em through spell-check and go home. Get to know your family again. Make love to your wife. Write that novel you got kicking around in your head. You know, the one about the intrepid Washington reporter with the courage to stand up to the administration. You know, fiction!
>
> *(Colbert, quoted in Greene 2011: 132)*

The Washington journalists could not fire Colbert, but a year later the association invited a humorist with a very different style to this annual dinner of media and political luminaries. Rich Little, famous a generation earlier for his congenial Ronald Reagan imitations, addressed the group, a nod to the less combative political humor of a previous era (Carr 2007). However, this guest from the comedic past was at best a comforting, stopgap measure for those who were being burned by the new style of take-no-prisoners political humor that now dominated the late-night comedy landscape. Despite that brief detour down memory lane, there would be no going back to the tamer past.

The New Late-Night Landscape

As Leno, Letterman, Stewart, and Colbert were making their marks, more traditional and less visible hosts came and sometimes went, mostly without making a long-term mark politically with their monologues. They have included, among others, Arsenio Hall, forever remembered for helping revive the scandal-scarred presidential candidacy of Bill Clinton; Conan O'Brien, whose numerous late-night slots included a brief and controversial stint as Jay Leno's would-be successor on *The Tonight Show*; and Seth Meyers, best known for his association with *Saturday Night Live* before he took over *Late Night* on NBC in 2014.

One decidedly political voice belongs to Bill Maher, a television survivor who proudly wears his liberalism on his sleeve. As discussed earlier, his *Politically Incorrect* talk show on ABC more than lived up to its name when, in the wake of the 9/11 attacks, he defended the terrorists against charges of cowardice and lobbed it instead at the U.S. military for "lobbing cruise missiles from 2,000 miles away. That's cowardly" (quoted in Bohlen 2001). The comment cost his show acrimony and advertisers, and it was cancelled at the end of the season. The next season, however, Maher started a weekly talk show titled *Real Time with Bill Maher* on HBO. It has remained on HBO's evening schedule ever since.

Two other voices with broadcast network slots honored political material mostly in the breach, even as they became more prominent in recent years – Jimmy Kimmel and Jimmy Fallon. Until the past few years, Kimmel has been known for his light material and focus on celebrities. Before the network late-night comedy gig, he was a host on the *Man Show*, a raunchy cable offering designed to appeal to the worst instincts of hard-partying fraternity members (Garber 2018). Once he landed his network opportunity, Kimmel would sometimes become intensely political, particularly where health care matters were concerned (Farnsworth and Lichter 2020).

Fallon, who worked at the "Weekend Update" anchor desk at *Saturday Night Live* earlier in his career, was a relative latecomer to the late-night talk scene, taking over *Late Night* on NBC in 2009. Five years later, following Jay Leno's retirement, he graduated to *The Tonight Show*. If anything, Fallon's early lack of interest in monologues featuring political material exceeded that of Kimmel. Fallon specialized in creating a genial milieu with light-hearted entertainment devices that include music, dance, impersonations, and games.

Finally, after two decades of late-night talk show dominance by Jay Leno and David Letterman, and 15 years after the emergence of Jon Stewart as a "fake news" host, there was a remarkable shuffling of the deck that in rapid succession produced new hosts of *The Tonight Show*, *Late Night*, and *The Daily Show*. In addition, ABC moved up the starting time of *Jimmy Kimmel Live* to allow Kimmel to compete directly with the flagship talk shows on CBS and NBC. In 2014, Leno retired, and Jimmy Fallon took over *The Tonight Show*. In May 2015, Letterman retired, and Stephen Colbert took over *Late Night*, while *The Colbert Report* ceased production. In August of the same year, Stewart retired from his late-night program; South African comedian Trevor Noah took over *The Daily Show* a month later. With all these changes, three of the four leading talk shows had new hosts in place just in time for the 2016 presidential election to begin.

These personnel changes produced corresponding long-term changes in the amount and focus of the political humor that they produce. In the following sections, we first examine the overall trends during presidential election years from 1992 to 2016 covered by the long-term CMPA dataset.

22 The Importance of Political Humor

We then discuss similar data from the 2020 election based on a new study by the CMPA. (The brief 2020 discussion here represents a preview for Chapter 3, which discusses campaign humor of 2020 in greater detail.)

Amounts and Targets of Political Humor

The targets and topics of late-night comedy were the subject of a long-term study by the CMPA. Starting in 1992, the CMPA examined over 100,000 jokes about politics and public affairs on several shows, including those hosted by Leno, Letterman, Stewart, and Colbert. All coding was done by students who were trained by the CMPA staff members. Coders had to attain a level of reliability of at least 80 percent agreement, and their coding continued to be spot-checked throughout the analysis.

The study found that political material on late-night television increased over time and reached its highest levels during presidential elections, when it eventually became a regular component of the campaign discourse. Accordingly, the next section focuses mainly on the targets of election year humor.

Table 1.1 shows the increase in political humor across recent decades. The most popular targets were almost always presidents and presidential candidates. As Table 1.1 shows, sitting presidents were the most frequently targeted individuals in 17 out of the 21 years included in this historical table. (As mentioned earlier, we focus on recent elections in subsequent chapters). Three of those exceptions took place in 1996, 2008, and 2012, when Republican presidential nominees Bob Dole, John McCain, and Mitt Romney exceeded the totals of the sitting presidents they sought (but ultimately failed) to replace. In addition, in 2001 outgoing president Bill Clinton edged out his successor George W. Bush. More generally, the presidential tickets of the two major parties combined to account for just under one-third (32 percent) of all political jokes in election years. Many of the remaining jokes were aimed at their defeated primary opponents.

The intensity of election campaigns, which dominate the news, and the need to come up with fresh material night after night feed into the tendency of comedians to accentuate a few personal characteristics of the contenders and relate the day's events to these qualities. The same is true of presidents, whose activities typically generate daily headlines. As the jokes feed on each other and echo characteristics often addressed more seriously in the news media, stereotypes emerge and are reinforced.

As noted above, Vice President Dan Quayle was the first major political figure whose public image developed largely through an interaction of bad press and late-night jokes. The comedians portrayed him as an outright fool, for example, "Reporters asked Dan Quayle what would be the

The Importance of Political Humor **23**

TABLE 1.1 Most Targeted Individuals on Late-Night Comedy, 1992–2012

	Most Targeted	N (percent)	Second Most	N (percent)
1992	George H.W. Bush	612 (16.3%)	Bill Clinton	421 (11.2%)
1993	Bill Clinton	440 (16.3%)	Ross Perot	75 (2.8%)
1994	Bill Clinton	552 (16.2%)	Ted Kennedy	85 (2.5%)
1995	Bill Clinton	397 (13.3%)	O.J. Simpson	220 (7.7%)
1996	Bob Dole	839 (17.5%)	Bill Clinton	657 (13.7%)
1997	Bill Clinton	808 (27.0%)	O.J. Simpson	260 (8.7%)
1998	Bill Clinton	1,717 (32.6%)	Monica Lewinsky	303 (5.8%)
1999	Bill Clinton	1,317 (29.1%)	Monica Lewinsky	342 (7.6%)
2000	George W. Bush	905 (18.3%)	Bill Clinton	803 (16.2%)
2001	Bill Clinton	657 (19.2%)	George W. Bush	546 (15.9%)
2002	George W. Bush	314 (10.1%)	Bill Clinton	193 (6.2%)
2003	George W. Bush	406 (15.2%)	Bill Clinton	241 (9.0%)
2004	George W. Bush	1,169 (22.3%)	John Kerry	505 (9.6%)
2005	George W. Bush	657 (20.4%)	Michael Jackson	439 (13.6%)
2006	George W. Bush	1,213 (18.9%)	Dick Cheney	430 (6.7%)
2007	George W. Bush	784 (15.0%)	Paris Hilton	256 (4.9%)
2008	John McCain	1,358 (10.2%)	George W. Bush	1,160 (8.7%)
2009	Barack Obama	936 (8.5%)	George W. Bush	466 (4.2%)
2010	Barack Obama	728 (7.6%)	Sarah Palin	298 (3.1%)
2011	Barack Obama	270 (6.9%)	Herman Cain	180 (4.6%)
2012	Mitt Romney	1,061(16.5%)	Barack Obama	401 (6.2%)

Shows included by year:
The Tonight Show (NBC) 1992–2012
The Late Show (CBS) 1992–2012
Arsenio (Fox) 1992–1994
Late Night (NBC) 1993–2009
Jon Stewart Show (MTV) 1994
Politically Incorrect (ABC) 1997–2001
The Daily Show (Comedy Central) 2003–2010, 2012
The Colbert Report (Comedy Central) 2007–2010, 2012

Source: CMPA

solution to global warming and he replied, 'central air conditioning'" (Letterman, quoted in Lichter et al. 2015: 72). His relative youth was sometimes brought into play by jokes that treated him as not ready for adulthood, for example, "Dan Quayle had a birthday this week. They had a huge party for him at Chuck E. Cheese" (Leno, quoted in *Media Monitor* 1991). While comedians surely welcomed Quayle as a highly valuable meal ticket, their jokes often dripped with disdain. As Leno put it, "People have said that every comedian's dream is to poke fun at Vice President Dan Quayle. I think it's every comedian's dream to poke fun at ex-vice president Quayle" (quoted in Lichter et al. 2015: 73).

24 The Importance of Political Humor

Any comedian who regarded Quayle as indispensable to his trade must have celebrated his successor as whipping boy in chief – Bill Clinton. Clinton arrived on the public stage wrapped in intimations of scandal, from which he never escaped for long. From Gennifer Flowers to Monica Lewinsky, fully half (50 percent) of all jokes about Clinton – more than 3,000 in all – dealt with his sexual behavior. Examples: "With Bill Clinton as president, I finally understand why they celebrate President's Day with a mattress sale" (Leno, quoted in Lichter et al. 2015: 55), when he cancelled a vacation to the Virgin Islands, Leno speculated, "Actually, the real reason, after Clinton left last year, no more virgins" (quoted in Lichter et al. 2015: 55). This vein of material normally proved so rich that, on a slow day for news that could be converted to political humor, Leno mused, "I wish Clinton would get another girlfriend. We need more jokes. Where is our president when I need him?" (quoted in Lichter et al. 2015: 56).

When George W. Bush replaced Clinton in the White House, the wellspring of presidential sexual humor abruptly dried up. Perhaps as a result, the late-night comedians seemed to have trouble saying farewell to Clinton. As noted above, in 2001 there were more jokes about Clinton, who left office on January 20 of that year, than there were about his successor. The lesson of 2001 for the late-night comics was that if there is little opportunity for current president sexual humor, one can always turn to former president sexual humor (Bush's totals also dropped during the final months of 2001 because comedians were loath to make fun of the president in the wake of the 9/11 terrorist attacks).

Even so, Bush brought his own set of comical characteristics to the job. These included occasional malapropisms and physical awkwardness. But he mainly gave comedians a chance to dust off their "stupid guy" jokes left over from the Dan Quayle era. Even though Bush was a graduate of Yale University and Harvard Business School, 38 percent of all Bush jokes – over 2,300 – referenced his reputed lack of intelligence. Example: When Bush fared poorly in the first presidential debate of the 2004 election, Letterman commented, "Experts are saying that if this was a game show, Bush would have gone home with a handshake and a quart of motor oil" (quoted in Lichter et al. 2015: 164).

Coverage of failed presidential candidates revealed similar patterns. For example, when Bob Dole ran for the president in 1996 at age 73, comedians quickly settled on his advancing years as the leitmotif of his candidacy. When Dole admitted that he dyed his hair to cover the gray, Leno commented, "It's like a Grecian formula kind of thing. Not the product you buy in the store. He actually got his from an ancient Grecian" (quoted in Lichter et al. 2015: 74). After Dole visited a kindergarten class, Leno remarked, "Dole stayed about fifteen minutes, then he had to leave because it was nap time – not for the kids" (quoted in Lichter et al. 2015: 155). All told, references to his age accounted for nearly two out of five Dole jokes (38 percent), while a secondary theme about his alleged moodiness accounted for an additional 12 percent of his jokes.

Comparable examples of jokes through stereotypes could be found for most of the major political figures over the past three decades. However, Barack Obama was at least a partial exception to this rule. As a candidate and as president, he was the target of fewer jokes than his predecessors were. Perhaps the first African American president represented a high-risk comedic minefield for the white humorists who dominated the nightly humor shows during his years in office. Notably, reporters also covered Obama more positively than they treated his predecessors (Farnsworth and Lichter 2011b, 2012a, 2012b, 2016). This relatively positive news made it more difficult for comedians to find personal characteristics around which to build a negative stereotype.

Accordingly, there was no single quality, or even set of qualities, that framed humor focusing on Obama. Indeed, many of the reputed "Obama jokes" turned out to be jokes about the reverence he received as a candidate and as a new president. For example, in his "fake news" report on Obama's trip to Israel, Jon Stewart reported that he "would be stopping in Bethlehem to visit the manger where he was born" (quoted in Lichter et al. 2015: 80). Obama's star eventually faded somewhat, and he followed his presidential predecessors in becoming the most joked-about individual from 2009 to 2011, albeit with lower joke totals than other recent chief executives during their years in the White House.

For the 21 years examined in Table 1.1 (1992–2012), presidents or presidential candidates ranked first every single year: seven years had George W. Bush at the top, and seven other years had Clinton ranked first. Obama, another two-term president, ranked first as the most joked-about figure in only three of his eight years as president. George H.W. Bush ranked first during his last year in office; the other top finishers were a trio of defeated Republican presidential candidates: Bob Dole, John McCain, and Mitt Romney.

In addition to his seven first-place finishes, Clinton ranked second as the target of late-night humor five times. George W. Bush had three second-place finishes, while O.J. Simpson, a football and film star who was acquitted of murder charges in a highly controversial trial, and Monica Lewinsky, America's most famous White House intern, ranked second in two different years.

Dan Quayle was not the only vice president targeted. Vice President Dick Cheney ranked second as a target of humor in 2006. While she was never

26 The Importance of Political Humor

vice president, 2008 Republican nominee and former Alaska Governor Sarah Palin ranked second in humor in 2010. Republican presidential aspirant Herman Cain did not even become a major party nominee, but he ranked second as a joke target in 2011.

Thus, apart from the occasional scandal-scarred celebrity, late-night humor has focused heavily on aspirants to and holders of national office. The case of Obama notwithstanding, the general experience of presidential candidates and presidents in office is clear from the examples cited above. When they make news, as they must, they are also providing material to late-night comedians. The talk show hosts, and their writers, take the daily headlines they generate and make these the basis of jokes that ridicule some aspect of a politician's personality, politics, lifestyle, or appearance.

Unlike their response to bad press, politicians cannot reasonably call for more fair or accurate coverage from talk show hosts. After all, the late-night comics are in the entertainment business, not the news business. Thus, whining about allegedly being picked on unfairly might just stimulate more of the same. The best politicians can do in this challenging environment is to accept an invitation to go on a host's show and demonstrate that they can take a joke (Kolbert 1992; Morris 2009). But they are still prisoners of a new order in political communication, particularly campaign communication, in which talk show monologues are one component of a generally unfriendly media environment that includes both news and entertainment.

Table 1.2 shows the relative percentage of jokes made about the two major party nominees during election years from 1992 to 2016. (The 2016 data for Trump and Clinton stops shortly after Election Day, on November 11, 2016.) Trump's total of 78 percent of jokes, compared to 22 percent for Hillary Clinton, represents the most one-sided distribution of jokes between the two major party nominees in the entire quarter century. However, Trump was only one percentage point ahead of Mitt Romney's 77 percent share, compared to Barack Obama's 23 percent, in 2008. The third greatest disparity occurred in 2004, when George W. Bush endured 70 percent of all jokes, compared to 30 percent for John Kerry. The next biggest difference was the 64 percent of jokes aimed at John McCain, compared to 36 percent for Obama in 2008, followed by George W. Bush's 62 percent versus Al Gore's 38 percent in 2000. Not surprisingly, the two Bill Clinton elections had the smallest partisan differences: George H.W. Bush's 59 percent versus Clinton's 41 percent in 1992 and Bob Dole's 56 percent compared to Bill Clinton's 44 percent four years later.

Thus, the tilt in jokes about Trump is not so one-sided in historical context as it is relative to other contenders in the 2016 election. The most consistent division was partisan – Republican candidates always attracted

The Importance of Political Humor **27**

TABLE 1.2 Proportion of Jokes about the Two Presidential Nominees, 1992–2016

	Republican			Democrat		Total Jokes
1992	George H.W. Bush	59%	B. Clinton	41%		1,033
1996	Dole	56%	B. Clinton	44%		1,496
2000	George W. Bush	62%	Gore	38%		1,451
2004	George W. Bush	70%	Kerry	30%		1,674
2008	McCain	64%	Obama	36%		2,126
2012	Romney	77%	Obama	23%		1,462
2016	Trump	78%	H. Clinton	22%		2,329

Shows included by year:
2016: *The Tonight Show* (NBC), *The Late Show* (CBS), *Jimmy Kimmel Live!* (ABC), *The Daily Show* (Comedy Central)
2012: *The Tonight Show* (NBC), *The Late Show* (CBS), *The Daily Show* (Comedy Central), *The Colbert Report* (Comedy Central)
2008: *The Tonight Show* (NBC), *The Late Show* (CBS), *The Daily Show* (Comedy Central), *The Colbert Report* (Comedy Central), *Late Night* (NBC)
2004: *The Tonight Show* (NBC), *The Late Show* (CBS), *The Daily Show* (Comedy Central), *Late Night* (NBC)
2000: *The Tonight Show* (NBC), *The Late Show* (CBS), *Politically Incorrect* (ABC), *Late Night* (NBC)
1996: *The Tonight Show* (NBC), *The Late Show* (CBS), *Politically Incorrect* (ABC), *Late Night* (NBC)
1992: *The Tonight Show* (NBC), *The Late Show* (CBS), *Arsenio* (Fox), *The Tonight Show* (NBC) 1992–2016
Note: Totals for 1992–2012 are based on entire calendar year in which election took place. Totals for 2016 cover January 1 to November 11.

Source: CMPA

substantially more jokes than their Democratic opponents do. Moreover, the gap became increasingly great over time, from less than a three-to-two margin in the earliest two elections to more than a three-to-one margin in the most recent two contests. Even Bill Clinton, whose behavior was like catnip to comedians, generated fewer jokes than his GOP opponents did in both 1992 and 1996. And there is a limiting factor on Trump's contribution to the partisan trend. With the tilt already up to 77 percent toward the Republican in the previous election, there was simply not much room for an additional increase without the monologues becoming all Trump all the time (as sometimes seemed to be the case).

Donald Trump, the Multimedia Phenomenon

More than almost any other political or business figure of his generation, Donald Trump was a media creation – and a largely self-made one at that. From his first appearances on the New York City real estate and late-night clubbing scenes four decades ago, Trump was the master of his own ceremonies (Bender 1983). He aggressively courted media attention and celebrity status at every opportunity, doing so with finely tuned media instincts that even battle-tested public relations operatives would envy (Borchers 2016, 2018; Geist 1986; Greenberg 2018). Trump commented regularly on the prominent issues of the day, whether those concerns had much to do with him or not, such as the infamous Central Park jogger assault case of the 1980s.

When his business and personal interests were more directly involved in those early years, Trump used the media to advance his reputation. This included needling city officials who did not act as he wished and pushing for tax breaks that allowed him to create large real estate developments bearing the family name. All the while, he was building his business empire (Pogrebin 1996). He promoted Trump products at every opportunity, offering an image of excess that stretched from his palatial apartment and elite golf resorts to his luxury yacht and private jet. When he was unsatisfied with the level of attention reporters devoted to him, he even used an alias ("John Barron") to provide morsels of his own jet-setting lifestyle to the gossip-hungry New York tabloids. Reporters looked the other way as Trump pretended to be someone else as he told stories about himself (Fisher 2018; Hurt 1993).

From the start, though, Trump had set his sights on drawing his self-portrait on a canvas larger than Manhattan. He aggressively sought to build a national brand for himself via appearances on late-night television and "shock jock" radio. He branded casinos, a university, steaks, wines, clothing, and an airline shuttle. He bought a professional football team, feuded with other real estate moguls, and regularly argued with *Forbes* magazine over how rich he really was. When all else failed in those early days, Trump used lawsuits to draw attention to his latest business ventures (or to change the subject when things were not going well).

Trump insisted his story be told in the media – and further insisted that he was the one to tell it. He and his coauthors wrote several best-selling books cataloging his rise, his financial challenges, and his revival – sporting his last name as the first word in the title (Trump with Leerhsen 1990; Trump with Bohner 1997; Trump with Schwartz 2004[originally 1987]). To increase book sales even further – as well as increasing the value of his personal brand – Trump publicly mused about running for president several times, years before his successful 2016 campaign (Hurt 1993).

Trump thus established himself as famous for being famous, even before the internet made that celebrity formula commonplace. In short, he went viral in the analog age, via the tabloids, glossy magazines, talk radio, and talk television (Fisher 2018).

To be sure, Trump's obsessive media-seeking behavior was a win-win proposition. Trump wanted the attention and the media wanted readers and viewers. Trump always offered a compelling story, and he was ratings gold when it came to television. NBC wisely created *The Apprentice* and then *The Celebrity Apprentice* as vehicles to highlight one of the nation's most media-savvy entrepreneurs. Trump TV was an immense commercial success, further building his reputation as a celebrity executive for those who already knew of him. For those who did not, these network television shows introduced Donald Trump to an even larger national audience of people who might spend money on his wine, his men's wear collection, and his steaks. They might even support his political ambitions someday.

Traditional news organizations were not the only media beneficiaries of Trump's presence in the national conversation. Such a relentless self-promoter represented a rich source of humor, both within New York City and for the nation. His aggressive, bombastic temperament and his willingness to appear in so many media formats made him ripe for parody and mockery long before he became a presidential candidate. Over the past three decades, Trump has been a familiar enough figure to be invited to joke with the hosts on late-night television talk shows. He took two celebrity star turns as a guest host of *Saturday Night Live*, for example, where he was frequently lampooned by actors imitating him.

For those who know only of Trump's presidential-era feuds with late-night comics, it may come as a surprise that he readily turned to those same outlets to help build his national brand years earlier. Trump, though, does not always dance with the one who brought him. As Trump began to move about the city's rarified social circles, he drew attention from the *New York Times*, which opened a 1976 feature story on him with these breathless sentences.

> He is tall, lean and blond, with dazzling white teeth, and he looks ever so much like Robert Redford. He rides around town in a chauffeured silver Cadillac with his initials, DJT, on the plates. He dates slinky fashion models, belongs to the most elegant clubs and, at only 30 years of age, estimates that he is worth "more than $200 million." Flair. It's one of Donald J. Trump's favorite words, and both he, his friends and his enemies use it when describing his way of life as well as his business style as New York's No. 1 real estate promoter of the middle 1970's. "If a man has flair," the energetic, outspoken Mr. Trump said the other day, "and is smart and somewhat conservative and has a taste for what people want, he's bound to be successful in New York."
>
> *(Klemesrud 1976)*

Such aggressive self-promotions continued in the 1980s, an era of turbo-charged capitalism embodied by the fictional Wall Street financier Gordon Gekko in *Wall Street* (1987), whose motto was "greed is good." In real life, the rising young developer Donald Trump could have given Gekko a run for his money (Pagliary 2016). Trump and his gilded lifestyle highlighted popular television entertainment programs of the day, including *Entertainment Tonight*, where the brash business executive's life was featured alongside mega-celebrities like Cher and former president Gerald Ford (Kerr 1984). The developer named an airline after himself, the Trump Shuttle, as well as Trump Air, a helicopter service, and he slapped his name on many of his buildings (Hurt 1993). Trump's national profile also expanded during these years via his ownership of the New Jersey Generals, part of the United States Football League (Eskenazi 1984; Geist 1984). When the renegade football league disbanded in 1985, Trump walked away with a financial loss estimated at $22 million (Hurt 1993). Trump then changed the subject by turning his attention to boxing, which fit in well with his existing investments in Atlantic City casinos – though the pivot did generate some media snark (Anderson 1987).

After having put his name on so many properties, Trump then sought to branch out into television. The syndicated game show, *Trump Card*, filmed at Trump's Castle in Atlantic City, gave contestants the opportunity to answer questions and thereby fill out an approximation of a bingo card (Carter 1989). When the show began airing in 1990, Trump said he was very optimistic: "I think it will be tremendously successful. We're trading on the glamour of the Trump Castle, the Trump Princess [his yacht] ... The Trump name has never been hotter" (quoted in Van Luling 2017). Despite the substantial publicity and the great interest from television producers, however, the show only ran for one season.

Trump's setbacks of the late 1980s did not deter him. He concentrated instead on his successes and planned a comeback. Trump the businessperson and New York City celebrity was prone to exaggeration, as he admitted in *Trump: The Art of the Deal*: "I play to people's fantasies. I call it truthful hyperbole. It's an innocent form of exaggeration – and a very effective form of promotion" (quoted in Swanson 2016).

Trump took risks, and he endured several bankruptcies of his businesses over the years, making him less a financial success story than he appeared to be in the media (Traub 2004; Swanson 2016). In good times and in bad, Trump was very effective at presenting himself as successful and well connected – a person of consequence in a city filled with celebrities. He was part of the establishment, to be sure, but also something of a renegade who lived an immensely posh lifestyle even as he exhibited a populist streak (Freedman 1987).

The Importance of Political Humor **31**

Trump secured iconic Big Apple status on December 10, 1988, when he and his first wife Ivana Trump, as played by Phil Hartman and Jan Hooks, provided the *Saturday Night Live* opening: "Live from New York, it's Saturday Night!" In that opening segment, the two Trump characters gave each other large, gold and jewel-encrusted, highly ostentatious presents (Tropiano 2013). The same two performers impersonated the Trumps again during the show's February 17, 1990, episode, when the divorcing couple argued over the distribution of Trump family assets (Tropiano 2013).

Trump's Media Instincts: Converting Crisis into Opportunity

One key strategy that also aided Donald Trump's rise to prominence in New York was his ability to see opportunities that would spring from injecting himself into ongoing news stories. In May 1989, a few days after New York City first learned of the horrific story of a white female jogger who was brutally attacked in Central Park, Trump took out ads in four of the city's daily newspapers arguing that the crime should lead to the reinstatement of the death penalty in New York State (Wilson 2002). The crime, which dominated the news of the city that spring, laid bare the city's often-simmering racial tensions. Years later, DNA evidence cleared the teenagers, who originally confessed to the crime under dubious circumstances and went to jail for years following their statements.. The new evidence identified instead a convicted murderer as the attacker (Wilson 2002). But Trump's efforts did feed into political pressure to restore capital punishment, and New York State passed a new death penalty law several years later (Halbfinger 1997).

In the 1990s and the decades that followed, Trump's desire for fame continued to take the form of media-oriented activities. There were the best-selling books, of course, which generated considerable national interest and attention. But the national marketing campaign was just getting started. He kicked off the 1990s with a *Playboy* cover photo and interview that he bragged about for a quarter century, even after becoming a Republican presidential nominee in 2016 in part through the support of conservative Christian voters (Wootson 2017).

At the core of Trump's rebranding as a connoisseur of beautiful women was Marla Maples, the former beauty pageant contestant who first became the "other woman" and then wife number two. Trump lavished attention on her, in part because he thought having a beautiful young woman on his arm reflected well on him (Brozan 1992). The breakup of Trump's first marriage drew the attention of *Saturday Night Live* on February 24, 1990, where Dana Carvey's "Church Lady" character scolded Donald Trump, then played by Phil Hartman, and Marla Maples, played by Jan Hooks,

32 The Importance of Political Humor

for their sinful ways, referring to the couple as a "satanic sandwich" (Tropiano 2013).

The eventual nuptials offered another opportunity for Trump to bask in the media attention he so intensely craved. It also reminded everyone about how this one-time outer-borough boy had arrived at the pinnacle of the New York society scene without a blue-chip pedigree. Late-night host David Letterman joked that Trump "was relieved to be settling down to marriage, so he could start dating again" (quoted in Purdum 1993). Howard Stern, the radio shock jock who often bantered with Trump on Stern's program and was a guest at the wedding, said on the day of Trump's nuptials: "It's probably in bad taste, but I give it four months" (quoted in Dullea 1993). In fact, the couple announced their decision to separate after less than four years of marriage (Weber 1997). About a year later, journalists reported that Trump was dating Melania Knauss, the Slovenian model who subsequently became Trump's third wife (Walder 1999).

His serial affairs and marriages were consistent with Trump's incautious approach to life. His willingness to appear on unrestrained entertainment programs and contribute to vulgar, demeaning commentary about women would create future problems for Trump. But in the years before the 2016 election, Trump felt quite comfortable talking like an aging frat boy, ranking women on their appearance and gleefully insulting those not up to his standards of physical perfection (Kaczynski and McDermott 2016).

Then came *The Apprentice*, which presented Trump even more forcefully before a national audience. The highly rated show was an excellent promotional vehicle for Donald Trump. It was a particularly effective way to reach people who knew little about New York or launching a business but knew an entertainer when they saw one. NBC shaped the show to make Trump the center of the action and the very model of a modern capitalist baron, shuttling around by helicopter and making hard business decisions every episode (Traub 2004).

The adulation, thanks to his television celebrity, came at a good time for the mogul, when his casino business was sinking in debt, leading to a chapter 11 bankruptcy filing (Segal 2004). But Trump's financial problems during these years were not the focus of Middle America, which loved the drama provided by the show and its star and cared little of whether Trump deserved the expertise accorded him on *The Apprentice*. As Eric Dezenhall, a Washington media crisis management firm executive, observed, "If your goal is to get people in the American heartland to watch your TV show, having outrageous hair and pink ties and using superlatives is a legitimate pathway to that goal" (quoted in Segal 2004).

Conan O'Brien Remembers Trump the Celebrity Guest

Longtime late-night TV host Conan O'Brien frequently featured Donald Trump on his show (then on NBC), starting in 1997 and continuing through Trump's years on *The Apprentice* on that same network. According to O'Brien, one of Trump's early appearances did not go well, and he left the stage in a huff. Moments before, O'Brien had asked how much money Trump had in his pockets at that moment, and Trump fished in his pockets and pulled out a condom (Doyle 2019). Trump vowed he would never be on the show again, O'Brien said, recounting that Trump told a producer as he stormed off the set: "That's the last time I'm gonna be on this f***ing show. He humiliated me in front of everybody" (quoted in Doyle 2019). He reconsidered and returned repeatedly to banter with Conan O'Brien in the years that followed.

For all the attention Trump sought via late-night comedy, including several subsequent appearances on O'Brien's show, the business executive appeared a sharp contrast from many political leaders who could laugh at themselves at least part of the time (Doyle 2019). As O'Brien said:

> To really have a sense of humor, you have to be able to laugh at yourself. You have to be able to see the human condition as absurd. Our funny presidents have always been able to see the inherent absurdity of it all. John F. Kennedy served in the Navy and saw how f**ked up the Navy brass was and how badly things were done. His illnesses as a kid helped educate him that life was a crapshoot and inherently ridiculous. I think that gave him a great, witty sense of irony. Lincoln famously found himself to be hideous and was the first one to make fun of himself, our most self-deprecating president. I think all of that is anathema to Trump. Trump's superpower is constantly believing in the infallibility of Trump. Humility is a weakness to him. Having performed two different White House Correspondents' Dinners and seen Clinton and Obama sit there and laugh at themselves, I don't think Trump can do that.
>
> *(O'Brien, quoted in Doyle 2019)*

While he could never self-deprecate like Lincoln did – and who among us could? – Trump may have developed a better sense of humor as the years went by. He first hosted *Saturday Night Live* on April 3, 2004, when he observed in his opening monologue, "It's great to be here at *Saturday Night Live*, but I will be completely honest, it's even better for *Saturday Night Live* that I am here," a riff on his large ego (Inside Edition 2015). That *SNL* episode – one of two that Trump hosted – included an advertisement for a fictitious chicken restaurant, "Trump's House of Wings." It featured

34 The Importance of Political Humor

Trump, dressed in a yellow suit and tie, dancing with cast members dressed up as chickens (Inside Edition 2015). That fake ad generated some controversy, and *SNL* removed it from some of its archives – though for reasons that remain unclear to this day (Inside Edition 2015).

Taken together, the Trump story is one of always moving forward toward getting what he wants, regardless of circumstances (Boot 2018). That made him irresistible to the late-night comics, even before Trump had all that much to do with running for president.

What Comes Next?

In this opening chapter, we have focused on political humor at key moments during the first half-century of late-night television comedy as well as the evolution of the presidency as a central figure of political satire and parody. We also set the stage for understanding the unique role that Donald Trump has played in the history of political humor.

Chapter 2 examines the rise of Trump as a focus of attention for both news and entertainment media during his successful 2016 campaign and the presidency that followed.

The 2020 presidential campaign is the focus on Chapter 3. In a year marked by the start of the COVID-19 pandemic and attacks on the political legitimacy of the nation's election system, Trump once again dominated the late-night political humor discourse. The comics offered political content that resembled mainstream election news coverage of presidential campaigns: very little policy-oriented commentary and a focus on strategy and personality.

In Chapter 4, we examine the first months of the Biden presidency and the first months of the Trump ex-presidency. As was the case for Bill Clinton in 2001, the new former president two decades later also remained a key late-night topic. The new president, Joe Biden, despite being a consistent target of ridicule across his years in the public, received comparatively little attention from these shows when compared to other presidents in their first years in office.

Chapter 5 examines *Gutfeld!* – the first truly successful late-night comedy program on Fox News. We consider the challenges conservatives have faced securing a beachhead on political satire in the years before 2021. We also compare the varying approaches of *Gutfeld!* and the competing nightly late-night programs during the fall of 2021, after the new show had secured its footing.

In Chapter 6, we examine public opinion surveys, analyses that demonstrate how growing numbers of voters, particularly younger ones, are focusing more on political humor as they learn about politics, and as they establish their political interests and opinions.

Our final chapter turns to the future of political humor. What might the comedians do during the remainder of the Biden presidency and how might their treatment of both Biden and Trump shape political humor as the late-night comics address subsequent presidents?

2

POLITICAL HUMOR AND THE RISE OF DONALD TRUMP THE POLITICIAN

Coauthored with Noah Gardner, Jeremy Engel, Deanne Canieso, and Shaelyn Patzer

By the 1980s, Donald Trump had succeeded in becoming one of the most famous names in New York City. Three decades later, he had become one of the most famous celebrities in the nation, the brash business titan who had become the focus of a hit television series built on his biography. Well before his 2016 presidential run, he began a pivot toward elective office. This chapter examines the shift of Trump from primarily a celebrity figure to one who is focused on politics, with special attention to how he was treated by the late-night comics during the 2016 campaign and the presidency that followed.

Trump Expands His Political Profile

In terms of his own brand of politics, Trump at first offered a somewhat inconsistent narrative. In the years before his 2016 presidential campaign, he had given money to Democrats as well as Republicans, and he changed his party registration back and forth (Ceaser et al. 2017). Trump considered running for office off and on over the years. He renewed his interest in politics during the Obama presidency, when he became a spokesperson for the "Birther" movement, which alleged without evidence that Barack Obama was not born in this country and therefore was ineligible to be president (Williamson et al. 2011).

The birther movement was hardly Trump's first entry into the political realm. Trump raised the possibility of being a presidential candidate as early as 1987. His theme at that time, one he would use when campaigning decades later, was that other nations had "ripped off" the U.S. by not paying their fair share of collective defense costs (Hurt 1993). While he

DOI: 10.4324/9781003283041-2

did not run then, news reports of his potential 1988 candidacy helped sell more copies of Trump's new book (Hurt 1993). He again teased a presidential campaign, this time when Trump and then-girlfriend Melania Knauss did a joint interview with Howard Stern in 1999 – a talk that also featured Trump bragging about his sex life (Walder 1999). Around the same time, Trump had a sit-down interview with Jay Leno on *The Tonight Show*, which honored his presence by playing "Hail to the Chief" as Trump's entrance music (Nagourney 1999). A *New York Times*/CBS News poll conducted in advance of the 2000 campaign found that 70 percent of Americans viewed him negatively, and so he again shelved the idea of running for president (Nagourney 1999, 2000).

Trump, Obama, and the Birther Rumor

When Barack Obama ran for president in 2008 and during Obama's tenure in office, Donald Trump, with the assistance of expanding and ever more influential social media outlets, spread the false rumor that Obama was not born in this country and therefore not eligible to be president (Chadwick 2013). Even after President Obama produced a birth certificate proving he was born in Hawaii, Trump's false claims continued to generate an enthusiastic response from Republican crowds and substantial attention from journalists (Abramowitz 2017).

In 2011, when Trump once again publicly flirted with the idea of becoming a presidential candidate, he surged in the polls and briefly seemed to be a viable challenger to Obama (Brooks 2011). He tweeted more than 200 times about President Obama in advance of the 2012 election, constructing an argument about why he should not be reelected – and repeated the debunked birther claim. Starting in April 2011, Trump provided a weekly commentary segment on *Fox and Friends*, where he offered his take on current political and business developments. He used his Fox News appearances to continue to promote the discredited "birther" claim, eventually improving his own electoral prospects (Bump 2019). In the end, Trump declined once again to run for office in 2012, but the exploratory efforts that year foreshadowed the approach that he would take in 2016: that of a brassy self-promoter who may play fast and loose with the truth but promises to shake up the system (Brooks 2011).

Since he was not a candidate in 2012, Trump remained a regular contributor to *Fox and Friends* until he declared for president in June 2015. That valuable media real estate provided several additional years of opportunities for the future presidential candidate to sell himself on the nation's leading conservative television outlet as the combative answer to Republican struggles to find a compelling, conservative presidential candidate (Bump 2019).

38 Political Humor and the Rise of Donald Trump the Politician

Obama Gets Even: The 2011 White House Correspondents Dinner

The White House Correspondents Dinner represents a rare public venue for a president to mock his critics in front of the country's most important political and cultural figures, as well as the national television audience tuning in to political Washington's premier social event. (Of course, the president is mocked in turn by a professional comedian selected for that very purpose.) At the Correspondents Dinner in April 2011, President Obama had a rare opportunity to return fire against Donald Trump, who was in the audience that night as a guest of the *Washington Post*. The president proceeded to make the most of the moment.

> "Donald Trump is here tonight," the comedian in chief said, grinning. "Now, I know that he's taken some flak lately, but no one is prouder to put this birth certificate to rest than The Donald. Now he can get to focusing on the issues that matter. Like, did we fake the moon landing? What really happened at Roswell? And where are Biggie and Tupac?"
>
> It was almost painful to watch, the juxtaposition of the president, flexing his new post-birther comedy chops, and the real estate mogul-cum-politician, grimacing at his table as Mr. Obama basked in his post-long-form-birth-certificate glow. "All kidding aside, we all know about your credentials and experience," Mr. Obama said, as people in the room either chortled or grimaced nervously, all depending on their proximity to Mr. Trump.
>
> In *Celebrity Apprentice*, Mr. Obama told Mr. Trump, teeth flashing, "the men's cooking team did not impress the judges from Omaha Steaks, but you recognized that this was a lack of leadership, so you fired Gary Busey." "These," Mr. Obama said, "are the kinds of decisions that would keep me up at night. Well-handled, sir. Well-handled."
>
> *(Cooper 2011)*

Throughout this pummeling from the president, Trump sat stone-faced (Cooper 2011). The developer turned media sensation would soon avenge his humiliation.

Trump Gets Even: Public Anger and Trump's Populist Challenge of 2016

While some earlier populist movements had some political success, in 2016 Trump succeeded where other populist efforts – including George Wallace, Ross Perot, Joseph McCarthy, and the John Birch Society – had not (Adorno et al. 1950; Craig 1993, 1996; Farnsworth 2001, 2003a, 2003b; Hibbing and Theiss-Morse 1995; Skocpol and Williamson 2012).

Trump's effective use of Twitter to attack the status quo resonated with many voters and helped him wrest the Republican nomination away from an experienced field of GOP governors and senators. He then defeated Democratic nominee Hillary Clinton, who had the bad luck to be an experienced political insider at a time when many voters yearned for an outsider who would shake up the system (Ceaser et al. 2017).

Conservatives, particularly religious ones, were in an extremely forgiving mood when it came to Trump, who vowed to reshape the federal judiciary to their liking (Ceaser et al. 2017). His departures from Republican orthodoxy on free trade and national security mattered little to them; nor did a personal lifestyle that hardly comported with Christian religious teachings. (At the time of his 2016 campaign, Trump was on his third marriage and for decades had enjoyed a lavish lifestyle that drew the attention of fame-worshippers everywhere but involved little attendance at religious services). "Trump was the people's billionaire, offering unashamedly what the average American wanted, a Trump steak or a night at a casino, or showing the kind of luxury people could only yearn for, like a personal airplane" (Ceaser et al. 2017: ix). As he reflected on the large, emotional crowds standing before him at campaign rallies, Trump came to think he was bulletproof. As he famously said in January 2016: "I could stand in the middle of Fifth Avenue and shoot somebody. And I wouldn't lose any voters. OK. It's like incredible" (quoted in MacWilliams 2016: 720).

Trump believed his supporters were very loyal, and he was right. He got into political troubles repeatedly during the 2016 campaign and yet survived unscathed (Sabato 2017).

With the expansion of social media's reach and visibility in the years leading up to 2016, voters faced a growing challenge to obtaining accurate information in a media environment populated by entrepreneurs promoting fake news for profit and Russian-backed hackers releasing misleading or false information about Hillary Clinton (Fisher et al. 2016; Green 2017). The tumultuous media environment was tailor-made for a candidate like Trump, who offered an increasingly apocalyptic message that would be amplified in a conservative media echo chamber that included Trump advisor Stephen Bannon (Benkler et al. 2017).

Earlier in the internet age, candidate Trump might have been a sideshow, a cranky idiosyncratic character with a bon mot or two and a high media profile, particularly with the late-night comics drawn to his larger-than-life persona. By 2016, though, the political ground had shifted a great deal. Rising populist anger, growing public partisanship, the high visibility of Fox News, and new peer-to-peer social media communication opportunities helped make him a winner.

40 Political Humor and the Rise of Donald Trump the Politician

TABLE 2.1 Comparing the Character of the Presidential Candidates, September 2016

(results in percentages)
Q. Thinking about the following characteristics and qualities, please say whether you think each applies or doesn't apply to Hillary Clinton/Donald Trump. How about – [randomize]?

	Applies to Clinton	Applies to Trump	Difference (Clinton–Trump)
Has the experience it takes to be president	69	29	+40
Would display good judgment in a crisis	54	39	+15
Can manage the government effectively	54	41	+13
Is likeable	50	38	+12
Cares about the needs of people like you	48	40	+8
Can get things done	60	56	+4
Can bring about the changes the country needs	41	41	0
Is a strong and decisive leader	56	57	−1
Is honest and trustworthy	33	35	−2
Stands up to special interest groups	46	52	−6
Is healthy enough to be president	60	77	−17

Source: Newport (2016)

One last point to consider before we dig more deeply into how the late-night comics treated Donald Trump the politician – how did the public view the candidate? As shown in Table 2.1, Democratic nominee Hillary Clinton bested him in many public evaluations during the 2016 campaign. In a September 2016 Gallup survey, for example, Trump had a 40-point deficit on the question of whether he had the experience to be president. He also ran double-digit deficits behind Clinton on whether respondents thought he would display good judgment in a crisis, manage the government effectively and was personally likeable. Trump's only double-digit advantage was on being healthy enough to be president. Taken together, these poll numbers speak to the uphill nature of the Trump campaign during the fall of 2016 and the magnitude of the public doubts concerning the future president as the election drew closer (Newport 2016).

While not good news for Trump, these survey results suggest a target-rich environment for the late-night comics: Trump's perceived inexperience, his gruff demeanor, his dishonesty, and his questionable judgment all offered ready opportunities for jokes.

After Trump's election, questions of who he was and how he would do as president became even more salient (Clement and Nakamura 2018). Fortunately, pollsters asked more detailed questions about public views of the new president focusing on why people said they liked or disliked Trump. In July 2017, for example, a Gallup survey compared a variety of public justifications for supporting or opposing the president. In this survey, 38 percent approved of Trump's presidency, while 56 disapproved (a margin that was surprisingly consistent throughout Trump's term in office). Roughly two-thirds (65 percent) of those who disapproved of Trump cited his personal characteristics, while only one out of six (16 percent) mentioned issues or policies (Newport 2017b). In contrast to the intense public focus on Trump's character, only 14 percent surveyed in 2009 mentioned Barack Obama's character and only 17 percent surveyed in 2001 mentioned character issues involving George W. Bush as reasons to oppose the job performance of those previous presidents (Newport 2017b). As we shall see in the remainder of this chapter, personal foibles and policy missteps are the bread and butter of political humor – and Trump always made sure humorists found the buffet well stocked.

Late-Night Humor and Presidential Campaign Comedy

Presidential campaigns are a time when even experienced politicians are at their most vulnerable. Senators and governors may enjoy exalted status because of their office and their reputations. But once they seek the presidency, even the most experienced and even-tempered official must engage in the desperate plea for votes that is the fate of presidential candidates. While the front-runners at the top of the pecking order may get the most media attention, they should expect the harshest media treatment of all (Farnsworth and Lichter 2011a).

The unpredictable and anxiety-filled maelstrom of presidential campaigns have long offered a rich buffet of material for late-night comedians. As political humor became a staple of late-night television talk shows, the comics increasingly aimed their fire at presidential campaign developments – if for no other reason than that there are more potential presidents to mock. For decades, presidents and presidential candidates have tried to navigate both the opportunity and the peril contained in political humor. Richard Nixon's appearance on "Laugh-In" during the 1968 presidential election was an early example of a candidate's efforts to improve a politician's image and perhaps bolster one's standing by appearing on evening comedy programs (Gould 1968; Lichter et al. 2015). In 1992, the year these entertainment venues came into their own as sources of political news, Ross Perot launched his independent candidacy

42 Political Humor and the Rise of Donald Trump the Politician

via appearances on *Larry King Live*, and Bill Clinton sought to win over younger voters by playing his saxophone on *Arsenio* (Davis and Owen 1998; Kolbert 1992). The late-night talk shows have remained prominent political platforms ever since.

Partly owing to Donald Trump's outsized personality and outrageous pronouncements, the talk show hosts had an unprecedented amount of material to work with during the 2016 campaign, and the line between campaign news and campaign humor became increasingly blurred. Taking a page from the cutting and often personality-oriented humor style of late night, Trump himself offered mocking asides about the personalities and physical appearances of his 2016 campaign rivals. These including attacks on Republican candidates Jeb Bush as "low-energy" and a "sad sack," Ted Cruz as "lying," "wacko" and a "loser," John Kasich as "pathetic" and "a total dud," Rand Paul as a "lightweight" who was "totally weird," and Marco Rubio as "little" and a "big loser" (Lee and Quealy 2019). Hillary Clinton, the 2016 Democratic presidential nominee (and the presumed front-runner throughout the nomination process) received particularly intense attacks from Donald Trump and his supporters. Trump mocked her as "crooked," prompting chants at his campaign rallies to "lock her up!" (Owen 2017).

Some scholars believe that late-night television talk shows, particularly *The Daily Show*, deserve to be considered as an alternative news source (Baym 2005). Late-night political humor has gained in attention and influence as people reduce their consumption of traditional media, such as daily newspapers and evening news shows on the broadcast television networks. This trend has been particularly pronounced among younger adults, many of whom turn to soft news as a major source of political information (Baumgartner and Morris 2011; Mitchell et al. 2014).

As a result, presidential candidates have increasingly treated these talk shows as a means of reaching potential voters who have little interest in traditional political news but are exposed to campaign information via infotainment programming. Candidates are trying to minimize the negative impact, or even seeking to "work the refs" of political comedy. By being willing to face grilling by the likes of Noah and Colbert, candidates can both build up credibility with viewers and perhaps even receive a softer treatment from the hosts themselves (Compton 2018).

How did these factors play out in the way late-night comedians treated the 2016 election? To find out, we first turn to the nominating phase of the presidential campaign. This part of the study includes 2,854 jokes the late-night comics made about political figures during the last four months of 2015 and the first four months of 2016. By the end of April, there was little doubt that the nominees would be Donald Trump and Hillary Clinton, despite increasingly desperate efforts by their remaining opponents to stem the tide. During this entire eight-month period, we tracked political jokes by Jimmy Fallon (*The Tonight Show* on NBC), Stephen Colbert (*The Late Show* on CBS), Jimmy Kimmel (*Jimmy Kimmel Live!* on ABC), and *The Daily Show*, the Comedy Central program with new host Trevor Noah. (We began tracking *The Daily Show* on September 28, when Noah formally took over from Jon Stewart.) The three broadcast network late-night shows consistently have had the largest audiences of any late-night talk shows airing more than once a week, while *The Daily Show* has been especially popular with young adults. We tracked both the traditional joke formats, the "one-liners," and the more extensive lead-in humor more commonly employed on Comedy Central's *The Daily Show*.

We then turn to the topics of late-night humor directed at the two major party nominees, extending the period of analysis through the general election. Specifically, we examined the treatment of Donald Trump and Hillary Clinton across more than a year of campaign discourse, starting on September 1, 2015, and ending on November 11, 2016, a few days after Election Day. (This slight extension past Election Day to the end of the week allowed us to capture the comedians' initial reactions to Trump's unexpected victory on November 8.)

Thus, we were able to compare the eventual party nominees against the larger landscape of their own party's contenders, and then against each other after they secured their nominations. The CMPA coded over 3,000 jokes about Clinton and Trump during the 2016 campaign cycle, analyzing each one for its policy, political, and/or personal content. (Many jokes covered more than one issue area.) College students, trained by senior staff, conducted the coding. Training continued until the coders attained

TABLE 2.2 Top Late-Night Joke Targets, 2015–2016 Nomination Campaign Cycle

Late 2015	*Jokes*	*Percentage*
1. Donald Trump	518	26.7%
2. Hillary Clinton	199	10.2%
3. Jeb Bush	146	7.5%
3. Ben Carson	142	7.3%
5. Bernie Sanders	97	5.0%
6. Barack Obama	77	4.0%
7. Chris Christie	49	2.5%
8. Ted Cruz	35	1.8%
9. Marco Rubio	29	1.5%
10. Carly Fiorina	23	1.2%
10. (tie) Bobby Jindal	23	1.2%

44 Political Humor and the Rise of Donald Trump the Politician

at least 80 percent reliability ratings. Videos of all relevant materials were examined rather than transcripts or captions, which can miss visual cues for punchlines. We also extend this analysis of political humor in a more qualitative dimension throughout the chapter, examining the content of a variety of once-a-week comedy programs during 2016 and 2017.

Political Humor and the 2016 Campaign

During the eight-month presidential nomination period examined here, presidential candidates dominated late-night humor. As shown in Table 2.2, during both late 2015 and early 2016, Donald Trump was the target of the late-night comedians' zingers aimed at politicians more than one time out of four. Hillary Clinton was second during late 2015 and fourth in early 2016. Bernie Sanders was second during early 2016, after ranking fifth during the final months of 2015. Ted Cruz was third during early 2016, a significant increase from his eighth-place finish during late 2015. Nine of the top ten political figures targeted in late 2015 were candidates for president. The one exception was President Obama, who ranked sixth. Obama also ranked sixth in the early 2016 rankings, and once again was the only name on the top ten list who was not a candidate for president during 2016.

Table 2.3 shows the late-night joke totals during the first four months of 2016, when the state-by-state nomination campaigns took place in earnest. Once again candidate jokes dominated, with 78 percent of the political jokes focusing on the presidential field. The results were very similar for the four comics during these four months, with candidates being the subject of the jokes between 76 percent and 79 percent of the time. [Further details on the late 2015 jokes can be found in Farnsworth and Lichter (2020)].

TABLE 2.3 Candidate Late-Night Joke Analysis, Early 2016

	Total Candidate Jokes									
	January		*February*		*March*		*April*		*Total*	
	# of Jokes	*%*	*# of Jokes*	*%*	*# of Jokes*	*%*	*# of Jokes*	*%*	*# of Jokes*	*%*
Fallon	118	77%	116	88%	106	72%	97	78%	437	78%
Colbert	104	84%	89	86%	63	63%	48	66%	304	76%
Kimmel	58	87%	89	78%	104	73	58	84%	309	79%
Noah	91	81%	92	89%	95	66%	89	82%	367	79%
Total	371	82%	386	85%	368	69%	292	78%	1417	78%

Of the 1,417 political jokes offered during those first four months of 2016, 1,036 (73 percent) were directed at the Republican field. During this four-month period, Noah's show devoted 64 percent of all jokes to Republicans, the highest level, and Fallon's show had the lowest percentage, with 53 percent of the jokes targeting Republicans. No more than one-quarter of the jokes were directed at the entire Democratic presidential field, with a high of 25 percent by Fallon and a low of 13 percent on *The Daily Show*. During all four months of early 2016, Trump consistently finished first, always well ahead of the pack.

Table 2.4 shows a detailed comparison of the humor directed at the two major party nominees during the general election phase of the campaign. Stephen Colbert told the most political jokes during the general election study period (from the start of the first major party convention on July 18 through November 11, a few days after the election). The pattern for three of the four late-night comics examined was consistent: 81 percent of Colbert's jokes focused on Trump, as compared to 80 percent of Noah's and 78 percent of Kimmel's. Fallon's famous head-rubbing and otherwise congenial September interview with Trump faced criticism for not being more critical (Merry 2016), and the data here show that Trump was treated with less hostility on *The Tonight Show* than on the offerings of the other networks. But even on Fallon's show, Trump was still the subject of far more ridicule than Clinton (64 percent versus 36 percent).

In addition to *whom* the comedians were joking about, we examined *what* they were joking about. Table 2.5 divides the jokes into three subject areas: policy content, nonsubstantive political content (such as political strategy and the horse race), and personal matters (such as the candidates' character and personality traits). We examined the jokes during three separate segments of the campaign: before the Iowa Caucus (September 1, 2015 through January 31, 2016), from the start of the nomination

TABLE 2.4 General Election Joke Totals, 2016

	Trump		Clinton		Total
	# of jokes	%	# of jokes	%	
Fallon	180	64%	101	36	281
Colbert	284	81%	65	19%	349
Kimmel	176	78%	50	22%	
Noah	199	80%	51	20%	
Total	**836**	**76%**	**267**	**24%**	**1103**

Note: Jokes were aired from the start of the first major party convention through the election, from 7/18/16 to 11/11/16.

Source: CMPA

46 Political Humor and the Rise of Donald Trump the Politician

TABLE 2.5 Topic Areas of Presidential Candidate Jokes, 2015–2016

	Before the Iowa Caucus (9/1/15 through 1/31/16)							
	All Jokes	*Policy*		*Politics*		*Personal*	
		# of jokes	*%*	*# of jokes*	*%*	*# of jokes*	*%*
Trump	672	58	9%	161	24%	605	90%
Clinton	161	9	6%	66	41%	150	93%
Total	833	67	8%	227	27%	755	91%

contests up to the start of the first nominating convention (February 1 through July 17, 2016) and from the start of the nomination conventions through the election and a few days beyond (July 18 through November 11, 2016). For both candidates during all three periods, personal matters dominated the humor: more than four out of every five jokes included some material regarding character, personality, or other personal traits, including 88 percent of the jokes focusing on Trump and 86 percent of those focusing on Clinton. Many of those jokes also focused on political calculations and the horse race, particularly in the late summer and fall, when 65 percent of jokes relating to Trump and 71 percent of the jokes relating to Clinton included references to political calculations. Political matters were notably less prominent in the preseason campaign jokes, referenced in only 24 percent of Trump's jokes and 41 percent of Clinton's.

Few jokes offered policy content: not once during those three periods did the frequency of jokes that focused on policy exceed one out of five. This is not particularly surprising (Niven, Lichter and Amundson 2003). One might expect the late-night comics to focus on personalities – human foibles are often rich veins for humor – and perhaps never more so with the larger-than-life personalities on the ballot in 2016. Even so, greater policy content in the jokes would provide more information for the surprisingly large number of voters who are using the late-night comedy shows as a source of campaign information (Baumgartner and Morris 2011).

The extent to which ongoing events shape the trajectory of humor is shown in Box 2.1, which offers some of the greatest hits of the late-night presidential campaign humor in 2016. While these selected jokes cannot convey the complete range of topics that shaped post-prime time snark, they demonstrate how closely aligned the day's headlines and the topics of late-night humor can be. (The jokes selected here are ones that would have enough staying power to retain some interest when appearing in print years later).

BOX 2.1 JOKES ABOUT CANDIDATE TRUMP, 2016

Character

Trump had some problems with the truth [at the previous debate]. Apparently, Trump made more than 34 comments that were either lies or misstatements. Clinton was tagged with four. No surprise. Before the debate, *Politico* analyzed a week's worth of Trump speeches and found that "Trump averaged about one falsehood every three minutes and 15 seconds." Which is damning. Though, on the plus side, you can use Trump's lies to tell if your microwave popcorn is done.

(Stephen Colbert, September 27, 2016)

Donald Trump, he spent the weekend campaigning and complaining. He's been cam-plaining, that is what he does. Tweeting up a storm how the election is rigged by the dishonest media and he's right. You can tell the media is rigged against Donald Trump because they keep putting microphones in front of him.

(Jimmy Kimmel, October 17, 2016)

[In reference to the Access Hollywood tape] Trump has broken almost every trick in the bag of scumbaggery. Trump's scandals now are like when the first black guy joined white sports, people were, like, I had no idea that was possible.

Trevor Noah, October 10, 2016

International Politics

Meanwhile, Vladimir Putin is shown on the cover of this week's *Time* magazine wearing an American "I voted" sticker. When Vladimir Putin saw the cover, he said, "It's funny because it's true."

(Jimmy Fallon, October 3, 2016)

Did you see there's a memo from a veteran spy that says Vladimir Putin has been supporting Donald Trump for five years. After hearing this, Trump said: [Trump impression] Oh my God, I forgot it was our anniversary. What do you get for five? Is it crystal? I hope it's not China.

(Jimmy Fallon, November 1, 2016)

The last 24 hours of Donald Trump has been an emotional roller coaster. You must be this crazy to ride. First, he was in Mexico, looking for an ally.

48 Political Humor and the Rise of Donald Trump the Politician

[Trump quote] "There are many improvements that could be made that would make both Mexico and the U.S. stronger and keep industry in our hemisphere."

That's not softening. Trump has always called for a wall between the hemispheres – and he will make the oceans pay for it.

(Stephen Colbert, September 1, 2016)

Trump Campaign

In North Carolina yesterday, a fight broke out at a Trump campaign rally. Either that or a Trump campaign rally broke out in a fight. I don't know which came first. A Trump supporter grabbed a protester by the neck and tried to hit him in the face. Things got so violent some people thought they were at a taping of *Dancing with the Stars*.

(Jimmy Kimmel, September 13, 2016)

I don't have to tell you folks that Donald Trump's not doing very well with African American voters. I especially don't have to tell you folks over there. Yesterday, at a rally in North Carolina, he once again brought the black community the message of hope that all is hopeless.

[Trump quote] "They are in the worst shape than ever, ever, ever."

For one thing, Donald Trump might become president.

(Stephen Colbert, September 21, 2016)

Box 2.1 includes observations that Trump was not honest (Colbert), not very smart (Colbert again), or that he was just a horrible person (Noah). These lines of commentary reflect the character-oriented conversation that was a key part of the political discourse during 2016, and topics that surveys showed were a key measure of evaluation of Donald Trump. While critics attacked Jimmy Fallon for not being hard enough on Donald Trump – in part a response to his hair-tousling interview that featured softball questions – Fallon was particularly effective in drawing attention to Russian President Putin's connection to the Trump campaign.

One unusual development during the 2016 campaign was the unruliness of the Trump campaign rallies. Trump himself campaigned as a highly divisive figure, attacking first his fellow Republicans and then Hillary Clinton with a venom that was unusually potent. While past candidates often said their rivals had bad policy ideas, rarely did they suggest their rivals were evil people or that they belonged in jail. In 2008, for example, Republican presidential nominee John McCain shut down a questioner at one of his town halls who vilified Barack Obama, saying that his opponent was a decent man (Ceaser et al. 2009). To be sure, McCain would never have permitted "lock him up" anti-Obama chants at his campaign rallies.

The exceptional level of anger expressed by Trump campaign supporters drew considerable attention from the comics as well as the mass media. Jimmy Kimmel drew attention to the violence at and around Trump rallies by wondering whether a fight broke out at a campaign rally, or a campaign rally broke out at a fight.

The Weekly Humor Programs and the 2016 Presidential Campaign

Saturday Night Live

Our discussion of how the late-night weekly comedy programs addressed the 2016 presidential campaign begins with *Saturday Night Live* (*SNL*), a show with a long tradition of political satire. Since the program's inception in 1975, its writers have sought to make light of the prevailing political issues of the time, with an ever-changing and talented cast bringing political figures to life in an unflattering and caricatured manner.

Several distinct circumstances set *SNL*'s coverage of Donald Trump apart from other programs. For instance, a notable casting change in early October 2016 marked a shift in the show's portrayal of Trump's candidacy. *SNL*'s mockery of Trump was initially more even-handed and less severe with Darrell Hammond's imitation of Trump than would be the case after Alec Baldwin took over the role. The program features various sketches, musical guests, and recurring skits, only a select few of which concern political matters. Of these segments, *SNL*'s "Cold Open" and "Weekend Update" most frequently dealt with contemporary politics during the 2016 campaign. Donald Trump was brought up sporadically in the former, as the sketch's format only allowed for quick one-liners. Far more regularly, Trump was profiled in "Cold Open," which allowed the show to offer extensive critiques several minutes in length.

Sketches featuring Trump in early 2016 were more disposed to criticize his supporters rather than him directly, including Trump endorser Sarah Palin, who was previously mocked by the show during her 2008 vice presidential campaign (*SNL* 2016a). Similarly, the *SNL* caricature of Trump supporter Scottie Nell Hughes, then a paid commentator on CNN, portrayed her as a ditsy pundit who offered absurd rationalizations of Trump's missteps (*SNL* 2016c).

The show also sought to make light of the casual racism that has characterized some members of Trump's base. In a mock political ad

50 Political Humor and the Rise of Donald Trump the Politician

for Trump, a handful of different "real Americans" contest the media's negative perception of Donald Trump and explain why they are voting for him. Each person appears to be engaging in menial, everyday activities, but it is revealed over the course of the ad that things are not quite what they seem. One person getting dressed later dons Nazi paraphernalia; another is ironing her Klansman robes. A third, initially framed as a painter, is writing "white power" on a house (*SNL* 2016b). The ad closes with the phrase, "racists for Donald Trump." Likewise, a sketch featuring Michael Che involves a spoof of a then-popular mobile game – in this version people attempted to catch "the rarest creature of them all," minorities at the Republican National Convention (*SNL* 2016d).

From the start, Alec Baldwin portrayed Donald Trump with mocking contempt (*SNL* 2016f). Even Baldwin's Trumpian accent was taken to a greater extent than that of Darrell Hammond. As the year progressed, the show began to rely more on direct personal insults, rather than mocking Trump through his supporters. In a faux presidential debate, Baldwin's Trump repeatedly refers to the African American moderator as "jazz man," speaking to Trump's alleged tone deafness and insensitivity regarding racial matters (*SNL* 2016e).

Even when dealing with the postelection 2016 reality of a Trump presidency, *SNL* went for the jugular. If anything, the show's writers took even greater pleasure in presenting the president-elect as moronic and childish. From November 2016 through the end of the year, Trump was depicted as stumbling from one blunder to the next as he prepared for life in the Oval Office. His lack of preparation for the presidency and his perceived low intelligence were targeted in one such sketch, where after discussing strategy with the Joint Chiefs of Staff, a concerned Trump, not knowing what ISIS is, asks Siri: "How do I kill ISIS?" (*SNL* 2016g). He was also shown delegating all tasks to his underlings and on one occasion even asking if he could be president just three days a week (*SNL* 2016h). *SNL* also began to insinuate that the president-elect was beholden to Vladimir Putin in some way, as allegations began to mount that the Trump campaign conspired with Russia to harm the Clinton campaign. In the program's 2016 Christmas special, Putin came down Trump's chimney as if he were Santa to express his overwhelming delight that "the best candidate, the smartest candidate, the Manchurian candidate" will soon be president (*SNL* 2016g).

Full Frontal with Samantha Bee

In keeping with the other comedy programs discussed here, the TBS show *Full Frontal with Samantha Bee* found ample material in covering the tumult of the Trump campaign. Bee brought to the table her own abrasive, crass brand of humor that stands in stark contrast to the situation-based *SNL*. She is by her own admission an unabashed liberal, and rarely held back in her criticisms of Donald Trump. Far more than *SNL* and *Last Week Tonight* (*LWT*), Bee was prone to jest in solidarity with her like-minded audience when confronted with the threats posed by Trump's candidacy.

Following the shock of the November 2016 election, she underscored the uptick in instances of intimidation and harassment of minority groups (*FF* 2016i). Indeed, much of her show's content considered the human impact of Trump's incendiary rhetoric throughout 2016 (FF 2016d). This unique agenda serves to build Bee's rapport with her liberal audience and gives her work a personal touch that endears her to like-minded consumers of late-night political humor. Additionally, her joining of vulgarity and news makes for unexpectedly pointed political commentary, as when she described the rise of Trump following his nomination by the Republican Party. "Trump isn't desecrating the Republican Party," she explained, "he's just peeling back the glossy exterior to reveal the hideous symbiont [i.e. the racist wing of the GOP] that has been lurking there for decades" (*FF* 2016a).

Samantha Bee's treatment of the Trump campaign was not simply limited to the man himself. In presenting unflattering profiles of some of the names touted for cabinet positions in the new administration following Trump's victory, Bee associated their various shortcomings with the man elected to the White House. She labeled this group of people a "parade of misfits, deplorables, zealots, and extremists" (*FF* 2016h).

Full Frontal is often interspersed with different types of segments, such as interviews, field pieces, and lengthy examinations of different news stories, providing several different avenues to vilify Trump supporters. One particularly humorous segment was a profile on "Latinos for Trump" founder Marco Gutierrez, known as the "taco truck guy." The piece repeatedly highlights what Bee sees as the absurdity and hypocrisy of Gutierrez's views, describing him as an "anti-Mexican immigrant Mexican immigrant" (*FF* 2016c). Samantha Bee was also prone to draw attention to the influx of white nationalist rhetoric into U.S. political discourse and the threat it poses to minorities, by extension disparaging Trump for embracing this aspect of the American electorate and his refusal to disavow white supremacy (*FF* 2016g).

Full Frontal's humor was heavily insult-based when covering Donald Trump's candidacy. Everything was fair game, from his physical appearance to his personality. It was not uncommon for Samantha Bee to intersperse her show with quick jabs at the so-called "orange supremacist at the top of the (Republican) ticket" (*FF* 2016a). After the election, Bee compared the

52 Political Humor and the Rise of Donald Trump the Politician

surprising outcome to a nation hacking up "a marmalade hairball with the whole world watching" (*FF* 2016e).

Bee was also prone to framing Donald Trump as childish and unintelligent. For instance, she repeatedly poked fun at how the GOP was tearing itself apart because it nominated a "sociopathic 70-year-old toddler" (*FF* 2016b), and even ran a mock investigative journalism piece where she suggested that Trump could not read (*FF* 2016d). She merged political humor with political commentary perhaps more than any other late-night comedian did. This framing became especially pertinent after Trump was actually elected president and Bee offered a window into the dysfunction about to consume the White House (*FF* 2016f).

Bee also bemoaned what she saw as Trump's willingness to tell whatever lies were necessary to serve his purposes, exclaiming that "one of the major questions being debated in our country today is whether it's okay for the president to lie his f**king face off 24 hours a day" (*FF* 2016j). Overall, Bee's postelection humor was centered on commiserating with her audience and underscoring how unconventional the Trump presidency was.

Last Week Tonight with John Oliver

Of the weekly comedy programs considered here, HBO's *Last Week Tonight with John Oliver* most closely resembles a traditional newscast. Oliver spends large portions of the show looking into a particular story or subject in some depth, rather than flitting from joke to joke as is the case with *SNL* and *Full Frontal*. *LWT* is certainly the most professionally argued of the three, with Oliver's lengthy policy-oriented segments often supplemented by real data. Oliver takes a more even-handed approach than do some other purveyors of late-night humor and is somewhat less overt in displaying his political persuasions. His insights, no matter how comically framed, are often designed to resemble the weight of traditional journalism rather than being simple throwaway lines.

Such was the case when Oliver tried to parse through Trump's immunity to the adverse effects of saying outrageous things on the campaign trail. During the campaign, Oliver observed, Trump had made not one but thousands of ludicrous statements, each of which would have been sufficient to disqualify him, yet every subsequent statement served to "blunt the effects of the others" (*LWT* 2016e). Oliver repeatedly sought to expose Donald Trump as a fraud and an unabashed racist, especially early in the year. "Donald Trump," he explained, "can seem appealing until you take a closer look; much like the lunch buffet at a strip club, or the NFL, or having a pet chimpanzee" (*LWT* 2016a). Oliver presented Trump's "border wall" proposal as being firmly motivated by racism and xenophobia, and he also sifted through the math behind the concept, concluding that it was extremely costly and ineffective in dealing with the immigration issues it was purported to fix (*LWT* 2016b).

Oliver also frequently outlined the various scandals and past mishaps that were a regular feature of Trump's candidacy. There was an entire segment devoted to detailing and weighing the different scandals that plagued both the Trump and Clinton campaigns. He asserted that the scandals surrounding Clinton were irritating rather than nefarious, and that "not being as bad as Trump [was] a low bar to clear" (*LWT* 2016f). Furthermore, in explaining to his audience the Trump Organization's history of vexatious litigation, Oliver listed every single cable television show featuring lawyers as major characters. The tally of the combined episodes of each show still didn't match the number of lawsuits the Trump organization filed in the last decade alone, prompting Oliver to exclaim, "Trump's lawsuits exceed the limits of the f*cking genre" (*LWT* 2016h).

Overall, the way in which John Oliver poked fun at Donald Trump involved less buildup and fewer drawn-out jokes. His style involved more frequent one-liner jokes designed to insult, ranging from making fun of Trump's appearance to attacking his disposition and his self-delusion (*LWT* 2016c). He too joked about Trump's skin tone, when he posed the question "where exactly are you from, because you look like you came out of the clogged drain at a Wonka factory" (*LWT* 2016h). Oliver also took a jab at Trump's philandering past when he said that "anything Trump's tiny fingers touch turns into an ex-wife or an abandoned casino" (*LWT* 2016h).

Most frequently, John Oliver harped on Trump's personality and psychology. He repeatedly framed Trump as a bigot, an egomaniac, and an all-around bad person, even going so far as to suggest he was in league with the devil. After the shock of the 2016 election, Oliver played a clip of reporters listing the Trump agenda, then interjecting: "it sounds like you are reading the to-do list on Satan's refrigerator, which of course Satan no longer needs now that hell has frozen over" (*LWT* 2016g). In the same vein, Oliver poked fun of Trump's use of the hit R.E.M. song "It's the End of the World" as a lead-in to a speech he gave on the Iran nuclear deal. "That is just too perfect," Oliver scoffed, "Trump may as well have been riding out on stage with the three other horsemen of the apocalypse" (*LWT* 2016d).

Taken together, it seems likely that the weekly programs were, if anything, even more anti-Trump than the weeknight shows in their comic material. Samantha Bee certainly made no bones about her detestation of Trump, and the formats of *SNL* (sketch comedy) and

54 Political Humor and the Rise of Donald Trump the Politician

Last Week Tonight (program length focus on a single topic) favored a focus on only one politician a night, and that politician was usually Donald Trump. There may also be a structural element involved. Three of the four weeknight shows we examined aired on broadcast television networks, which still require larger and more diverse audiences than cable programs in order to survive. You need higher ratings to avoid cancellation on CBS than you do on TBS. And HBO's audience of subscribers frees politically oriented hosts like John Oliver (and Bill Maher) from worrying about advertisers. Of course, *SNL* airs on NBC, but its political sketches are just one piece in a diverse mix of comedy sketches. All in all, the weekly talk shows we examined add to the overall impression that late-night comedy during the 2016 campaign was an anti-Trump zone.

How POTUS Played on Late Night, 2017

Once a new president takes office, comedians can focus their attention on a single political figure. No longer are they looking at the two major party nominees and the occasionally colorful running mate, not to mention the cast of characters who sought the presidential nomination at the start of an election year. The transition from campaigning to governing does not mean the laughs stop coming; it means the laughs start focusing on the victorious candidate and his plans for the new administration. In the case of the Trump, his chaotic campaign and chaotic presidency provided a great deal of material to consider (Parker 2016, 2018).

Once in office, presidents pay considerable attention to the late-night humorists who are paying so much attention to them. Of course, few presidents have devoted as much energy to attacking the late-night comics as did former President Trump. During his time as a candidate and as president, he routinely sought to reshape the critical late-night narrative by engaging in Twitter feuds with late-night comics on Twitter. Alec Baldwin, who impersonated Trump on *Saturday Night Live*, became a particular *bête noir* (Borchers 2017a, 2017b; Itzkoff 2018). Given these dustups, Trump drew more attention to his comedic critics than they could ever produce on their own. Even though Trump's own mocking, insulting style is not unlike the cutting barbs of late-night comedy, he just cannot let things go. After one particularly irritating week, for example, Trump said that Alec Baldwin's Trump imitation "stinks" and "just can't get any worse" (Lee and Quealy 2019).

Trump is hardly the first president to try to redirect late-night humor to his advantage, but his behavior offers a powerful contrast with the way his predecessors reacted to comedic mocking. During his time in office, President Obama focused on shaping the news narrative by interacting with comedians, even willingly participating in efforts to generate laughs on his own. He famously appeared on *The Tonight Show* to "slow-jam" the news with Jimmy Fallon, and he sat down on *Between Two Ferns* to trade insults with comedian Zach Galifianakis before promoting greater youth enrollment in the Obama health care program (Farnsworth 2018; Hopper 2017; Martinelli 2016; Scacco and Coe 2016).

Of course, Obama had a big advantage on these programs. His politics more closely aligned with those of his hosts than did the views of recent Republican presidents. The subject of his slow jam was student loans, and the audience was a highly receptive group of University of North Carolina students. In retrospect, the sketch foreshadowed the much-criticized mutual admiration that Trump shared with certain Fox News commentators during his presidency.

Nonetheless, this rapport with humorists was not unique to Obama. In 1975, during the first season of *Saturday Night Live*, President Gerald Ford tripped and stumbled down the stairs when disembarking from Air Force One. The TV networks showed the event and rising young *SNL* comedian Chevy Chase repeatedly parodied Ford's stumble as a pratfall. Ford admitted to watching the show and even being entertained by it. He later reflected, "On occasion, I winced. But, on the other hand, Betty and I used to watch *Saturday Night Live* and enjoyed it. Presidents are sitting ducks, and you might as well sit back and enjoy it" (quoted in Lichter et al. 2015: 46). Three presidencies later, George H.W. Bush even invited Dana Carvey, his *SNL* impersonator, to a holiday party for the White House staff. That day, the two shared the lectern and the laughs to the delight of Bush's team, which a few weeks earlier had lost the 1992 presidential election (Rosenwald 2018).

In some ways, late-night humor is more consequential for presidencies than for presidential candidates. While elections determine who gains power, the presidency determines how they use (or abuse) it. In addition, the winner brings with him (so far) a completely new cast of characters, from appointees to family members, as well as a new set of issues and policies.

To understand how this running dramedy played out in late-night comedy routines during 2017, we coded the 6,337 late-night political jokes by Kimmel, Fallon, Colbert, and Noah that aired from January 23 (the Monday after Inauguration Day) to December 31, 2017. Once again, we also compared these findings to a qualitative study of the three weekly comedy shows we examined in the previous section of the chapter.

56 Political Humor and the Rise of Donald Trump the Politician

The Nightly Humor Programs, 2017

The first year of Trump's presidency generated consistently negative public approval numbers, with much of the public frustration with Trump continuing to focus on matters of character (Newport 2017b). Against that backdrop of public negativity, it should come as no surprise that Donald Trump dominated the late-night humor discourse during his first year as president (Farnsworth and Lichter 2018).

Before delving into the data, it is important to note the changing role that late-night hosts sometimes claimed for themselves during the Trump presidency. For decades, these shows have not offered much policy content beyond some topical jokes in the opening ten minutes or so of the program. Most of the airtime on these programs involved chats with celebrities and with the occasional political figure, but even then, the content generally remained light. While the number of jokes, and the harshness of the topics, increased considerably over the years, there remained little deep discussion of policy matters, perhaps because producers believed that getting into policy specifics in a late-night program would drive away viewers seeking a little rest and relaxation before bed.

Then along came Jimmy Kimmel and Republican efforts to repeal the Affordable Care Act. On September 19, 2017, in his opening monologue for ABC's "Jimmy Kimmel Live!" Kimmel departed from the usual string of jokes about celebrities, current events, and public affairs to issue a point-by-point criticism of health care insurance legislation pending in Congress. He concluded by exhorting his studio and television audience to lobby against the legislation: "So if this bill isn't good enough for you, call your congressperson." *Politico* later calculated that Kimmel devoted 24 minutes of airtime in three nights to defeating the Republican bill designed to repeal the Obama health care law (Diamond 2017).

Heard in its entirety, Kimmel's commentary sounds considerably more like parts of a stump speech than a laugh fest. In any event, Kimmel's engagement with health care legislation illustrates the extent to which the juncture of news and entertainment in politics can quickly expand to encompass the juncture of political advocacy and entertainment. In fact, a *Newsweek* story asserted that Kimmel "has proved to be the nation's most effective critic of the Graham-Cassidy bill that was designed to repeal and replace the Affordable Care Act" (Nazaryan 2017).

Neither Johnny Carson nor Jay Leno would ever have made such a personal appeal regarding such a divisive political issue, nor would either have discussed it in the deeply personal terms Kimmel employed. Kimmel's public policy activism during the Trump years also focused on exhortations regarding school gun violence after the mass shootings in Las Vegas and Parkland, Florida (Garber 2018). Media reports of Kimmel's policy influence in the health care debate are indicators of the communication techniques of agenda setting and priming, as Kimmel linked his own infant son's need for expensive heart surgery to such insurance problems as coverage of preexisting conditions and lifetime caps on coverage (Farnsworth and Lichter 2020).

The way the comics treated Trump during his first year as president fed into a media narrative about the politicization of late-night entertainment, in particular, the frequent focus of comedians on Donald Trump and his administration. For his part, Trump blasted talk show hosts with all the fervor that he applies to denouncing the news media, demanding equal time to balance the comedians' "one-sided" treatment of his administration (Associated Press 2017). As Bill Carter, a former *New York Times* reporter of late-night entertainment, put it, "There's no example of any kind of sustained attack like this on a politician ... There's a horde of writers writing jokes about Donald Trump every single night" (quoted in Rutenberg 2017).

A generation ago, late-night hosts did not want to go too far and risk offending Middle America. Now the tables have turned. These days, these hosts face criticism, both (from conservatives) for being too partisan in their remarks and (from liberals) for not being partisan enough. This happened to Jimmy Fallon during the 2016 general election, after he had Trump as a guest and did a routine that culminated with him tousling Trump's hair. After a deluge of articles and social media posts that accused him of "normalizing" Trump, a contrite Fallon insisted that he had intended not to "humanize" his guest but to "minimize" him, saying that people "have a right to be mad" at his 2016 interview with Trump (quoted in Andrews 2017). Despite the public apology, Fallon's ratings suffered following his congenial treatment of Trump (Kolbin 2017).

Of course, Trump is the latest in a long line of media bashers on the right side of the political spectrum. Republicans and conservatives, for whom demonizing the "liberal news media" is a long-standing staple of their rhetorical repertoire, have long complained about its counterpart among Hollywood liberals, including the hosts of late-night talk shows (Dagnes 2012). But the criticisms prior to 2016 were mostly intermittent and episodic, in contrast to the steady drumbeat of Trump's attacks on the late-night comics during the 2016 campaign and the presidency that followed (Farnsworth and Lichter 2020).

In fact, our content analysis suggests that, like the news media, late-night comedy during 2017 threatened to feature all Trump, all the time. Table 2.6 shows Trump was the focus of almost half of all political jokes (3,128 out of 6,337, or 49 percent) on the top four late-night programs during his first year in office. Trump's staggering total of jokes exceeded the rest of the top 20 joke targets combined. Finishing a very distant second

58 Political Humor and the Rise of Donald Trump the Politician

TABLE 2.6 Leading Targets of Late-Night Humor, 2017

Donald Trump	3,128
Policy Issues	208
Trump Administration*	166
Sean Spicer	162
Roy Moore	160
Donald Trump Jr.	108
Congressional Republicans*	106
Jeff Sessions	104
Melania Trump	96
Mike Pence	80
Anthony Scaramucci	73
Hillary Clinton	71
Steve Bannon	69
Kellyanne Conway	58
Ted Cruz	50
Vladimir Putin	49
Barack Obama	48
Jared Kushner	43
Congress*	41
James Comey	40
Michael Flynn	39
Eric Trump	37
Paul Ryan	36
Betsy DeVos	35
Voters	35
Paul Manafort	35
Rex Tillerson	34
Kim Jong-un	34
Ivanka Trump	31
Mitch McConnell	30

Note: Only individuals and institutions that were the subject of at least 30 jokes are included here.

* General categories are used for jokes that focus on the institution rather than a specific individual. Jokes that name individuals are coded as jokes directed at that individual.

N = 6,337. Totals include late-night jokes aired during January 23–December 31, 2017 on *Jimmy Kimmel Live*, *The Daily Show with Trevor Noah*, *The Late Show with Stephen Colbert*, and *The Tonight Show with Jimmy Fallon*

was a cluster of policy issues, which attracted a combined 208 jokes. The Trump administration collectively generated 166 jokes. The individual who garnered the most laughs after Trump was his former Press Secretary Sean Spicer, who was the subject of 162 jokes on the four programs.

Only eight individuals or topics were the subject of more than 100 jokes during the year, and other than policy issues, and those eight included

Trump himself, members of the Trump family, and other Republican officeholders and candidates. In fifth place was Roy Moore, a Trump-endorsed Republican Senate candidate in Alabama who lost after allegations emerged about his interactions with teenage girls when he was in his 30s. Presidential son Donald Trump, Jr. took sixth place; First Lady Melania Trump ranked ninth. Attorney General Jeff Sessions ranked eighth, while Vice President Mike Pence ranked tenth.

Defeated presidential candidate Hillary Clinton was the top-rated Democrat, ranking 12th, behind Anthony Scaramucci, who briefly served as White House Communications Director, and just ahead of Steve Bannon, a top Trump political advisor. Former President Barack Obama was the second highest Democrat, ranking 17th with 48 jokes, just behind Russian President Vladimir Putin.

Critics have long faulted network television for focusing on the executive branch and providing relatively little attention to the other branches of government in its news reports (Farnsworth and Lichter 2006). Our data here reveal that late-night humor does little better in covering the range of governmental actors in Washington. For the current and potential members of the legislative branch, the most jokes (160) targeted defeated Senate candidate Roy Moore. Congressional Republicans in general ranked seventh with 106 jokes, while Republican Texas Senator Ted Cruz ranked 15th, with 50 jokes. Congress as a collective ranked 19th with 41 jokes, while House Speaker Paul Ryan (R-WI) and Senate Majority Leader Mitch McConnell (R-KY) were the subject of 36 and 30 jokes, respectively.

The judicial branch was even less likely to be in the sights of the late-night comics. Neil Gorsuch, nominated and confirmed to the Supreme Court during Trump's first year in office, was the leading member of the judicial branch in terms of late-night humor, ranking 35th with 23 jokes during 2017. No other member of SCOTUS ranked among the top 60 subjects of late-night humor. Since the justices as individuals generally receive news coverage only during their nominations, confirmations, and resignations, late-night comics probably find these largely unknown figures to be a poor source of humor for a mass audience.

On a monthly basis, Donald Trump once again dominated, finishing first in the humor sweepstakes during every single month of 2017, with at least double the joke totals of the second-place finisher every single month of his presidency that year (Farnsworth and Lichter 2020). Sean Spicer, Trump's first presidential press secretary, quickly became a key target of the comics. Scandalous behavior could also propel one higher in the ranking, as was the case for Trump-endorsed Senate candidate Roy Moore of Alabama. Statements from victims that Moore pursued teenagers for dates while in

60 Political Humor and the Rise of Donald Trump the Politician

his 30s made him the second-ranked source of humor in November and December of 2017, for example (Farnsworth and Lichter 2020).

Donald Trump also dominated the late-night jokes when each humorist is examined individually. As shown in Table 2.7, all four programs

TABLE 2.7 Leading Target Frequency by Program, 2017

	Kimmel	*Noah*	*Colbert*	*Fallon*	*Total*
Donald Trump	598 (54.5%)	689 (46.3%)	1,151 (46.3%)	690 (54.5%)	3,128
Issues	26	85	70	27	208
Trump Admin*	26	34	75	31	166
Sean Spicer	42	26	60	34	162
Roy Moore	38	32	71	19	160
Donald Trump Jr.	13	9	77	9	108
Congressional Rep*	7	35	55	9	106
Jeff Sessions	14	24	50	16	104
Melania Trump	31	17	14	34	96
Mike Pence	9	15	23	33	80
Anthony Scaramucci	4	9	39	21	73
Hillary Clinton	14	15	13	29	71
Steve Bannon	1	14	48	6	69
Kellyanne Conway	15	9	23	11	58
Ted Cruz	10	25	5	10	50
Vladimir Putin	9	7	12	21	49
Barack Obama	12	19	9	8	48
Jared Kushner	16	10	15	2	43
Congress*	5	11	16	9	41
James Comey	2	10	23	5	40
Michael Flynn	3	10	23	3	39
Eric Trump	2	12	13	10	37
Paul Ryan	0	18	11	7	36
Betsy DeVos	3	0	7	25	35
Paul Manafort	1	7	24	3	35
Voters*	6	15	10	4	35
Total	**1097**	**1487**	**2487**	**1266**	**6337**

Note: Only the subjects of at least 35 jokes are included.

* General categories are used for jokes that focus on the institution rather than a specific individual. Jokes that name individuals are coded at the individual level.

Totals include late-night jokes aired during January 23–December 31, 2017 on *Jimmy Kimmel Live*, *The Daily Show with Trevor Noah*, *The Late Show with Stephen Colbert*, and *The Tonight Show with Jimmy Fallon*.

provided at least eight times as many jokes about Trump as any other topic, institution, or individual during 2017.

Despite their general similarities, these are not four cookie-cutter late-night humor programs. Indeed, it is important to examine these programs as separate entities. For example, Jimmy Fallon has been seen as less critical of Trump than the other late-night hosts, particularly Stephen Colbert (Hartung 2017; Itzkoff 2017; Merry 2016; Poniewozik 2017), and different hosts have different orientations to political comedy, as we illustrate below.

In addition to telling more jokes overall and more jokes directed at Trump than his three leading competitors, Colbert has focused far more on the Trump family and the Trump governing team. His 75 jokes on the Trump administration were double the number of any one of the other three programs examined here, as were his 50 jokes on Attorney General Sessions. His 77 jokes on Donald Trump, Jr., far outpaced the other three hosts, with Kimmel's 13 jokes in second place. Colbert likewise found much mirth to share regarding White House political advisor Stephen Bannon, the subject of 48 jokes on his program, as compared to 14 jokes on *The Daily Show*.

Of course, other programs had other targets of particular interest. Trevor Noah regularly turned to Sen. Ted Cruz (R-TX), the source of 25 jokes on *The Daily Show*, which represented more than double the number of jokes told about that failed 2016 candidate when compared to each of the other three shows. Noah also offered more jokes about Obama than the other programs, perhaps because the other three hosts, who are white, might have been less comfortable joking about the first African American president. Noah's program also focused more on policy matters than did the other late-night programs.

For Fallon, who saw his ratings drop in response to what some viewers felt was a too favorable treatment of Trump during the 2016 campaign, spent 2017 offering more humor directed at former presidential candidate Hillary Clinton, Russian President Vladimir Putin, and Vice President Mike Pence than his nightly comedy competitors did. The continued Clinton attacks offered a way to retain some of *The Tonight Show* viewers who might not respond to the sharper treatment of Trump on Fallon's show during 2017.

The joke data suggest that Fallon was responding to audience pressures, as the percentage of political jokes he provided regarding Trump during 2017 accounted for 55 percent of his political jokes, a higher percentage than either Colbert or Noah, each of whom focused on Trump in 46 percent of their political jokes. Kimmel matched Fallon, with 55 percent of his political jokes aimed at the president during 2017. Colbert's sheer number of jokes about Trump dwarfed those told by the other three hosts, but

62 Political Humor and the Rise of Donald Trump the Politician

Fallon's total number of Trump jokes was almost identical to Noah's. Even so, Fallon's increasingly critical treatment of Trump jokes in 2017 may have had less of an impact on his ratings than his relatively cozy approach to Trump during the 2016 campaign, a matter that generated considerable media attention at the time. You only get one chance to make a first impression, and Fallon's more generous treatment of Trump during 2016 apparently reduced his audience share during these polarized times, and his shift in 2017 would not be noticed by those who had already stopped watching the program.

Kimmel, whose program received considerable attention during 2017 as he talked about health care in the context of his sick infant son (France 2017), did not emphasize policy that much in his jokes during Trump's first year in office. (Kimmel's emotional, personal, and lengthy discussion about his family's health crisis contained relatively little humorous content, and therefore was the source of few jokes here. The CMPA coding system did pick up the occasional zinger during Kimmel's emotional personal appeals, however.) Kimmel's 26 jokes relating to policy matters were far below the totals on Noah's and Colbert's programs during 2017.

Many of the jokes that focused on Trump and the Trump White House had significant policy dimensions, even though the main target of the humor was the president rather than the policy itself. Among joke topics identified in Table 2.8, all four humorists found Russia a more compelling policy matter for humor than any other issue, as that topic ranked first for each of the four comedians. Stephen Colbert, who had more policy-focused humor than the other three hosts did, joked about Russia as much as all three other hosts combined. (This topic included Russian interference in the 2016 elections and Trump's postelection coziness with Russia.) Colbert and Noah had notably more policy-oriented humor than did Kimmel and Fallon.

Once again, there were some significant differences in choices made by the different programs. While all four hosts joked about racism, Jimmy Fallon offered only three jokes, a fraction of those offered by the other three hosts. (That pattern of limited discussion of racial matters might connect with those viewers who appreciated Fallon's less contentious history with Trump as a presidential candidate). Noah focused more attention on the alt-right, the political movement that triggered a fatal clash in Charlottesville, Virginia during August 2017. That event promoted Trump to talk about "very fine people on both sides" of the riot there, one of Trump's more controversial presidential pronouncements during his first year in office (Blake 2019).

TABLE 2.8 Policy Topics by Program, 2017

Topic	Kimmel	Noah	Colbert	Fallon	Total
Russia	64	154	324	84	626
Sex	46	65	94	30	235
Health care	23	57	83	26	189
North Korea	36	9	40	14	99
Racism	23	13	35	3	74
Immigration	11	11	40	12	74
Taxes	3	22	19	15	59
Border wall	10	16	12	14	52
Climate change	4	19	10	6	39
Alt-Right	1	19	1	0	21
Budget	0	3	13	0	16
Election	3	4	5	0	12
Puerto Rico	0	0	9	0	9
Terrorism	0	6	2	0	8
Net neutrality	0	2	6	0	8
Marijuana	1	1	0	6	8
Opioids	3	3	0	0	6
Gun control	0	3	1	1	5
Grand Total	**230**	**413**	**701**	**214**	**1558**

Note: Only topics that were the subject of five or more jokes were included here.

N = 6,337. Totals include late-night jokes aired during January 23–December 31, 2017 on *Jimmy Kimmel Live*, *The Daily Show with Trevor Noah*, *The Late Show with Stephen Colbert*, and *The Tonight Show with Jimmy Fallon*.

Some of these comedic choices correspond to the policy issues of greatest public concern, as revealed in surveys taken at that time (Newport 2017a). Americans said then that their main policy concerns included health care and the budget, a difficult-to-explain topic that nevertheless generated a significant amount of political humor. While hunger, homelessness, and crime were issues of great public concern in the survey, these topics seem even less transferable to humor than budgetary matters.

But not all did. While it ranked first in terms of policy topics employed in political comedy during Trump's first year as president, Russia does not appear among the major concerns of voters in the 2017 Gallup survey (Newport 2017a). Rarely does one see much comedic attention to issues that do not have some connection to current public opinion or news coverage.

64 Political Humor and the Rise of Donald Trump the Politician

---

BOX 2.2 JOKES ABOUT PRESIDENT TRUMP, 2017
TRUMP CHARACTER

- To make sure Trump reads his daily briefings for this trip, sources say that for this trip, National Security Council officials have strategically included Trump's name in "as many paragraphs as we can because he keeps reading if he's mentioned." That is a true story. Apparently, the only thing that can overcome Trump's short attention span is his crippling narcissism. But, of course, if they want to explain that to him, they'll have to call it his crippling Trumpicism.

Stephen Colbert, May 19, 2017

- Good afternoon. Before the fake news media reports any more inaccuracies, the White House would like to clarify, Secretary of State Tillerson did not call the President a "moron." He also did not call him any of the following: idiot, bonehead, nincompoop, imbecile, empty jack-o-lantern, suntanned ham loaf, so stupid he got his hair stuck in a cotton candy machine and called it a hairstyle, dumb dumb, dumb [bleep], [bleep] for brains, or racist sweet potato. Thank you. We'll have an update on this tomorrow.

Jimmy Kimmel, October 4, 2017

- At a dinner last night, President Trump told Republican senators that if they didn't vote for the health care bill, they'd look like dopes. And he combed his neck hair over the top of his head and walked away with his tie dragging on the floor.

Jimmy Fallon, July 18, 2017

- Wow, guys. You see what's happened? Trump used to be the carefree rich guy, and now he and Obama have switched lives. It's like they got hit by lightning while peeing in the same fountain. Or maybe like Trump made a wish on a monkey's paw while he was being peed on. All I know is there was pee involved. That's all I'm saying.

Trevor Noah, February 7, 2017

- On Tuesday, Brooke Shields appeared on Andy Cohen's *Watch Andy Cohen Happen Live* and told this story about Donald Trump asking her out in the 1990s.

[Shields quote] "He called me right after he'd gotten a divorce, and he said, 'I really think we should date because you're America's sweetheart and I'm America's richest man, and the people would love it.'"

Really? That was his pickup line? No wonder he prefers women who speak English as a second language.

Stephen Colbert, October 6, 2017

- "Here [Trump] is on Howard Stern bragging about how he handled STDs in the New York dating scene":

[Interview quotes] Trump: "It is a dangerous world out there, it's scary, it's like Vietnam, sort of like –"

Stern: "It is, it's like your personal Vietnam, isn't it? You've said that many times."

Trump: "I feel like a great and very brave soldier."

I know it sounds bad, and it is, but he's right. Sex with Trump is like Vietnam. It's a bungled operation launched on false pretenses without a satisfying ending.

Stephen Colbert, October 23, 2017

Trump and Russia

- Trump is not worried about the testimony of Sally Yates or the testimony of former intelligence director James Clapper, tweeting: "Director Clapper reiterated what everybody, including the fake media, already knows – there is 'no evidence' of collusion with Russia and Trump." Um, Mr. President, a little tip: When you put "no evidence" in quotes, it really makes you seem "Innocent."

Stephen Colbert, May 9, 2017

- This is pretty big, though. Yesterday, White House officials said Russia targeted election systems in 21 states last year. Trump was furious. He said, "I paid for all 50."

Jimmy Fallon, June 22, 2017

Trump and Health Care

- While they've pulled the bill, Republicans say they're going to come back with something better. So, they're going to – what do you call it? – repeal and replace their bill. And there's a lot of blame to go around. In fact, today, *The New York Times* said Donald Trump "Faltered in his role as a closer." Yeah, usually, he's a great closer. Just look at his casinos.

Stephen Colbert, June 28, 2017

- Trump told reporters he was being unfairly judged because he's only been in office six months and people are expecting him to deliver a health care bill. And he has a point. I mean, where did anyone get the idea that passing health care was going to be easy?

Jimmy Kimmel, July 20, 2017

- For the last 24 hours, Donald Trump has been the President of busy town. This morning, he signed an executive order to get rid of some key provisions of Obamacare. For instance, the care part.

Stephen Colbert, October 12, 2017

Box 2.2 offers a sample of late-night presidential humor offered during 2017 regarding a range of topics, including many that related to Trump's character and his physical appearance. The jokes listed are not representative samples, but rather this selection provides a flavor of the some of the lines of mockery that humorists employed. Several of these clips are particularly harsh. For example, on October 4, 2017, Jimmy Kimmel used the debate over whether then-Secretary of State Rex Tillerson called Trump a "moron" as an opportunity to launch into a very intense list of all the other insults that could be lobbed at the president. The humorists also mocked the president's sexism and his narcissistic remark that trying to avoid sexually transmitted diseases in the New York City dating scene of his youth represented his own personal Vietnam.

Box 2.2 provides some policy-oriented jokes relating to three key subjects of presidential humor during 2017, including relations with Russia and North Korea. These Russia-related jokes, and many others not included in this list of barbs, presumed at least some members of the Trump team were guilty long before the Mueller investigation was completed – or even before Michael Flynn, a former general who served briefly as Trump's national security advisor, admitted to lying to the FBI regarding contacts with the Russians (Leonnig et al. 2017).

The Weekly Humor Programs

Like their daily humor program brethren, hosts of the weekly comedy programs found Trump to be a highly attractive target for their humor during 2017. A close reading of these three prominent once-a-week shows demonstrates that they generally offered quite similar material to the comedy shows examined earlier, which are broadcast four or five times a week.

One potential problem that weekly shows faced, particularly when compared to the nightly comics, was that the barrage of daily news often added to an immense amount of material deserving attention during the seven days between episodes. As a result of the news deluge, they had to boil down this immense amount of joke-worthy material with enough time to provide context and offer humorous content.

Saturday Night Live

We start our discussion of the 2017 content of the once-a-week programs with *Saturday Night Live*, the dean of weekly late-night political humor (Parkin 2018). By using Twitter to criticize Alec Baldwin's imitation of him as unfunny, Trump elevated the show's salience to contemporary political conversations (Waisanen 2018). As with the other weekly late-night shows, the rapid pace of the news cycle became a subject for some humor, such as when Colin Jost remarked, "I know I said this last week, but this week was crazy" (*SNL* 2017j). Some of the news stories covered by "Weekend Update" were President Trump's executive orders on immigration (*SNL* 2017c), Republican attempts to repeal and replace the Affordable Care Act (*SNL* 2017g), U.S. military strikes in Syria (*SNL* 2017h), developments in the various investigations of the Trump campaign (*SNL* 2017j), and relations with North Korea (*SNL* 2017i).

SNL's sketches, in contrast to the rapid-fire commentary of "Weekend Update," would sometimes nod at recent events but generally focused more on mocking the individuals involved in these news stories. News coverage was certainly not the purpose of these sketches. Rather, news stories framed the sketches. For example, when the U.S. Court of Appeals for the Ninth Circuit challenged the legality of President Trump's immigration executive order, *SNL* produced a sketch in which Trump, as portrayed by Alec Baldwin, challenged the appeals court ruling on the reality court show *The People's Court* (*SNL* 2017d). Another example is a sketch showing Trump making a surprise visit to the home of Trump's former campaign manager Paul Manafort, produced after the real-life Manafort was charged with a number of crimes by Special Counsel Robert Mueller (*SNL* 2017l).

68 Political Humor and the Rise of Donald Trump the Politician

Like *Full Frontal* and *Last Week Tonight*, *SNL* mostly relied on personal insults for its jokes about Trump and his administration. *SNL* continued to find plenty of humor in Trump's physical appearance. "Weekend Update," for example, joked about Trump's weight. When Trump ended his remarks on his executive orders on crime by saying, "A new era of justice begins, and it begins right now," the hosts of "Weekend Update" joked that he spent the next 20 minutes struggling to squeeze into a Batman costume (*SNL* 2017e). *SNL*'s sketches expanded on the mocking of Trump's physical appearance through Alec Baldwin's portrayal. Baldwin emphasized and exaggerated aspects of Trump's appearance as a form of mockery, squinting his eyes and pushing out his lips in extreme versions of Trump's facial expressions. Baldwin also mimicked Trump's hunched over posture, as well as his hand gestures.

As was the case on the other late-night shows, *SNL* sometimes framed Trump as a bigot, a misogynist, an egomaniac, and a fool. One sketch, entitled "Through Donald's Eyes," suggests that Trump's self-obsession and insecurity are so intense that they alter his perception of the world (*SNL* 2017f). The sketch shows a day in Trump's life through his eyes, beginning with Trump awakening and watching a Fox News anchor on TV saying "Huge, huge success. Fantastic. Victory. Landslide. Fox News" (*SNL* 2017f).

SNL's sketches also targeted numerous people surrounding Trump. Kate McKinnon portrayed Kellyanne Conway, counselor to President Trump, as a somewhat sinister character obsessed with appearing on television. In one memorable example, Conway's character is crossed with the evil clown Pennywise from the film *It* as she attempts to lure a reporter into a sewer (*SNL* 2017k). Melissa McCarthy portrayed Press Secretary Sean Spicer as a liar wearing an ill-fitting suit in parodies of White House press briefings (*SNL* 2017b).

Another recurring character in *SNL* sketches about the first year of the Trump presidency was Russian President Vladimir Putin, played by Beck Bennett. Sketches featuring Putin generally suggest that the Russian president was largely responsible for Trump's election and that the president is under Putin's control (*SNL* 2017a). These sorts of jokes aim to undermine the legitimacy of Trump's presidency while also striking at Trump's ego by suggesting he is not in control. Since Putin often appears in these sketches without a shirt, he also represents a macho contrast to the flabby Trump.

Full Frontal

As was the case with the other comedy programs examined here, *Full Frontal* sought to cover many of the major news stories in the first year of the Trump presidency. The show tackled the executive orders on immigration (*FF* 2017c), the investigations into Russian interference in the 2016 election (*FF* 2017f), various attempts by congressional Republicans to pass a health care reform bill (*FF* 2017i) and the firing of FBI Director James Comey (*FF* 2017i).

At times, the show's struggle to get through all of the week's key items was apparent. The opening news roundups of some episodes sped through several news stories within just a few minutes. While the nightly talk shows were able to give certain news stories more coverage, the limitations of *Full Frontal*'s weekly format became obvious as Bee was forced to rush through the news. In fact, the rapid pace of the news cycle became the subject of jokes itself, such as when Bee joked only a few weeks after Trump's inauguration that he had managed to complete his first 100 days in office in just 19 (*FF* 2017d).

Full Frontal also featured profiles of various members of the Trump administration such as Sebastian Gorka, who worked briefly as a presidential aide (*FF* 2017g), White House Chief of Staff John Kelly (*FF* 2017l), and Trump's daughter and advisor Ivanka Trump (*FF* 2017e) – an administration Bee described as a "batsh*t telenovela" (*FF* 2017k).

As a host, Samantha Bee is forthright with her political views. She is essentially the Rachel Maddow of late-night humor – very openly liberal, as evidenced by her attendance at and positive coverage of the Women's March (*FF* 2017b). Bee also makes her personal politics clear in the way she discusses President Trump and his agenda. In her coverage of the first year of the Trump presidency, Bee had no kind words for the president or his policies. She was consistently critical of Trump's words, actions, and proposals.

Full Frontal's humor demonstrated that Bee considered everything about Trump, from his physical appearance to his personality and behavior, as fair game. Bee mocked his weight through the extensive use of unflattering pictures (*FF* 2017l) and described his walking style as "lurching" (*FF* 2017h). *Full Frontal* frequently portrayed Trump as a bigot and misogynist, as well as intensely insecure, fearful, and childish. For example, Bee described the Trump presidency as an "experiment in toddlerocracy" (*FF* 2017j). In a jab at Trump's perceived insecurity, Bee repeatedly suggested that he might not be in charge at the White House. Following Trump's inauguration speech, Bee joked that then Chief Strategist Steve Bannon was providing "more Nazi code than Enigma" (*FF* 2017a).

Trump's behaviors, past and present, also provided *Full Frontal* with a great deal of comedic material. When U.K. Prime Minister Theresa May visited the White House during Trump's first months as president, she was pictured holding her host's hand while descending a set of stairs.

70 Political Humor and the Rise of Donald Trump the Politician

This prompted Bee to comment, "Honestly, Theresa May is lucky all he grabbed was her hand" (*FF* 2017c).

Bee also focused on Trump's past business practices to generate humor. When he threatened to withhold federal funds from cities that declared themselves "sanctuary" locations for illegal immigrants, Bee made a joking reference to Trump allegedly not paying contractors who had completed work for him: "Well, he did say he'd run the country the same way he runs his business" (*FF* 2017d).

Full Frontal even tapped into very specific, odd features of Trump's personality for humor. His preference for well-done steaks served with ketchup was brought up repeatedly for mockery (*FF* 2017f). Bee even joked about the illegibility of Trump's signature, likening it to a "polygraph malfunction" (*FF* 2017c). All of the above listed subjects for jokes about Trump demonstrate just how insult-based *Full Frontal*'s humor was during the first year of the Trump presidency.

Last Week Tonight

LWT prefers to move beyond the indexing norm of the nightly political humor shows, which have little time or inclination to develop the sort of investigative content commonly offered on Oliver's HBO program (Fox 2018; McKain 2005). Oliver at least touched on many major news items in the opening news roundup of each episode, though these segments frequently rushed through several stories within the span of a few minutes. Like *Full Frontal*, the pace of news stories itself became a subject for jokes on *Last Week Tonight*, such as when Oliver joked that Trump, "seems to be bending the space-time continuum in order to fill a week with more news than it can scientifically contain" (*LWT* 2017g).

In the longer segments, Oliver offered extensive coverage of a number of stories relating to the Trump presidency. He dedicated substantial time to stories like the proposed American Health Care Act of 2017 (*LWT* 2017b), Trump's decision to remove the U.S. from the Paris Climate Accord (*LWT* 2017e), and developments in the U.S.'s relationship with North Korea (*LWT* 2017h). He also reported on the investigation of possible collusion between the Trump campaign and the Russian government, a scandal that Oliver dubbed "Stupid Watergate" (*LWT* 2017d). *Last Week Tonight* also covered stories that had less direct connections to Trump, including an examination of the state of the U.S. coal industry that Oliver tied to Trump's promises to help the industry (*LWT* 2017f).

Oliver occasionally found humor in simply pointing out the inherent absurdity of something. This style of humor frequently was used when discussing President Trump's stream-of-consciousness speeches (*LWT* 2017a, 2017i). Of course, insult-based jokes are the bread and butter of late-night political humor, regardless of format. Oliver was true to form, mocking various aspects of Trump's physical appearance, including his weight and skin tone. For example, when President Trump announced via Twitter his intention to ban transgender people from the U.S. military, Oliver joked that the lengthy gaps between the three tweets making this announcement occurred because Trump was finishing his breakfast of "deep-fried Big Macs and mashed Doritos" (*LWT* 2017g).

As was done on the other programs examined here, Oliver generally portrayed Trump as a bigot, a misogynist, and an egomaniac. Oliver, like Bee, joked about Trump being like a child, such as when he remarked after playing a clip of a Trump speech notable for its incoherence, "I don't speak 'Toddler Psychopath'" (*LWT* 2017c). Oliver also joked about Trump seeming unhinged, such as claiming that Trump has the temperament of a wet cat (*LWT* 2017h). He also mocked Trump for seeming out of touch, as seen in jokes about Trump's awkward attempt to pantomime coal mining at a rally (*LWT* 2017f).

Last Week Tonight also made numerous jokes about Trump's apparent lack of knowledge and experience upon entering office. After observing that Trump seemed to be a regular viewer of morning cable news shows, Oliver announced that he had purchased ad time during those same shows to broadcast ads to provide useful information such as an explanation of the nuclear triad and the difference between weather and climate (*LWT* 2017a). The show reprised this joke in the last episode of the year, announcing a new series of ads explaining to Trump the error of his own public statements. The ads noted that it is dangerous to look directly at a solar eclipse (Trump did precisely that), and that the Virgin Islands has a governor, not a president (another Trump gaffe). These jokes all served to portray Trump as an inexperienced fool (*LWT* 2017i).

Conclusion

As a candidate and as a president, Donald Trump dismissed presidential norms. His prolific use of Twitter and his great interest in employing personal attacks on his critics made him popular with his base (Schier and Eberly 2017). Everything about Donald Trump that seems larger than life – his gilded lifestyle, his private resorts and golf courses, his abandonment of policy consistency in favor of being able to declare momentary victories – all allow humorists to have a field day. If the calm, cool, self-controlled introvert Barack Obama was a profound challenge for late-night comedy writers several years ago, then Trump was their dream come true.

During the 2016 presidential campaign, the heavier focus on Republican than Democratic candidates continued for another presidential election cycle, and the emphasis on personality over policy remained unchanged as well. On the other hand, the sheer volume of jokes about Trump was certainly unprecedented; even Bill Clinton was never so frequent a target during his election campaigns (Lichter et al. 2015). In addition, there seemed more of an edge to much of the humor, as the comedians' distress and disdain toward the Donald sometimes seemed palpable. For example, in one routine Colbert tried to "connect the dots" among Trump's ideas and behavior on a blackboard and ended up drawing a swastika. But even this was in line with highly negative news coverage of Trump that included discussions of whether it was appropriate to call him a fascist or compare him to Hitler. Thus, Trump posed a challenge to comedians, as he did to journalists. Even when making light of Trump, there was a dark edge to the outpouring of late-night comedy.

As our findings demonstrate, late-night comedians found a huge payoff during the 2016 campaign and during the first year of the Trump presidency. Regardless of format, frequency, and host style, mocking Trump became a growth industry for late-night humor. With obvious glee, the current generation of last night comedy hosts have torn into Trump from a multitude of directions: They make fun of his physical appearance, his clothing style, his chaotic administration, his policy ignorance, inconsistency in his statements, his neediness, his narcissism, and his volatile temperament.

Media observers who have examined these comedy shows have noted important differences in their treatment of the new president during 2017. As discussed earlier, no one seems to have changed more than Fallon between the 2016 campaign and the soft treatment of a fellow NBC star from *The Apprentice* – and 2017, Trump's first year as president (Farnsworth et al. 2018, Itzkoff 2017; Merry 2016; Poniewozik 2017). While much of the late-night audience skews young and liberal, Fallon offers a slightly different product: one a bit more hospitable to a segment of the audience less critical of Trump than viewers drawn to the blistering barrage and extreme harshness of the anti-Trump jokes most notably offered by Trevor Noah and Stephen Colbert.

As we shall see in the upcoming chapter, Trump continued to offer rich veins of comedy gold for the late-night comics during his 2020 reelection campaign.

Early 2016	Jokes	Percentage
1. Donald Trump	587	32.3%
2. Bernie Sanders	205	11.3%
3. Ted Cruz	151	8.9%
4. Hillary Clinton	115	6.3%
5. Jeb Bush	104	5.7%
6. Barack Obama	94	5.2%
7. Ben Carson	62	3.4%
8. Marco Rubio	61	3.4%
9. John Kasich	43	2.4%
10. Chris Christie	34	1.9%

Source: CMPA

Republican Candidate Focus

	January		February		March		April		Total	
	# of Jokes	%	# of Jokes	%	# of Jokes	%	# of Jokes	%	# of Jokes	%
Fallon	83	54%	84	64%	75	51%	51	41%	293	53%
Colbert	72	58%	57	55%	48	48%	38	52%	215	54%
Kimmel	38	57%	69	61%	79	55%	44	64%	230	58%
Noah	75	67%	77	75%	79	55%	67	62%	298	64%
Total	**268**	**59%**	**287**	**64%**	**281**	**53%**	**200**	**53%**	**1036**	**57%**

Democratic Candidate Focus

	January		February		March		April		Total	
	# of Jokes	%	# of Jokes	%	# of Jokes	%	# of Jokes	%	# of Jokes	%
Fallon	35	23%	32	24%	28	19%	44	35%	139	25%
Colbert	31	25%	19	18%	13	13%	8	*	71	18%
Kimmel	17	25%	16	14%	40	14%	8	*	61	16%
Noah	16	14%	12	12%	15	10%	19	18%	62	13%
Total	**99**	**22%**	**79**	**17%**	**76**	**14%**	**79**	**21%**	**333**	**18%**

*Fewer than ten jokes in the category for a comic for that month, too few for analysis.

Note: Some political jokes relate to more than one candidate and cannot be classified as clearly directed toward one party or another.

Source: CMPA

From the Iowa Caucus to the Start of the Party Conventions (2/1/16 through 7/17/16)

	All Jokes	Policy		Politics		Personal	
		# of jokes	%	# of jokes	%	# of jokes	%
Trump	844	114	14%	359	43%	802	95%
Clinton	222	31	14%	140	63%	193	87%
Total	1066	145	14%	499	47%	995	93%

Party Conventions through General Election (7/18/16 through 11/11/16)

	All Jokes	Policy		Politics		Personal	
		# of jokes	%	# of jokes	%	# of jokes	%
Trump	836	156	19%	547	65%	662	79%
Clinton	267	19	7%	190	71%	222	83%
Total	1103	175	16%	737	67%	884	80%

Full Campaign Period (9/1/15 through 11/11/16)

All Jokes		Policy		Politics		Personal	
		# of jokes	%	# of jokes	%	# of jokes	%
Trump	2,351	325	14%	1,059	45%	2,058	88%
Clinton	657	59	9%	396	60%	565	86%
Total	3008	384	13%	1455	48%	2633	87%

Note: Percentages do not sum to 100 because jokes can refer to more than one topic area.

Source: CMPA

3

POLITICAL HUMOR AND THE 2020 PRESIDENTIAL CAMPAIGN

Coauthored with Kate Seltzer and Sally Burkley

The Symbiotic Nature of Late-Night Comedy and U.S. Politics

As the years leading up to the 2020 election demonstrated, political humor has become an increasingly important part of American political discourse. As usage of traditional media declines, and as political humor becomes increasingly present on social media, the political commentary of late night has become more common on the late-night comedy programs – and that mocking content has become an important part of contemporary political discourse beyond those programs. In addition, political humor has also become harsher over time, reflecting the increasingly combative political culture of our era. Never has this been truer than during the years when Donald Trump commanded the center stage of American politics, as he did from the start of his 2016 presidential campaign through his years as president and beyond.

The 2020 presidential campaign offered a new opportunity to consider presidential candidates and political humor. While Donald Trump was unopposed for his Republican renomination, the incumbent president was never out of focus when it came to late-night comedy. On the Democratic side, Joe Biden, who had long been a source of political humor during his days as a long-winded senator and as a relatively uninhibited and loquacious vice president, faced off against a variety of Democratic candidates, including the iconic Bernie Sanders, the independent senator from Vermont who drew considerable comedic attention during his failed effort to secure the Democratic presidential nomination in 2016.

DOI: 10.4324/9781003283041-3

76 Political Humor and the 2020 Presidential Campaign

How did these factors about political humor and presidential candidates play out in the way late-night comedians commented upon the 2020 presidential election? To find out we examine the content of political humor throughout the 2020 campaign. During the nomination part of the campaign, we tracked political jokes by Jimmy Fallon (*The Tonight Show* on NBC), Stephen Colbert (*The Late Show* on CBS), Jimmy Kimmel (*Jimmy Kimmel Live!* on ABC), and *The Daily Show*, the Comedy Central program with host Trevor Noah. The three broadcast network shows had the largest audiences of any late-night talk shows broadcasting more than once a week, while *The Daily Show* has been especially popular with young adults. We tracked both the traditional joke formats, the "one-liners," and the more extensive lead-in humor more commonly employed on Comedy Central's *The Daily Show*. Financial considerations required a trimming of the nightly humor data collection during the 2020 general election campaign, when we examined political jokes offered only by Fallon and Colbert.

For the nomination phase of the 2020 contest, we examined late-night comedy jokes of those four nightly shows from September 11 to October 17, 2019, and from January 13 to April 9, 2020. Taken together, these four comedy programs offered 3,327 jokes relating to the presidential campaign during these two periods of the candidate nomination cycle. The first nomination period represents a time when the candidates are trying to introduce themselves to the electorate before the start of the primaries and away from the busy holiday season. The second nomination period corresponds to the time when the nomination contests are underway. By April 9, the end of the 2020 nomination study period, there was little doubt that former Vice President Joe Biden would be the Democratic nominee. (There had never been a serious chance that Republicans in 2020 would fail to renominate incumbent Donald Trump).

During the fall general election campaign season, we analyzed 1,688 political jokes on NBC's and CBS's late-night comedy offerings that aired between August 24, 2020 and October 26, 2020 and during November 2, 2020, through November 13, 2020. The latter period included days on either side of the 2020 Election, which was held on November 3. As has been the case throughout this project, we analyzed these jokes for their policy, political, and/or personal content. (Many jokes covered more than one issue area.)

As we did during our studies of late-night comedy discussed in Chapter 2, we undertook both quantitative and qualitative studies of political humor during the nomination and general election campaign periods on three once-a-week programs: *Saturday Night Live (SNL)*, *Full Frontal with Samantha Bee*, and *Last Week Tonight with John Oliver*. None of these programs employ the rapid-fire comedic monologue format

Political Humor and the 2020 Presidential Campaign **77**

that is common among the four nightly programs, so a more qualitative approach suited those very different programs.

The two campaign periods examined here from the 2020 presidential campaign cycle regarding political humor represent an updating of the CMPA historical database, which includes more than 100,000 jokes by hosts on popular late-night TV shows from 1992 to 2021. This database includes not only jokes about political figures but also those directed at government and social institutions, such as churches and the military, as well as jokes that addressed a social or economic problem, like inflation, gay rights, or climate change. Due to limited resources, however, this study of the 2020 campaign was limited to jokes directed at individual political figures during select periods from late fall of 2019 to late 2020. In addition, as noted earlier, the general election portion of the campaign cycle involved the analysis of fewer nightly humor programs than were examined during the nomination phase of the 2020 campaign.

Nightly Late-Night Comedy and the 2020 Nomination Campaign

In Table 3.1, we look at the number of jokes told by these four nightly humorists during the earlier study period of the 2020 nomination campaign cycle (September 11 to October 17, 2019). The Democratic Party may have had one of the largest and wide-ranging fields of party candidates ever to suit up for the Iowa Caucus, but that did not matter a bit to the late-night comics. For them, nothing the Democratic candidates could do would compete with President Trump. Of the 1,425 jokes the four comics told during that period, only 154 (11 percent) related to the Democratic contest and its many candidates. The pattern of an overwhelming focus on Trump appeared for all four of the nightly late-night comics examined here during this part of the nomination cycle. It occurred even though he faced no Republican opposition for renomination, a sharp contrast from the large field of Democratic contenders.

TABLE 3.1 Candidate Late-Night Joke Analysis, Late 2019

Total Candidate Jokes				
	September	*October*	*Total*	*Total Percent*
Fallon	103	99	202	14%
Colbert	281	248	529	37%
Kimmel	208	237	445	31%
Noah	134	115	249	17%
Total	726	699	11425	99%*

78 Political Humor and the 2020 Presidential Campaign

BOX 3.1 SAMPLES OF POLITICAL HUMOR DURING THE 2020 NOMINATION CAMPAIGN TRUMP

Melania had a candlelit dinner tonight because it's dark in the tunnel she's digging. A personal record for most tweets in the day since he became president, he tweeted 140 times today, not one of those times was about his anniversary.

(Jimmy Kimmel, January 22, 2020)

[President Trump has] made us all confused and nervous. (Laughter) You're like an Uber driver who has taken our country way off the Google maps route, and at first, we hoped you just knew a short cut, but then you opened your mouth, and we realized you're insane. Now we're trapped in here with you, and we just have to hope we don't die on the way to a birthday party we didn't even want to go to. Also, you're taking us to the wrong Kansas City.

(Stephen Colbert, February 3, 2020)

Democratic Candidates (Collectively)

It doesn't make sense. They need to pare this down. It's like the menu at the Cheesecake Factory. There's too much to choose from. Let's go through the Cheesecake Factory and the candidates ... They are all trying to defeat the world-famous pumpkin cheesecake Donald Trump.

(Jimmy Kimmel, October 15, 2019)

There were 12 candidates on stage, an all-time record, which is a little weird. Candidates aren't supposed to multiply as the debates go on, so, please, America, remember to have your candidate spayed or neutered! We can't handle any more!

(Trevor Noah, October 15, 2019)

Sanders

(Post-Senate impeachment trial) So, there it is, okay. It is official: Nothing means anything. Right is wrong. Up is down. Missouri is Kansas. (Laughter) Now we know that asking a foreign power to interfere in our election is the new normal. The Democrats have no choice but to do the same thing. (As Bernie) 'Russia, if you're listening. I could really use that pee-pee tape. Milk, milk, lemonade. Around the corner, justice is made!

(Stephen Colbert, February 5, 2020)

Political Humor and the 2020 Presidential Campaign **79**

Here's another fact: the most similar illness to the Coronavirus is the 1918 Spanish flu fiction, or as Bernie Sanders put it, "worst summer ever."

(Jimmy Fallon, March 11, 2020)

Biden

Joe Biden took a selfie with an elevator attendant the other day and the moment is going viral. Take a look at this. Aww. [Audience aws] When the woman asked, "Do we need the flash?" Biden was like, "No, I got my teeth."

(Trevor Noah, January 22, 2020)

Impeachment

Republicans basically treat Trump like white people treat their dog, you know, sure, pooped on the floor and bit the neighbor's kid, but who can stay mad at that face? Who can stay mad at that face? Is he just one of the quid pro quo? He was a quid pro quo? Who wants a quid pro quo? Are you the quid pro quo?

(Trevor Noah, February 3, 2020)

Pelosi appointed seven impeachment managers who will prosecute the case against Trump. I don't know if that was a good idea. I mean, when you pick seven, aren't you begging Trump to give them dwarf nicknames from Snow White? [Laughter] "There's congressman dopey, sleepy, grumpy." [Laughter] Can we see a photo of Pelosi and the seven managers? I know it doesn't seem like much, but compared to last night's debate that looks like the cast of "Dolemite."

(Jimmy Fallon, January 15, 2020)

The materials also include a letter from Giuliani to Ukrainian President Zelensky requesting a meeting in his capacity as personal counsel to President Trump, and with Trump's knowledge and consent. (Audience reacts) Yes, two words not generally associated with President Trump: Knowledge and consent.

(Stephen Colbert, January 15, 2020)

Meanwhile, Trump is in Switzerland for the World Economic Forum, over 4,000 miles away from Washington. Apparently when he asked his lawyers, "How can I help?" They handed him a plane ticket.

(Jimmy Fallon, January 21, 2020)

80 Political Humor and the 2020 Presidential Campaign

Coronavirus

[SC] "Vice President Mike Pence. He addressed a growing concern for Americans: The cost of testing and treatment." [video of Pence] "All of our major health insurance companies have now joined with Medicare and Medicaid and agreed to waive all co-pays, cover the cost of all treatment for those that contract the coronavirus." [SC] "What a cool idea! It's like Medicare but ... for all. (Laughter) That's really – that would be kind of cool."

(Stephen Colbert March 11, 2020)

We're going too, for the foreseeable future. So, you people, this audience tonight, you are one of the last audiences I will have. You are all collector's items. Have yourselves notarized.

(Stephen Colbert, March 11, 2020)

Box 3.1 offers an assortment of jokes from these four late-night comedy shows. As noted in Chapter 2, Jimmy Fallon lost his position atop the ratings following what some viewers considered to be his too-friendly treatment of candidate Trump during the 2016 campaign (Hartung 2017; Itzkoff 2017). Four years later, it was clear that Fallon has retained his lighter-on-politics approach to late-night comedy during a presidential campaign, particularly when compared to his fellow late-night hosts. Overall, Fallon told far fewer jokes about the presidential race than did the other three nightly comics examined here. His 202 jokes represented only 14 percent of all the 2020 election jokes during that period. Stephen Colbert, who ranked first among these four comics in the audience ratings and in the number of jokes made relating to the upcoming election, offered 529 comedic remarks on the campaign during this same period. Colbert's total was more than double Fallon's total.

Similar patterns emerged when we separated the jokes based on whether they focused on Democratic or Republican candidates. All four hosts focused overwhelmingly on Trump and the Republicans. Colbert ranked first and Fallon last overall, as well as in both the Republican and Democratic subset of jokes during these parts of the 2020 nomination cycle.

The same patterns were identified in Table 3.1, which covered part of the nomination process on late-night comedy during 2019, appear in Table 3.2, which covered late-night comedy's attention to the presidential nomination contests during early 2020. Once again, we see an intense focus on Trump and the tiny amount of attention the late-night comics paid to the Democratic field. Only 296 of 1916 election-related jokes

(15 percent) on these four late-night programs focused on the Democratic candidates between January 13 and April 9, 2020, even though there was a very competitive election going on during these months. Colbert again had notably more political jokes than the other three hosts examined here did, and Fallon again had the least. During this period, though, Kimmel and Noah provided similar levels of attention to the presidential nomination season, each ranking in roughly the middle of the pack.

Table 3.3 illustrates the continued intense late-night comedic focus on Trump, even as the Democratic presidential candidates were heading into

TABLE 3.2 Candidate Late-Night Joke Analysis, Early 2020

Total Candidate Jokes

	January	*February*	*March*	*April*	*Total*	*Total Percent*
Fallon	146	72	60	4	282	15%
Colbert	313	156	96	102	667	35%
Kimmel	157	97	130	82	466	24%
Noah	172	108	147	74	501	26%
Total	788	433	433	262	1,916	100%

TABLE 3.3 Late-Night Candidate Joke Targets, Late 2019

September 2019		*October 2019*		*Total*	
Donald Trump	617	Donald Trump	646	Donald Trump	1,263
Bernie Sanders	28	Bernie Sanders	11	Bernie Sanders	39
Joe Biden	26	Joe Biden	10	Joe Biden	36
Elizabeth Warren	6	D Candidates*	8	D Candidates*	8
Kamala Harris	3	Tom Steyer	4	Tom Steyer	6
Nancy Pelosi**	2	Tulsi Gabbard	3	Kamala Harris	5
		Beto O'Rourke	2	Tulsi Gabbard	4
		Kamala Harris	2	Bill de Blasio	2
		Bill de Blasio	2	Amy Klobuchar	2
		Amy Klobuchar	2	Andrew Yang	2
		Andrew Yang	2	Beto O'Rourke	2
		Cory Booker	2	Cory Booker	2
				Elizabeth Warren	2
				Julian Castro	2
				Nancy Pelosi**	2

Note: Only candidates with more than one joke in a given period are listed.
* Jokes relating to the entire Democratic field of candidates.
** Not a presidential candidate in 2020, but the focus of at least one 2020 campaign joke. Analysis period runs from September 11 to October 17, 2019.

Source: CMPA

82 Political Humor and the 2020 Presidential Campaign

the contentious 2020 nomination contests. During the final three weeks of September 2019, only three presidential candidates received more than one joke aimed at them: Donald Trump with 617 jokes, as compared to 28 jokes focusing on Vermont Senator Bernie Sanders and 26 about Joe Biden. In the October portion of the study period (October 1–17, 2019), the emphasis remained nearly all Trump all the time, as the president was subject to 646 jokes, as compared to 11 focused on Sanders and 10 focused on Biden. Eight jokes targeted the Democratic field collectively. Two long-shot candidates, Tom Steyer, a hedge fund manager and environmentalist, and U.S. Rep. Tulsi Gabbard of Hawaii, ranked fifth and sixth, with four and three jokes, respectively. (They would go on to finish sixth and seventh in the 2020 New Hampshire Primary before abandoning their campaigns).

President Trump also dominated the political content of the late-night monologues during early 2020, as demonstrated in Table 3.4. During the period between January 13 and April 9, 2020, the late-night comics lobbed 1,410 jokes at Trump. Not a single Democratic candidate received 100 jokes during that period. Only three Democratic presidential candidates topped 40 jokes: 80 for Sanders, 68 for Biden, and 41 for Michael Bloomberg, the former New York City mayor and media billionaire. Next in line for the Democratic Party were former Mayor Pete Buttigieg of South Bend,

TABLE 3.4 Late-Night Candidate Joke Targets, Early 2020

January 2020		February 2020		March 2020		April 2020		Total	
Trump	657	Trump	303	Trump	230	Trump	220	Trump	1,410
Sanders	40	Biden	45	Biden	13	Sanders	12	Sanders	80
Bloomberg	20	Sanders	27	Sanders	8	Biden	5	Biden	68
Booker	11	Bloomberg	21	Obama**	2			Bloomberg	41
Klobuchar	10	Buttigieg	18					Buttigieg	25
Pelosi**	10	Klobuchar	6					Klobuchar	16
Buttigieg	7	Romney**	4					Booker	11
Schiff**	6	Steyer	3					Pelosi**	10
Warren	5	Yang	2					Warren	8
Biden	5	Warren	2					Steyer	6
Steyer	3							Schiff**	6
								Romney**	4
								Yang	3
								Obama**	2

Note: Only candidates with more than one joke in a given period are listed.
* Jokes relating to the entire Democratic field of candidates.
** Not a presidential candidate in 2020, but the focus of at least one 2020 campaign joke.
Analysis period runs from January 13 to April 9, 2020.

Source: CMPA

Indiana, who enjoyed some media hype and some success in Iowa before his campaign faltered, and U.S. Senator Amy Klobuchar of Minnesota, with 25 and 16 jokes, respectively. Trump led in all four months of the early 2020 jokes, outpacing the runner-up in these rankings by a 10-to-1 margin in three of the four months examined here. The exception was during February, when Trump's margin over Joe Biden was only 6-to-1. As expected, the number of presidential candidates who were subject to late-night mockery shrank along with the field as the weeks passed by in early 2020.

In Table 3.5, we summarize the results from the entire nomination study period, the more than 3,000 political jokes on these four shows during the two analysis periods: September 11 to October 17, 2019 and January 13 to April 9, 2020. Even though the Democratic Party

TABLE 3.5 Late-Night Candidate Joke Targets, 2019–2020 Nomination Study Period

	Number of Jokes	Percentage of Total Election Jokes (N = 3,046)
Trump	2,673	80%
Sanders	119	4%
Biden	81	3%
Bloomberg	42	1%
Buttigieg	26	1%
Klobuchar	19	1%
Booker	13	*
Pelosi**	12	*
Warren	10	*
Steyer	10	*
D candidates***	9	*
Schiff**	6	*
Yang	5	*
De Blasio	4	*
Gabbard	4	*
Romney**	4	*
Harris	3	*
Julian Castro	2	*
Beto O'Rourke	2	*
Obama**	2	*

Note: Only candidates with more than one joke in a given period are listed.
* Less than 0.5 percent.
** Not a presidential candidate in 2020, but the focus of at least one 2020 campaign joke.
*** Jokes relating to the entire Democratic field of candidates.

Analysis period runs from September 11 to October 17, 2019 and from January 13 to April 9, 2020.

84 Political Humor and the 2020 Presidential Campaign

could choose from a large field of highly experienced candidates, these candidates received very little attention in the late-night monologues. These four comedians told 2,673 jokes about Trump, or 80 percent of all comedy relating to the presidential campaign during the part of the nomination campaign examined here. In contrast, Sanders was the only Democratic candidate who was the subject of more more 100 humorous remarks during the same study period. Excluding Trump, the comics judged Bernie Sanders the most appealing candidate for humor, as he received 119 jokes, or 4 percent of the total. Biden, the eventual nominee, ranked third overall and second to Sanders among the Democratic field, with 81 jokes. Lagging were some also-ran candidates: Bloomberg ranked fourth with 42 jokes, Buttigieg fifth with 26 jokes, and Klobuchar sixth with 19 jokes.

Sanders, with his intense emotional appeals, rumpled demeanor, and strong New York accent, was easier to imitate and to make humorous remarks about than was Biden, whose highly organized 2020 public presentation largely overshadowed his gaffe-prone past. As a more mainstream political figure than Sanders (as well as more inhibited in demeanor than the Vermont senator, particularly during the 2020 campaign), Biden was less appealing as a subject for humor. Indeed, even after the November election, as Biden prepared to become president, *Saturday Night Live* continued to struggle with finding an effective imitator of the man who had become the president-elect (Andrews-Dyer 2020).

In 2016, the late-night comics focused on Trump but sometimes invested more attention on a candidate who spent a lot of money or who seemed to generate more attention from the media than support from the voters. Former Florida Governor Jeb Bush was a prominent example of a Republican underperformer that year, as was Dr. Ben Carson, whose uncommonly low-energy campaign triggered mockery on late night (Farnsworth and Lichter 2020). Both received a good deal of attention on late-night comedy for their failings, but of course not nearly as much attention as Trump received for his campaign.

For 2020, a similar pattern emerged regarding the humorous condition measured by the gap between expectations and performance. This common source of late-night political comedy was filled by Bloomberg, who committed to record campaign spending that did not generate much voter support, and by Buttigieg, whose small-town mayoral career did not produce all that much voter enthusiasm as the primary process moved beyond the early states. Another candidate who failed to match the preseason hype, former Congressman Beto O'Rourke of Texas, did not receive all that much mocking, perhaps because he faded so quickly.

Political Humor and the 2020 Presidential Campaign **85**

TABLE 3.6 Key Policy Topics of Late-Night Political Comedy during the 2019–2020 Nomination Period

Jokes about COVID-19 That Also Served as Public Service Announcements *(March 1 to April 9, 2020)*	
Jimmy Kimmel Live	179
The Daily Show with Trevor Noah	160
The Late Show with Stephen Colbert	192
The Tonight Show Starring Jimmy Fallon	24

While there are some powerful similarities between how late-night comedy treated the 2016 and 2020 nomination contests, the policy environment was very different in two ways: the opening months of 2020 included the rise of a nationwide health emergency relating to the coronavirus as well as President Trump's first impeachment trial (the second impeachment trial took place after Trump left office in January 2021). As shown in Table 3.6, these policy matters during the 2020 campaign season helped drive attention toward President Trump, who had been the key focus of late-night comedy since he started his 2016 presidential campaign more than four years earlier.

At first, the late-night comics sought to include some public service information relating to COVID-19 in their late-night comedy. (In March 2020, when many parts of the country first entered some form of lockdown, the U.S. infection rates and death counts relating to COVID-19 were far smaller at that point than they would become later in 2020). Jimmy Kimmel, who focused on the proposed repeal of the Affordable Care Act on several shows during Trump's first year in office, again focused on health care, telling more COVID-related jokes that focused on Trump than did the hosts of the other three shows. Colbert, though, told more COVID-related jokes that offered a public service announcement component than the other comics. Kimmel ranked second in the public announcement aspect of pandemic humor. In both COVID-related categories, Fallon was a distant fourth among the late-night hosts, offing a tiny fraction of the humor relating to the pandemic.

Trump's first impeachment trial, which began on January 16, 2020, and concluded with his acquittal by the U.S. Senate on February 5, 2020, did not last long. But it did generate significant comedic attention on late-night television. Colbert was particularly focused on this theme, as he offered more than twice as many impeachment-related jokes as did any of the other leading comics. Once again, Fallon and his *The Tonight Show* – which generally focuses more on less-political content – was a distant fourth.

86 Political Humor and the 2020 Presidential Campaign

The Weekly Humor Programs and the 2020 Nomination Campaign

Saturday Night Live

For more than four decades, *Saturday Night Live* has offered humor and satire, largely through character portrayals of real political figures and imagined citizens reacting to political events. As in previous election cycles, *SNL* primarily used the "cold open" and the segment "Weekend Update" to satirize the field of presidential candidates. The opening segment, which runs for several minutes in length, allowed for extensive development of caricatures of the top primary candidates. It also provided a platform for political figures to interact in imagined settings that would not ordinarily occur and for the show to blend separate headlines of the week into one sketch.

SNL's December 21, 2019 parody of a Democratic debate featured surprise appearances from candidates who had at that point dropped out of the race, as well as from Alec Baldwin's Donald Trump. In this sketch, Maya Rudolph as Kamala Harris wanders onto the stage with a martini to mourn the lack of diversity on the debate stage and to show Americans "how good you could have had it" (*SNL* 2019). Later in the sketch, Cecily Strong reprised her role as Tulsi Gabbard (who had not qualified for that debate) in order for the show to poke fun at the congresswoman's "present" vote on the House's first articles of impeachment against Donald Trump (Folley 2019). That opening segment concluded with an appearance from Trump (Baldwin) and House Speaker Nancy Pelosi (Kate McKinnon), who riffed on the articles of impeachment news of the week. In a similar fashion, a February 2020 cold open imagined a scenario where Vice President Mike Pence held a press conference to discuss COVID-19 updates, only to have the event hijacked by various Democratic candidates (*SNL* 2020b).

In general, *SNL*'s primary coverage focused on candidates' character and personality traits, rather than on specific policies. Its jokes highlighted the horserace nature of the campaign, reflecting news coverage patterns (Patterson 2016a, 2016b). In another pattern common to campaign news, *SNL* also emphasized conflict, at different times playing up the feud between Massachusetts Senator Elizabeth Warren and Bernie Sanders, and emphasized another dispute, this one between Klobuchar and Buttigieg.

The show reprised two popular political caricatures from the 2016 election cycle. Alec Baldwin's portrayal of Trump was featured heavily throughout the coverage: his orange makeup, pursed lips, and exaggerated voice readily mimic Trump's mannerisms, and the show routinely presented him as narcissistic, foolish, a liar, and a crook (and not a particularly successful one). In both debate cold opens referenced here, Larry David – with a loud, thick New York accent and exaggerated gesticulations, and an uncanny physical resemblance to the Senator – portrayed Sanders as being old, out of touch, and angry at everything from the thermostat to corporations to his iPhone (*SNL* 2020a).

One continuing challenge that the show faced was how to portray former Vice President Joe Biden, the eventual Democratic nominee. A series of actors, including Jason Sudeikis, Woody Harrelson, and John Mulaney, played Joe Biden with varying degrees of resemblance and critical success during the nomination cycle, and Jim Carrey briefly portrayed Biden later in 2020 (Andrews-Dyer 2020). Carrey didn't last all that long as a Biden impersonator, either, as *SNL* struggled throughout 2020 to establish a plan for making fun of Biden.

During the nomination period, these performers seemed less focused on imitating his mannerisms and appearance, focusing instead on drawing attention to his rambling speech patterns and sometimes awkward behavior. Along these lines, the performers generally played him as bumbling and mildly incoherent, with a tendency to sneak up behind unsuspecting people in an off-putting way. When Sudeikis as Biden was asked if he was concerned about his poor performance in the Iowa caucus, he answered "I'm not worried at all, because by the time we get to South Cackalacky, Joe Biden's gonna do what Joe Biden does best: creep up from behind" (*SNL* 2020a).

Kate McKinnon's version of Elizabeth Warren, on the other hand, came off as exceedingly smart, if a little overenthusiastic and wonkish – "Last debate I gave you policy TMI and now I am ready to walk it back," McKinnon said as Warren at *SNL*'s mock PBS debate (*SNL* 2019). Warren was also portrayed as both appealing to and being reflective of a specific trope of white, highly educated, tote bag carrying, NPR-listening women. "I tend to really connect with New England moms who own big dogs and rock a fleece vest seven days out of the week," McKinnon said (*SNL* 2020a). And: "PBS is my safe word" (*SNL* 2019).

In contrast, Buttigieg was portrayed as a robotic candidate, generally lacking in personality. The show also repeatedly riffed on Buttigieg's inability to connect with non-white voters. When asked his appeal among the diverse Democratic electorate, Colin Jost as Buttigieg says, "I know that I sound like a bot that has studied human behavior by watching 100 hours of Obama speeches. So, let's get #WhiteObama trending, and, please, not ironically" (*SNL* 2020a). The next day, #WhiteObama was in fact trending on Twitter, and the hashtag stuck, with the joke recycled by other late-night hosts as well (Wagtendonk 2020).

Meanwhile, Amy Klobuchar was played as uniquely boring candidate, with "carefully rehearsed Midwestern mom jokes" (*SNL* 2019), who was consistently bitter at not performing better throughout the race. Perhaps her most noteworthy characteristic, according to the segments,

88 Political Humor and the 2020 Presidential Campaign

was her competition with Pete Buttigieg for the position of moderate Midwestern candidate. "Stay out of my center lane, b –" said *SNL* alum Rachel Dratch as Klobuchar. "I'm from Minnesota so I will cut you … in line at Target, son" (*SNL* 2020b). The rivalry between the two Midwestern candidates was routinely played up throughout the show's coverage of the primary.

Full Frontal with Samantha Bee

Full Frontal, as in the 2016 election cycle, pulled no punches in its pointed, sometimes vulgar commentary during the 2020 nomination season. Even though she presented herself as partisan, Samantha Bee demonstrated that she considered the events and candidates of the 2020 Democratic nomination period were fair game for mockery. Throughout Bee's treatment of the contest, she took the opportunity to speak directly to her liberal audience and encourage unity within the party. Like *SNL* writers, Bee also spent time mocking candidates based on their distinctive personalities (or lack thereof), but she also made it abundantly clear that she would ultimately back the Democratic nominee no matter what and urged her viewers to do the same.

To further her dominant message of party cohesion, Bee sometimes criticized the size of the Democratic presidential field. In a segment titled "Run for Senate, God damn it," she urged low-polling candidates like Colorado Governor John Hickenlooper, who did win a 2020 Senate election, and Montana Governor Steve Bullock, who would go on to lose a 2020 Senate election (Hulse 2020), to drop out of the presidential race in favor of Senate campaigns they might actually have a shot at winning. "Winning the presidency would be great, but real change is impossible unless the Senate changes hands too," Bee said in a June 2019 clip (*FF* 2019a). Similarly, speaking directly to unpopular candidates, later in the month she put out the call for would-be Democratic presidential nominees to drop out of the race on her show, promising a "kick ass, drop out party" including a cake of their choosing and a list of acceptable reasons for stepping aside: " 'spending more time with my family,' 'party unity,' or 'I am Tulsi Gabbard' " (*FF* 2019b).

Although Bee emphasized the importance of supporting the eventual nominee, she did not hold back in her criticism of various candidates. Throughout the 2020 nomination cycle, Biden was often the butt of jokes (although the basis for some of those jokes was just verbatim playbacks of Biden's own words). After the Iowa debate in January, Bee referred to "iPhone 4 user Joe Biden['s]" lackluster performance as hailed by critics as "awake, standing, and are you okay?" (*FF* 2020a). The joke was followed by clips of Biden stumbling through several debate responses. A different segment described Biden as "fine" right before showing a clip of him mixing up his wife and sister (*FF* 2020b). In general, *Full Frontal* treated the liberal Sanders more favorably: after Super Tuesday, Bee described the race between the last remaining candidates – Sanders and Biden – as "a race between unapologetic progressive values and the color beige" (*FF* 2020b).

In a segment relating to a debate, Bee joined other comics in taking aim at Bloomberg's seemingly pointless campaign. She also satirized the other candidates: there was "Minnesota Senator and co-worker who would report you for leaving early, Amy Klobuchar," the "guy who wants you to know he was at the club last night, Tom Steyer"; and "mom and dad" Elizabeth Warren and Bernie Sanders. She dismissed Buttigieg's campaign entirely: "also appearing at the debate was Pete Buttigieg. Moving on" (*FF* 2020a).

Bee additionally criticized media outlets like CNN for pushing the horserace and infighting narrative of the Democratic primary (Moran 2020). For instance, one *Full Frontal* segment scolded the media for dramatizing Warren's perceived handshake snub toward Sanders at a debate shortly before the Iowa Caucus. The incident in question came in the wake of Warren publicly calling out Sanders for saying in 2018 that he did not believe a woman could win the presidential election, a claim which he denies. After the debate, where both candidates were pointedly asked about the event, Warren appeared to reject Sanders's extended handshake. "That's it?" Bee asked, incredulous. "That's what's dominated our national discourse for 36 hours? Two great candidates who are a little sad and disappointed with each other over a misunderstanding?" (*FF* 2020a).

Bee directly called out both the debate moderators and the networks' talking heads for encouraging personal infighting within the Democratic field, arguing that the conversation and inevitable criticisms, particularly so late in the campaign, should be much more policy-oriented.

> If we're having fights, they should be about how to protect reproductive rights and how to fight gun violence … I promise I will vote for that uncanny valley resident [Biden] if he's the nominee because there is only one wrong choice this November.
>
> *(FF 2020a)*

Although Bee describes herself as "a really respectful interviewer," she said that unlike in years past, she had real difficulty getting candidates to appear on her show. These same candidates made frequent appearances on

90 Political Humor and the 2020 Presidential Campaign

other late-night comedy shows, a factor which might have influenced her commentary (Lewis 2020). Nonetheless, though Bee had plenty of criticisms for the politicians running for president, she consistently advocated for an increasingly polarized party to unify behind the overarching goal of removing Trump from office.

Last Week Tonight with John Oliver

The formatting of *Last Week Tonight* allows for host John Oliver to present in-depth analyses of political issues, rather than relying on fast-paced jokes that cover a variety of topics as quickly as possible. This very distinct approach to political humor is often data-driven and includes real-world statistics and evidence. His treatment of the 2020 nomination campaign was consistent with this approach, as he routinely outlined the specific policy beliefs of individual candidates. But Oliver does not present an evening newscast: his in-depth segments on serious topics were frequently interspersed with jokes about candidates' personal traits and his own evaluations.

Perhaps the best example of his approach to a topical issue is his treatment of Medicare for All. In that segment, Oliver discussed how Warren and Sanders had both put out versions of a single-payer health care system and how many moderate Democrats were wary of such a system. Oliver first painted a bleak picture of the current system, where 27 million people are uninsured, an additional 44 million are underinsured, and the majority of people who file for bankruptcy cite medical expenses as the primary reason. Oliver highlighted the three most commonly cited concerns about Medicare for all: cost, wait times, and choice. He made the point that nobody knows whether those factors will balance each other out, but said that even if the cost went up, it would be worth it. Oliver spoke very highly of Sanders's plan, which includes vision, dental, long-term care, and drugs, calling it "incredibly generous … it's more generous than the policy of any single payer country on Earth" (*LWT* 2020a).

Oliver then intensely criticized Buttigieg's alternative, saying that it would leave so much of the current insurance infrastructure and all its problems intact and would not do enough to address the major healthcare issues. He equated this to being offered "a shit sandwich, or a slightly smaller shit sandwich with guac – I'll take the second one if you're asking, but honestly the lack of guac wasn't my main concern" (*LWT* 2020a).

Oliver was particularly contemptuous of Mike Bloomberg. Like Bee, Oliver criticized news outlets for focusing on the wrong thing regarding the billionaire former mayor of New York City. In a critique of a CNN report that described Bloomberg as someone who could take you to the prom in the best-looking gown with the biggest flowers, Oliver quipped: "Nobody is hoping Mike Bloomberg will take them to the prom." Oliver then acknowledged that like a would-be prom date, Bloomberg is painfully awkward, looks uncomfortable in a suit, and has "big virgin energy" (*LWT* 2020b).

Oliver also took aim at Bloomberg's history as a big-city mayor, when he oversaw the massive expansion of "stop and frisk" policing. Oliver said the policy, which overwhelmingly affected minorities, represented "a decade of constant harassment." Oliver went on to show clips of Bloomberg being entirely unrepentant, indeed saying that the racial profiling did not go far enough. Bloomberg only apologized when he had something to gain from doing so, that is shortly before he started running for president in a Democratic primary, Oliver observed (O'Connor 2020).

Overall, Oliver continually focused on the real-world (and often very human) impacts of specific events and figures within the Democratic primary. He did not ordinarily weigh in on the daily or even weekly events of the Democratic debates, primary elections, and candidate drama, but instead covered broadly the significant policy dynamics and characters of candidates seeking to be president.

Nightly Late-Night Comedy and the 2020 General Election Campaign

As noted earlier in the chapter, financial and time concerns required limiting our analysis of the political humor during the 2020 general election phase to only the two nightly humor shows. We selected the late-night shows on CBS (Stephen Colbert) and NBC (Jimmy Fallon) because those two shows have been around longer than their competitors. In addition, they frequently finish first and second in the ratings, with Colbert securely in the lead and Fallon, the previous leader, fighting it out with Kimmel for the runner-up slot. They are also arguably the two most distinctive shows among the four, with Colbert focusing most heavily on political humor and Fallon using more pop culture material. Finally, the two shows are frequent subjects of media attention and of research examining previous election cycles (Farnsworth and Lichter 2020).

The political humor offered by Colbert and Fallon during the fall election campaign season is summarized in Table 3.7. The period examined includes August 24 through October 28, 2020, roughly the traditional campaign season, and jokes told around and after Election Day, from November 2 to November 13, 2020. The coverage on these humor programs was the most one-sided we have seen in decades of examining political humor. That was

92 Political Humor and the 2020 Presidential Campaign

TABLE 3.7 Candidate Late-Night Joke Analysis, General Election 2020

Total Candidate Jokes

	August	%	September	%	October	%	November	%	Total
Colbert	154	100%	307	58%	435	60%	125	55%	1,021
Fallon	No shows	n/a	227	42%	289	40%	151	45%	667
Total	154	9%	534	32%	724	43%	276	16%	1,688

Republican Candidate Focus

	August	%	September	%	October	%	November	%	Total
Colbert	150	100%	299	58%	421	60%	117	46%	987
Fallon	No Shows	n/a	220	42%	276	40%	138	54%	634
Total	150	9%	519	32%	697	43%	255	16%	1621

Democratic Candidate Focus

	August	%	September	%	October	%	November	%	Total
Colbert	4	100	8	53	14	58	8	38	34

true for both programs: Colbert told 1,021 jokes during this period, and 987 of them were focused on the GOP. Fallon told 667 jokes, with 634 of them focused on Republicans. The 34 Democratic-focused jokes told by Colbert and the 30 Democratic-focused jokes told by Fallon represented tiny shares of the political mirth (3.3 percent and 4.5 percent, respectively). Colbert told consistently more jokes during most of the campaign season, but Fallon had more political humor to offer in the part of November we examined, around the time of the election and immediately after it.

When one takes the number of jokes told about other Democratic and Republican figures out of the comparison, we see that political humor during the fall of 2020 was (once again) nearly all Trump all the time. The two comics told 1,619 jokes about Trump and 49 about Biden, a 97 percent to 3 percent ratio.

Trump's dominance in political humor during the campaign season dominated every month of the survey period, as shown in Table 3.8. In the parts of August, September, October, and November that we examined, Trump's advantage was well over 10-to-1. For the last week of August, when only Colbert was offering new content, the level was 50-to-1. Joe Biden did rank second to Trump in each of these four periods, while former President Obama ranked third, with six jokes devoted to him during the entire period. Russian President Vladimir Putin was the subject of three jokes, as was former Democratic presidential candidate Bernie Sanders.

BOX 3.2 SAMPLES OF POLITICAL HUMOR DURING THE 2020 GENERAL ELECTION CAMPAIGN POLICY

So, we've reached the point where Donald Trump is dictating our health regulations. That's why the new suggested serving for chicken is bucket.
(Stephen Colbert, August 26, 2020)

That was a pretty crazy press conference. At one point, Trump went off on a rant attacking military leaders because when you're in a scandal about calling soldiers names, the best offense is to antagonize their bosses. Trump was like: "this goes all the way to the top, people, whoever is the chief of all the commanders."
(Jimmy Fallon, September 8, 2020)

Even Joe Biden is like, "Trust me. Being vice president is not essential work." [Laughter] That's right, the coronavirus is spreading through the coronavirus task force. [Laughter] But don't worry, the White House is now forming a task force to figure out what went wrong with the task force.
(Jimmy Fallon, October 27, 2020)

Of course, refusing a peaceful transition implies a violent transition. I don't want that. I majored in theatre. The only fighting experience I have is stage combat. I do have a black belt in pretending to punch you. Trump's threats to disregard the results of the election alarmed top Democrats, who swiftly unleashed their most powerful weapon: Stern tweeting. Chuck Schumer posted, "President Trump: You are not a dictator and America will not permit you to be one."
(Stephen Colbert, September 24, 2020)

Political

And this is crazy [about the Covid vaccine on the brink of being approved shortly after the election]. You're not gonna believe what the vaccine is: sunlight and bleach. That's gotta sting right? That's gotta sting how much does this burn Trump? That's like your wife divorcing you, and then in next day she wins the power ball. And then marries Timothee Chalamet.
(Jimmy Fallon, November 9, 2020)

Oh, my God! He [Obama] got hotter. Our country's ex-boyfriend got hotter. Is he doing Peloton? Look at his butt. Put that in tennis shorts! Why

94 Political Humor and the 2020 Presidential Campaign

did we ever stop dating this guy? He's swishing three pointers in church shoes while our new boyfriend needs two hands to drink water.

(Jimmy Fallon, September 15, 2020)

Trump has prioritized reruns of *The Andy Griffith Show*, which ran from 1960 to 1968. Not to be outdone, Biden started advertising on the "Train entering the station" channel. (As Biden) "I was on that train. Got into a fistfight with one of the Lumiere brothers. Release the director's cut! Come on, Jacques!"

(Stephen Colbert, October 28, 2020)

Personal

(As Biden) 'That's right, we're Goin' for it, Jack! Everything's bigger in Texas! Remember the Alamo ... Also, remember where I put my glasses – never mind, they're in front of my eyes. Always the last place you look. Come on!

(Stephen Colbert, October 29, 2020)

That's right Kamala Harris will be taking over for Mike Pence. It's rare these days for a human to take over the job of a robot.

(Jimmy Fallon, November 9, 2020)

(As Trump) 'Look, I get the planet better than anyone. It's blue and it's green, heaven is up, hell is down, it's shaped like a meatball, and the whole thing revolves around me.'

(Stephen Colbert, October 28, 2020)

Now, remind me, which candidate had a chunk of white stuff fly out of their nose last week? [Laughter] (As Trump) 'That's right we're going to make – [sniff] America – [sniff] great – [sniff] again, again.'

(Jimmy Fallon, September 15, 2020)

Box 3.2 provides some examples of the different kind of political humor levied at the candidates during the general election season. As has been the case in the past, nearly all of the jokes contain political and personal dimensions. Rarely does policy make the cut. The relatively infrequent Biden jokes often make references to his age, even though he is only a few years older than Trump. Trump jokes often focused on his alleged narcissism and laziness.

Political Humor and the 2020 Presidential Campaign **95**

TABLE 3.8 Top Late-Night Joke Targets, Pre- and Postelection 2020

August		September		October		November	
Donald Trump	150	Donald Trump	519	Donald Trump	697	Donald Trump	253
Joe Biden	3	Joe Biden	12	Joe Biden	16	Joe Biden	18
Barack Obama*	1	Chuck Schumer*	1	Vladimir Putin*	3	Barack Obama	4
		Nancy Pelosi*	1	Mike Bloomberg	2	Bernie Sanders	1
				Bernie Sanders	2	Kamala Harris	1
				Ocasio-Cortez*	1		
				Barack Obama*	1		
				Hilary Clinton *	1		
				Kamala Harris	1		

Table 3.9 puts the extreme nature of the Trump focus into context. When compared to late-night comedy's treatment of presidential candidates in previous presidential elections (including Trump's own 2016 campaign), the unprecedented 2020 late-night assault on the incumbent president becomes apparent. The focus on Trump – 96 percent of the jokes about either presidential candidate in 2020 were about the incumbent president – broke the record for the most-one sided treatment of a presidential candidate on late-night comedy programming. The election cycle of 2020 recorded a far higher percentage than the old record from four years earlier, when 78 percent of the jokes focused on Trump.

The presidential campaign content of 2020 marked the eighth consecutive campaign in which more jokes were told about the Republican nominee than the Democratic nominee. The four percent of jokes devoted to Biden was roughly one-sixth of the percentage of jokes devoted to Hillary Clinton, the Democratic nominee who faced Trump in 2016. Biden's four percent likewise was a fraction of the jokes directed towards Barack Obama during his first campaign for the presidency in 2008, when he was the subject of 36 percent of the late-night jokes. Biden was the Democratic Party's vice presidential nominee that year, and again in 2012, and a far less significant target.

As we noted earlier, our 2020 content analysis was slimmed down because of financial and time pressures. Our analysis of the general election period of 2020 contains two late-night programs, not our usual group of four nightly late-night shows. In addition, we were only able to analyze any of those comedy programs for roughly six months, a fraction of the time analyzed during previous election years. All previous years contained in Table 3.9 had included analysis of political humor on for

96 Political Humor and the 2020 Presidential Campaign

TABLE 3.9 Proportion of Jokes about the Major Party Presidential Nominees

(Election Years, 1992–2020)

	Republican		Democrat		Total Jokes
1992	G.H.W. Bush	59%	B. Clinton	41%	1,033
1996	Dole	56%	B. Clinton	44%	1,496
2000	G.W. Bush	62%	Gore	38%	1,451
2004	G.W. Bush	70%	Kerry	30%	1,674
2008	McCain	64%	Obama	36%	2,126
2012	Romney	77%	Obama	23%	1,462
2016	Trump	78%	H. Clinton	22%	2,329 [partial year]
2020	Trump	96%	Biden	4%	3,146 [partial year]

Shows included by year:

2020: The Tonight Show (NBC), *The Late Show* (CBS), *Jimmy Kimmel Live!* (ABC) [nomination season only], *The Daily Show* (Comedy Central) [nomination season only]

2016: The Tonight Show (NBC), *The Late Show* (CBS), *Jimmy Kimmel Live!* (ABC), *The Daily Show* (Comedy Central)

2012: The Tonight Show (NBC), *The Late Show* (CBS), *The Daily Show* (Comedy Central), *The Colbert Report* (Comedy Central)

2008: The Tonight Show (NBC), *The Late Show* (CBS), *The Daily Show* (Comedy Central), *The Colbert Report* (Comedy Central), *Late Night* (NBC)

2004: The Tonight Show (NBC), *The Late Show* (CBS), *The Daily Show* (Comedy Central), *Late Night* (NBC)

2000: The Tonight Show (NBC), *The Late Show* (CBS), *Politically Incorrect* (ABC), *Late Night* (NBC)

1996: The Tonight Show (NBC), *The Late Show* (CBS), *Politically Incorrect* (ABC), *Late Night* (NBC)

1992: The Tonight Show (NBC), *The Late Show* (CBS), *Arsenio* (Fox), *The Tonight Show* (NBC) 1992–2016

Notes: Totals for 1992–2012 are based on entire calendar year in which election took place. Totals for 2016 cover January 1 to November 11.

Totals for 2020 cover less than six months of the year: January 13–April 9 [nomination season – four shows]; August 24–October 28 and November 2–13 [general election season – two shows].

programs across the entire 12 months, except for 2016, which contained a four-program analysis of about 10.5 months. Despite this substantial reduction in the 2020 humor analysis, we nevertheless found that this abbreviated and reduced study identified more political humor directed at the presidential election than any full-year presidential election analysis going back to 1992.

The Weekly Humor Programs and the 2020 Election Campaign

Saturday Night Live

During the general election campaign, a lot of the Trump commentary took place during "Weekend Update" segments. Rather than simply offering a string of one-liners, these faux evening news segments included longer and more serious discussions regarding the election. For example, the hosts repeatedly lamented about how "we cannot do another four years of Trump," referencing his insistent damage to the country. Furthermore, they would offer outright support for Biden by calling him the nation's "Designated Driver" (*SNL* 2020d) and other positive statements.

The "Cold Open" sketches remained a bit more even-handed in terms of satire. In contrast, the more talking that was added to the "Weekend Update" segments over the course of the fall, the more potently anti-Trump the show became. The news format allows for more expression of opinion as there is no overt mockery or acting, but rather simply straight commentary.

In a fall campaign segment, aired on October 3, 2020, the "Cold Open" mocked the first, interruption-filled presidential debate. As the show began, it started with a black screen which stated, "We thought it was important to see it again, since it might be the only presidential debate. And it was pretty fun to watch. As long as you don't live in America" (*SNL* 2020c). This statement presents a sense of shame and disappointment in the debate, and overall, in the election. In this segment, *SNL* was not promoting one candidate and putting the other down, but rather expressing overall sadness for the funny yet largely uninformative debate. This tone of disappointment in the elections is pervasive throughout *SNL*'s other skits as well. When displaying the Trump and Biden town halls, *SNL* portrayed both candidates as avoiding taking clear policy positions and perhaps not being all that sharp (*SNL* 2020e). Nevertheless, the undertones surrounding each candidate differed in their severity.

SNL criticized Trump and Pence directly as racist and characterized Trump specifically as moronic and careless. During the "Cold Open" segment that focused on the vice presidential debate, Pence was called the "white devil" (*SNL* 2020e) and during the Town Hall campaign event "Cold Open" segment, a pretend audience member called out to inquire if the lady dancing behind Trump was "a token black supporter or just Candice Owens" (*SNL* 2020e). Across his appearances during the fall campaign season, Alec Baldwin also made sure to emphasize a caricature of Trump not refusing the support of the "good ol' boys" and white supremacy during the second debate (*SNL* 2020f).

98 Political Humor and the 2020 Presidential Campaign

Unlike other people being caricatured on the show, it seemed as though *SNL* did not have to reach very far to generate material for the Trump segments. The writers took what Trump had said and exaggerated the portions where he appeared foolish and crass. During the *SNL* "Town Hall" campaign event cold open, Trump constantly called the host "woman" and during both that segment and one that followed later in the show, Trump consistently pronounced any woman's name wrong (*SNL* 2020e). Trump also talks to the host of the second debate as if she were a waitress at a restaurant, portraying him as moronic and disrespectful to women.

While *SNL* showed clear animosity toward Trump, *SNL* portrayed Biden as a caring person and the superior candidate by having him always wearing a mask when entering the stage, and as trying to rise above the division in the country (*SNL* 2020f). But the show nevertheless mocked several of his mannerisms. With Jim Carrey portraying Biden, every physical action was exaggerated and overly focused on facial expressions. It was almost as if the old rubber-faced "Fire Marshall Bill" character that Carrey had played on the 1990s hit comedy show *In Living Color* had aged and mellowed – at least a bit – into a senior citizen running for president (Hayes 2020).

During both the debates, Carrey as Biden would be making frustrated but smiling faces, trying to hold in his apparent rage at Trump (*SNL* 2020c, 2020f). In the segment relating to the second debate, Carrey as Biden asked the moderator if he could slap Trump anytime he continued over the allotted time (*SNL* 2020f). This gave an air of anger and lack of control to the show's Biden characterization.

While both Trump and Biden were mocked as somewhat clueless and old, Trump jokes were more focused towards his rude attitude. In contrast, Biden was portrayed along the lines of an "adorable" old man trope. During the segment relating to the "Town Hall" campaign event, when he was dodging questions and rambling, Carrey as Biden changed costumes into an outfit that recalled Bob Ross, the understated host of a long-running public television show on painting, and then into one for Mr. Rogers, the gentle host of a long-running children's show (*SNL* 2020e). The "audience" was of course confused and wanted to hear Biden's answers, but the program framed Biden as a sweet old man possibly too kind for politics by dressing him up as the extremely benign Ross and Mr. Rogers characters.

Overall, *SNL*'s cold open skits mocked both Trump and Biden for similar reasons but differed in the tone and severity of mockery. Neither were mocked primarily for their policy positions, but more so for their age, appearance, and actions.

Full Frontal with Samantha Bee

While *SNL* often provided crass humor when it mocked the candidates, Samantha Bee once again offered an even darker vision of contemporary 2020 politics, one that demonstrated her liberal sympathies without apology. Prior to COVID-19, Bee tended to play off of the audience at her tapings, but due to the pandemic she could not, as her show was not taped in front of an audience during the Fall 2020 campaign. Rather, it felt even more like a news segment as she spoke toward the camera rather than a studio audience. The "news host" feeling of those episodes was furthered by a lack of laugh track or background sounds in general. When Bee would make a joke, she would simply continue talking rather than pause for a laugh or interaction. Her sharp attacks on Trump were heightened in contrast to the lack of criticism of Biden. Pairing her direct unabashed criticism with an even more news-like fashion heightened the sense of political commentary rather than slapstick comedy.

In her overview and criticism of the first debate, Bee compared the debate to a dysfunctional Thanksgiving dinner with distant relatives, as it had "very little substance and a lot of yelling" (*FF* 2020c). Bee directed her criticism of the event squarely at Trump. She said that based on the debate it is even more evident that Trump is deeply racist and that he entirely mishandled COVID-19 and the relevant scientific findings (*FF* 2020c). Bee extended her criticism to moderator Chris Wallace, the host of *Fox News Sunday*. Bee, who often has found a good deal to criticize when it comes to Fox News, complained that Wallace would not fact check the president and let the president spread lies, or in her earthy terms "mist the air with complete and total bulls**t" (*FF* 2020c). This differs from *SNL*'s depiction of Wallace, where he was treated less critically to focus the *SNL* attack on the president. This segment shows Bee's framing of a general broad dislike for the whole process and conservatives, as Wallace is from right-leaning Fox News, as well as directly at Trump.

Unlike *SNL*, Bee offered little criticism of then-candidate Biden. She framed Biden as innocent and kind amid Trump's raging fury during the first debate stating, "Biden responded with the sweetest lil' comebacks you ever did see" (*FF* 2020c). She also calls him, "Joe, friend" (*FF* 2020c) before continuing on to offer the smallest bit of criticism, saying he should "toughen up next time" (*FF* 2020c).

Bee's later episodes continued the same theme, where she focused on lambasting Trump and generally framed Biden as the congenial old man, and Democrats in general as heroes (*FF* 2020e, *FF* 2020g). Her focus on disliking Trump and supporting Biden is present even after the election. During her Thanksgiving special, she states that "it's been an unexpected,

100 Political Humor and the 2020 Presidential Campaign

sweet surprise to watch Joe Biden win a little more every day. As if we defeated the last boss that's been tormenting us for years" (*FF* 2020f). The use of "we" directly connects her with the audience, and the framing of Trump as a video game villain forms a unity around a common antithesis, with a common hero as well.

Overall, Samantha Bee's show was consistently critical toward Trump, often employing crude language. She didn't really direct much criticism at the Biden campaign, and when discussing her stories, she did not rely heavily on facts (*FF* 2020d). Her attacks seemed somewhat more direct in the fall than they had been during the nomination season. Prior to the format changes mandated by COVID-19, Bee bantered with the audience more. As a result, the show became more intense during the fall of 2020, when she chose to talk alone to a camera.

Last Week Tonight with John Oliver

On the *Last Week Tonight* show, John Oliver generally recaps the important events of the week with his own quippy, intense style. When presenting stories, he sits at a table with a screen projected next to him highlighting the topic and key features under discussion. At first this format may not appear to be a comedy show. He frequently fact checks stories and supplements them with sources, but the humor comes in with his tone and commentary. *LWT* differs from *SNL* as it primarily has the news-style format and differs from Samantha Bee in being more fact-based in orientation.

John Oliver's show generally operated by presenting news segments from that week, and then fact checking and commenting on the segment with pop culture references. For example, on his discussion of mail-in voting, he cites the exact number of ballots that had been mailed in by the day of his show and then plays the Fox News story that showed Trump's deliberate campaign to undermine the legitimacy of these ballots and Trump's own ambiguity about leaving office if he were to lose the 2020 contest (*LWT* 2020c).

Rather than making conventional jokes regarding Trump's appearance, as some other comics did, Oliver focused on what Trump and his supporters said, and on their actions. For example, when the vote counting was taking some time, Oliver pointed to the fact that Trump's supporters were chanting "stop the count" in some states and chanting "count the votes" in other states at the same time (*LWT* 2020d). He commented that the intense and conflicting preferences of Team Trump, which varied depending on whether the incumbent was ahead or behind in the state's vote count at a

Political Humor and the 2020 Presidential Campaign **101**

given time, must be confusing the voter counters inside. Oliver also points to Trump's Twitter timeline, consisting of "a whole run of tweets flagged as disputed or misleading" (*LWT* 2020d).

Oliver also criticizes the Republican Party in general, specifically focusing on their record in campaigns. "First, let's acknowledge that there's nothing new in Republicans attempting to depress turnout" (*LWT* 2020c). Oliver highlighted the Republican history of voter suppression and how now we have just seen them brought to light and also discusses ways to prevent voter suppression. This augmented his anti-Trump tone with Republican criticism, but in a way designed to be informationally productive.

Sometimes he employed insults, though. After the election was finalized, Oliver labeled Trump an "asshole" for not stepping down and conceding like a "normal" person would after an electoral defeat and said that he was more so disappointed in the political leaders who continued to support him, like Secretary of State Mike Pompeo (*LWT* 2020e). He made a snide joke about America's top diplomat, stating, "your whole job is to denounce coups" (*LWT* 2020e), and then expressed his disappointment in others who continued to support Trump after his defeat was clear. Oliver's commentary during the campaign showed Oliver's dislike for Trump, but also offered a sadness for the system overall. While the attacks were not directed equally at both Trump and his followers, Oliver expressed disappointment over the actions of Trump supporters as a group, not over their ideology.

Once the vote counting was concluded, Oliver took a moment to recognize his joy regarding the outcome.

> I would love to make fun of this, but unfortunately, I have no time for losers ... I am starting to focus on the negatives and be cynical about what a Biden presidency could or is even going to try to achieve, but before we get to anything negative at all, let me just give us all a quick moment with no caveats of celebration.
>
> *(LWT 2020d)*

While Oliver primarily took aim at Trump and his supporters, he also provided some criticism toward Biden during the campaign. At the very start of his October 5, 2020 show, he showed a get-out-the-vote public service announcement designed to encourage African American turnout. The PSA urged voters to vote locally and "get your booty to the polls" because an individual vote can make a difference (*LWT* 2020c). After the PSA ends, Oliver states it is a "better message than Joe Biden's Team's" (*LWT* 2020c).

102 Political Humor and the 2020 Presidential Campaign

Oliver also critiqued reporters. When CNN's Don Lemon was pressing a voter counter on when the counting would finish, Oliver stated "he doesn't f**king know, Lemon! Leave the man alone!" (*LWT* 2020d).

Overall, Oliver has a very professional factual tone to his show. His commentary does show some of his opinions, specifically his dislike of Trump, but he supported his opinions with facts and figures that countered Trump's statements. Oliver does provide criticism to both candidates; he focused on Trump more during the election cycle, but he said that he plans to criticize Biden and his actions once he becomes president.

Conclusion

Our study of the attention late-night comics paid to politicians during the 2020 presidential campaign confirms the impression that Donald Trump remained in a class by himself as a target of the late-night comics. In a pattern consistent with that of the campaign jokes of four years earlier, Trump ranked first on the comedic hit list by a wide margin – and did so month after month. The blustery billionaire remained a rich source of material for comedy, and that fact varied little depending on the state of the Democratic field or the distance on the calendar from Election Day. Regardless of which candidate had done well in the previous caucuses and primaries, the late-night humorists remained as focused on Trump as they were during 2016. Of course, the political environment of 2020 did contain some distinct features, among them the first U.S. House vote to impeach Trump and the subsequent Senate acquittal occurred in early 2020. That process was followed closely by the rise of COVID-19. The start of the pandemic was followed, in turn, by the administration's missteps in responding to the biggest health care crisis in decades. Indeed, it would have been odd if Trump had not been the focus of considerable late-night attention during these very unusual months of his presidency. But the distance between the comedic attention paid to Trump and to Democratic candidates for the president is vast indeed.

Both the nightly comedy shows, and the weekly programs, found Trump an appealing target, during both the Democratic nomination campaign period and the general election that followed. When the humorists turned to the Democratic presidential candidates, they often had more to say about Biden or Sanders than the candidates further back in the pack. The humorists struggled to make the 2020 version of Biden all that funny, particularly when compared to the high-energy counterpoint of Bernie Sanders, his chief rival for the 2020 Democratic presidential nomination. The humorists also settled on similar lines of commentary regarding candidates further back in the field. The long-shot candidates triggered

Political Humor and the 2020 Presidential Campaign **103**

some mirth on these programs for arguably exaggerated descriptions of who they were, including the intense policy-wonk (Warren), the clueless and not all that liberal billionaire (Bloomberg) and the young man – like the puppet Pinocchio – who dreams of being fully human (Buttigieg).

In Chapter 4 we examine the political humor of 2021, asking whether the voters' selection of Joe Biden as the 46th president – and his Inauguration to that office – helped reduce the imbalance that for the last half-dozen years has focused on candidate and then President Trump.

Republican Candidate Focus

	September	*October*	*Total*	*Total Percent*
Fallon	85	97	182	14%
Colbert	240	233	473	37%
Kimmel	182	226	408	32%
Noah	114	94	208	16%
Total	621	650	1271	99%*

Democratic Candidate Focus

	September	*October*	*Total*	*Total Percent*
Fallon	12	2	20	13%
Colbert	41	15	56	36%
Kimmel	26	11	37	24%
Noah	20	21	41	27%
Total	105	49	154	100%

Percentages not sum to 100 because of rounding down.
Analysis period runs from September 11 to October 17, 2019.

Source: CMPA

Republican Candidate Focus

	January	*February*	*March*	*April*	*Total*	*Total Percent*
Fallon	110	35	23	1	169	12%
Colbert	268	119	36	82	505	36%
Kimmel	154	79	82	74	389	27%
Noah	134	78	82	63	357	25%
Total	666	311	223	220	1,420	100%

Democratic Candidate Focus

	January	February	March	April	Total	Total Percent
Fallon	36	37	3	0	76	26%
Colbert	45	37	15	10	107	36%
Kimmel	2	18	5	6	32	11%
Noah	38	30	9	4	81	27%
Total	122	122	32	20	296	100%

Analysis period runs from January 13 to April 9, 2020.

Source: CMPA

Jokes about COVID-19 Relating to Trump and Trump Administration Responses
(March 1 to April 9, 2020)

Jimmy Kimmel Live	142
The Daily Show with Trevor Noah	125
The Late Show with Stephen Colbert	117
The Tonight Show Starring Jimmy Fallon	19

Jokes about President Trump's First Impeachment*
(January 13 to February 29, 2020)

Jimmy Kimmel Live	117
The Daily Show with Trevor Noah	112
The Late Show with Stephen Colbert	268
The Tonight Show Starring Jimmy Fallon	69

* Trump's first impeachment trial began in the Senate on January 16, 2020 and concluded with Trump's acquittal on February 5, 2020.

Source: CMPA

	August	%	September	%	October	%	November	%	Total
Colbert	4	100%	8	53%	14	58%	8	38%	34
Fallon	No shows	n/a	7	46	10	42%	13	62%	30
Total	4	6%	15	23%	24	38%	21	33%	64

General Election Joke Totals: Percent Trump v. Percent Biden

	Trump	%	Biden	%	Total
Colbert	985	61%	23	47%	1,032
Fallon	634	39%	26	53%	687
Total	1,619	97%	49	3%	1,667

Note: The data examine jokes told on *The Tonight Show* (NBC) and *The Late Show* (CBS) from August 24, 2020 to October 28, 2020 and November 2–13, 2020.

Source: CMPA

Overall

August–November 2020	Jokes	Percentage
Donald Trump	1,619	87%
Joe Biden	49	3%
Barack Obama**	6	*
Bernie Sanders	3	*
Vladimir Putin**	3	*
Chuck Schumer**	2	*
Kamala Harris	2	*
Mike Bloomberg	2	*

August–November 2020	Jokes	Percentage
Donald Trump	1,619	97%
Joe Biden	49	3%

* Less than 0.5 percent.

** Not a presidential candidate in 2020, but the focus of at least one 2020 campaign joke.

Note: Only candidates with two or more jokes are reported here. The data examine jokes told on *The Tonight Show* (NBC) and *The Late Show* (CBS) from August 24, 2020 to October 28, 2020 and November 2–13, 2020.

Source: CMPA

4

LATE-NIGHT POLITICAL HUMOR AND THE TWO PRESIDENTS OF EARLY 2021

Coauthored with Sally Burkley

The combustible nature of Donald Trump's departure from office in January 2021, together with his continuing efforts in the years that followed to claim without evidence that the 2020 election was stolen, provided a steady source for material for late-night comics who have targeted Trump's years in public life like no other previous president. An examination of the key targets of the humor revealed that the four long-running nightly entertainers examined in this project (Stephen Colbert, Jimmy Fallon, Jimmy Kimmel, and Trevor Noah) paid considerable attention to Trump and relatively little to Joe Biden, the actual president as of January 20, during the early months of 2021. Three influential once-a-week comedy programs [*Saturday Night Live (SNL)*, *Full Frontal (FF)*, and *Last Week Tonight (LET)*] examined in this project likewise offered a great deal of material on the former president in comparison to his Democratic successor. Using a content analysis of nightly host monologues and a qualitative study of a variety of once-a-week comedy programs during early 2021, as well as past content analyses of late-night presidential humor going back to the George H.W. Bush presidency, this chapter examines both short-term joke patterns about the two presidents during the start of that tumultuous year, as well as the long-term patterns relating to presidential humor.

Political Humor during a Troubled Presidential Transition and Beyond

In this study, we examined late-night comedy jokes of those four nightly shows from January 18, 2021 to April 30, 2021, a period that

DOI: 10.4324/9781003283041-4

included Biden's Inauguration and his first months as president, as well as former President Trump's departure from Washington and his second impeachment trial. Taken together, these four comedy programs offered 4,423 jokes relating to political figures and topics during early 2021. That volume of one-liners represents an exceptionally large volume of political humor. For the nomination phase of the 2020 campaign, as we discussed in Chapter 3, those same four shows produced 3,327 jokes relating to the presidential campaign over an even longer study period – from September 11 to October 17, 2019 and from January 13 to April 9, 2020. What the two very different political environments had in common, though, was an overwhelming focus of these political humorists on Donald Trump.

We analyzed the jokes from early 2021, as we have done for previous chapters, to determine the target of the humorous remarks on those nightly shows. We then analyzed these jokes for their policy, political, and/or personal content. We also undertook a qualitative study of political humor during early 2021 on three once-a-week programs: *Saturday Night Live, Full Frontal with Samantha Bee*, and *Last Week Tonight with John Oliver*. None of these programs employ the rapid-fire comedic monologue format that is common among the four nightly programs, so a more qualitative approach is better suited for them.

This study of political humor during the early months of the Biden presidency represents an updating of The Center for Media and Public Affairs (CMPA) historical database, which includes more than 100,000 jokes by hosts on popular late-night TV shows from 1992 to 2021. This database includes not only jokes about political figures but also those directed at government and social institutions, such as churches and the military, as well as jokes that addressed a social or economic problem, like inflation, gay rights, or climate change. Due to limited resources, however, this chapter focuses on the treatment of political figures during the early months of 2021. We will talk more in Chapter 5 about the content of these late-night shows later in 2021. In Chapter 5 we focus on examining a new conservative comedy program on Fox News: *Gutfeld!* We also couple that analysis with data from the four nightly shows we routinely examine during that same period of analysis. *Gutfeld!* first aired as a regular weeknight program containing political humor on April 5, 2021 (Roig-Franzia 2022), near the end of the early 2021 humor content study period employed in this chapter regarding those four nightly shows.

Nightly Late-Night Comedy and the two Presidents of Early 2021

In Table 4.1, we look at the number of jokes told by these four nightly humorists during the winter and spring of 2021 (January 18, 2021 to

108 Late-Night Political Humor and the Two Presidents of Early 2021

TABLE 4.1 Leading Targets of Late-Night Humor, Early 2021

Donald Trump	1,697
Joe Biden	457
Mike Lindell	249
Matt Gaetz	191
Ted Cruz	179
Marjorie Taylor Greene	157
Andrew Cuomo	148
Mike Pence	143
Republicans*	94
Mitch McConnell	87
Rudy Giuliani	84
Donald Trump Jr.	51
Lindsey Graham	46
Madison Cawthorn	45
Joe Manchin	44
Vladimir Putin	40
Kevin McCarthy	32
Eric Trump	30
Mitt Romney	37
Bernie Sanders	39
Rioters*	35
Kevin McCarthy	32
Eric Trump	30
Anthony Fauci	23
Chuck Schumer	22
Sarah Sanders	20
Rick Santorum	19
Ron DeSantis	18
Caitlin Jenner	17
Ron Johnson	16
Barack Obama	16
Fox News*	15
Melania Trump	15
Chris Christie	13
Jim Jordan	12
Lou Dobbs	12
Greg Abbott	11
Ron Paul	11
Bill Cassidy	11
John Borrasso	10
Adam Kinzinger	10

Total N = 4,423.

Note: Only individuals and institutions that were the subject of at least ten jokes are included here.

* General categories are used for jokes that focus on the institution or a group rather than a specific individual. Jokes that name individuals are coded as jokes directed at that individual.

Totals include late-night jokes aired during January 18–April 30, 2021, on *Jimmy Kimmel Live*, *The Daily Show with Trevor Noah*, *The Late Show with Stephen Colbert*, and *The Tonight Show with Jimmy Fallon*.

Source: CMPA

April 30, 2021). Even a new president who promised a major departure from the policies and the governing approach of his predecessor could not compete with that predecessor when it came to being the focus of late-night comedy. Of the 4,423 jokes they offered about politics and political figures during that roughly three-month period, only 457 of them (10.3 percent) related to President Biden. Trump, in contrast, was the subject of more than three times as many barbs: 1,697 jokes or 38 percent of the political jokes offered on these shows during this period.

This intense focus on Trump extended beyond the former president himself. The next four top targets of political humor included some of the most ardent public defenders of Trump's false claim that Democrats stole the 2020 presidential election. Mike Lindell, an online marketer of bedding products (commonly known as the "My Pillow Guy") before he began focusing on promoting the false stolen election claim, ranked third as the subject of 249 jokes. The next three positions were occupied by some of the most vocal Trump allies in Congress: Rep. Matt Gaetz (R-FL), with 191 jokes; Sen. Ted Cruz (R-TX), with 179 jokes; and Rep. Marjorie Taylor Greene (R-GA), with 157 jokes.

Then-New York Governor Andrew Cuomo (D) ranked seventh among the top comedy targets of early 2021. During that time, he was fighting allegations of inappropriate behavior, including sexual harassment and groping, that had been reported by current and former aides (Ferré-Sadurní 2021). Matters of personal misconduct often provide extensive material for late-night comics, as demonstrated by the late-night treatments of former presidents Bill Clinton and Donald Trump, who each frequently faced mockery regarding their treatment of women (Farnsworth and Lichter 2020). As for Cuomo, the governor resigned in August 2021, following months of trying to contain the damage the scandals were causing to his administration (Kerr and Blackstone 2021).

Biden and Cuomo were the only two Democrats in the top ten of leading targets of political humor during early 2021. Sen. Joe Manchin (D-WV), a conservative Democratic senator often the target of ire from the party's liberals, ranked 15th as a leading subject of mirth, and third among Democrats, as the subject of 44 jokes. Between Cuomo and Manchin were former Vice President Pence (143 jokes), Republicans generally (94 jokes), Senate Republican Leader Mitch McConnell of Kentucky (87 jokes), Trump lawyer and former New York City Mayor Rudy Giuliani (84 jokes), and first son Donald Trump Jr. (51 jokes), along with others in the Trump orbit. Russian President Vladimir Putin was the top-ranked person from outside the U.S. on the list of top targets of political humor, with 40 jokes, and the only non-American to receive ten or more jokes on these late-night programs during the study period.

110 Late-Night Political Humor and the Two Presidents of Early 2021

Being Biden, or a member of the Democratic Party, meant one was far less likely to be the subject of late-night mockery. Pence was the subject of 143 jokes, while his successor as Vice President, Kamala Harris, was the target of only six jokes. While the House and Senate Republican leaders both made the top 20 as political humor targets during early 2021, Senate Democratic Leader Schumer ranked 25th, with 22 jokes. House Speaker Nancy Pelosi (D-CA) was the subject of only two jokes during the period. (This comparison demonstrates that humor does not always follow power, though the partisan differences may correspond to the ideological perspectives offered on the programs. Democratic majorities controlled both chambers of Congress during 2021 and 2022, but that party's leaders were less interesting to the late-night comics than the Republican elected officials serving in the minority on Capitol Hill).

The same partisan pattern emerges when examining family connections. Melania Trump, the former first lady, was the subject of 15 jokes, while there was only one joke directed at First Lady Jill Biden across those four programs. There were more jokes about the Trump children, who were vocal defenders of their father's efforts to stay in office despite losing the election: Donald Trump Jr. was the subject of 51 jokes; Eric Trump was the subject of 30 barbs; and there were eight jokes about first daughter Ivanka Trump, a top White House aide to her father.

In contrast, there was only one joke during early 2021 about Hunter Biden, who may have been engaged in some controversial if not problematic activities in the private sector (and in his personal life) during recent years (Goldman et al. 2020). The Biden son, it should be noted, did not become part of his father's administration, but he was a frequent target of conservative attacks over his international business interests and the alleged contents of a laptop computer that made its way into the hands of Republican operatives (Goldman 2020).

The relatively modest attention that the Biden son received from the late-night comics is in sharp contrast to the attention President Trump and the Republicans in Congress sought to direct to Hunter Biden's business dealings and his laptop computer, which according to Republicans contained incriminating information that could hurt the Biden family (Goldman 2020; Goldman et al. 2020).

When one looks at the month-by-month patterns of political humor on these four shows one sees how little Trump's transition to a former president redirected the focus of these comics away from him. On late night, it was almost as if Trump was still at the White House after his term ended on January 20, 2021. As shown in Table 4.2, Trump ranked first as a source of political humor during the second half of January, and during the entire months of February, March, and April. During the second half of January, Trump had a more than five-to-one advantage over every other

Late-Night Political Humor and the Two Presidents of Early 2021 **111**

TABLE 4.2 Leading Targets of Late-Night Humor by Month, Early 2021

January		February		March		April	
Donald Trump	528	Donald Trump	499	Donald Trump	449	Donald Trump	221
Joe Biden	85	Ted Cruz	144	Joe Biden	144	Mike Lindell	201
Rudy Giuliani	34	Joe Biden	98	Andrew Cuomo	121	Matt Gaetz	159
Marjorie Taylor Greene	31	Marjorie Taylor Greene	87	Republicans*	63	Joe Biden	119
Lindsey Graham	22	Mike Pence	46	Madison Cawthorn	45	Joe Manchin	42
Total	922		1,274		1,198		1,029

Total N = 4,423

Note: The total numbers include many targets not listed here.

* General categories are used for jokes that focus on the institution or group rather than a specific individual. Jokes that name individuals are coded at the individual level.

Totals include late-night jokes aired during January 18–April 30, 2021, on *Jimmy Kimmel Live*, *The Daily Show with Trevor Noah*, *The Late Show with Stephen Colbert*, and *The Tonight Show with Jimmy Fallon*.

Source: CMPA

subject of humor, as compared to a more than three-to-one advantage over every other target in February and March. April was the only month examined where the results were close between the first- and second-ranked targets of humor. During that month, Trump was the subject of 221 jokes and Trump's political ally Mike Lindell was the subject of 201 barbs. Rep. Gaetz was a distant third, with 159 jokes.

Though he became president on January 20, 2021, Joe Biden never dominated the political humor conversation during early 2021. (Of course, it may be better for a president's political fortunes not to receive a lot of attention from the late-night comics). The new president ranked second as a source of political humor in January and March but ranked third in February (behind Trump and Sen. Cruz), and fourth in April (behind Trump, Mike Lindell, and Rep. Gaetz). Few other Democrats cracked the political humor monthly rankings as Republican partisan figures remained the dominant targets throughout early 2021. The only Democratic targets that joined Biden in the monthly joke rankings were scandal-plagued New York Governor Cuomo, who ranked third in March, and independent-minded Sen. Joe Manchin of West Virginia, who ranked fifth in April.

Table 4.3 demonstrates that the intense late-night comedic focus on Trump was common across the four late-night programs we analyzed. Jimmy Kimmel had both the largest number of political jokes (2,085) and

112 Late-Night Political Humor and the Two Presidents of Early 2021

TABLE 4.3 Leading Target Frequency by Program, Early 2021

	Kimmel	Noah	Colbert	Fallon	Total
Donald Trump	934	414	228	121	1,697
[Percentages]	[45%]	[32%]	[33%]	[37%]	
Joe Biden	71	228	60	98	457
Mike Lindell	241	0	8	0	249
Matt Gaetz	89	32	70	0	191
Ted Cruz	80	76	5	18	179
Marjorie Taylor Greene	101	24	32	0	157
Andrew Cuomo	27	107	14	0	148
Mike Pence	91	35	6	11	143
Republicans*	0	0	76	18	94
Mitch McConnell	18	54	15	0	87
Rudy Giuliani	60	9	5	11	84
Donald Trump Jr.	50	1	0	0	51
Madison Cawthorn	0	45	0	0	45
Joe Manchin	0	42	2	0	44
Lindsey Graham	12	24	4	0	40
Bernie Sanders	19	8	3	9	39
Vladimir Putin	0	0	18	21	39
Mitt Romney	3	33	0	1	37
Total	**2,085**	**1,311**	**697**	**330**	**4,423**

Totals include late-night jokes aired during January 18–April 30, 2021, on *Jimmy Kimmel Live*, *The Daily Show with Trevor Noah*, *The Late Show with Stephen Colbert*, and *The Tonight Show with Jimmy Fallon*.

Note: Only the subjects of at least 35 jokes are included. The total numbers include many humor targets not listed here.

* General categories are used for jokes that focus on the institution rather than a specific individual. Jokes that name individuals are coded at the individual level.

Source: CMPA

the largest number of jokes about Trump (934), representing 45 percent of all political jokes Kimmel told during the study period. The other three programs also offered far more on Trump than any other political figure, with percentages of jokes aimed at Trump ranging from 32 percent to 37 percent of all jokes aimed at political figures.

Kimmel's program stood out in another way as well, with its intense focus on Trump allies. Kimmel told 241 jokes about pillow marketer turned "stop the steal" activist Mike Lindell. Stephen Colbert was the only other comic to offer even a single joke during the study period that related to Lindell, who was the target of eight Colbert jokes. Kimmel told 101 jokes about Rep. Marjorie Taylor Greene, roughly two-thirds of the total jokes focused on her across these four shows. Kimmel also told more than two-thirds of the total jokes the four comics offered about Rudy Giuliani, the former New York City mayor turned Trump's lawyer, and about Donald Trump Jr.

Indeed, the results of Table 4.3 suggest that the humorists, apart from their consistently harsh treatment of Trump, went in very different directions in their search for laugh lines during early 2021. Trevor Noah focused far more on the troubles of New York Governor Cuomo and the political activities of Republican Senate Leader Mitch McConnell of Kentucky than did his colleagues. Noah also stood apart with his greater focus on Sens. Mitt Romney (R-Utah) and Joe Manchin (D-WV) during his late-night monologues. Stephen Colbert and Jimmy Fallon had a lot more to say about Putin than did the other two hosts. Colbert seemed particularly inclined to joke about Republicans collectively, compared to his colleagues.

Once again, the content of Jimmy Fallon's program presents an interesting contrast when compared to that of his fellow late-night comics. While the percentage of Fallon's jokes about Trump were higher than the percentages of jokes about political figures told by Noah and Colbert, Fallon told far fewer political jokes overall – less than half the jokes each of the other three late-night comics examined here told about political figures.

Fallon's unusually light touch to political humor during early 2021 was not a new trend on *The Tonight Show*. Jimmy Fallon lost his position atop the late-night ratings following the 2016 campaign and what some viewers considered to be his too-friendly treatment of candidate Trump during that contest (Hartung 2017; Itzkoff 2017). Over the years that followed, Fallon retained his light-on-politics approach to late-night comedy, particularly when compared to his fellow late-night hosts (Farnsworth et al. 2021). The same pattern of difference that appeared in previous studies of late-night humor in 2016 and 2020 also appeared in early 2021, as shown in Table 4.3.

As one would expect, Fallon was less one-sided in his treatment of the two presidents of 2021 than were his late-night counterparts. Even though he had by far the smallest number of political jokes of the four comics, he offered the largest percentage of Biden jokes. Furthermore, the percentages aimed at the two presidents of 2021 were relatively close on *The Tonight Show*: 37 percent of Fallon's jokes were directed at Trump (121), as compared to 30 percent of his jokes aiming at Biden (98). In contrast,

Biden was the target of roughly 17 percent of the political jokes told by Noah, and less than 10 percent of the political jokes told by the other two comics. The Fallon and Noah numbers regarding the two presidents of early 2021 were relatively close in comparison with the other two comics, with a less than two-to-one margin on those shows. The number of Trump jokes versus Biden jokes exceeded three-to-one on the programs hosted by Kimmel and Colbert.

Another area of sharp disagreement among the hosts was the volume of attention paid to the January 6, 2021, insurrection during our study period, which began nearly two weeks after the assault on the U.S. Capitol. Overall, there were 678 jokes about the attack during our study period, or about 15 percent of the total political jokes offered during early 2021. Jimmy Kimmel delivered 303 jokes about the incident, and Stephen Colbert provided 291. Both were in sharp contrast to the other late-night comics: Jimmy Fallon offered 52 jokes on this matter, while Trevor Noah delivered only 32. The attack on the Capitol, a radical departure from the tradition of peaceful transfers of power in this country, represented a major political and cultural development. But some comics clearly found it less of a subject for late-night mirth that did others.

Few incidents in the recent decades of U.S. politics can compare with the developments of January 6, 2021, which continue to be the subject of investigations and prosecutions years after the violent, failed attempts to keep Trump in office. Even so, the late-night comics sometimes have focused intensely on major political developments involving presidents in the past. Bill Clinton, whose personal behavior gave rise to many jokes about his sexual behavior, was the subject of more than 1,500 jokes about his misconduct during his eight years as president – and his subsequent years as a former president (Farnsworth and Lichter 2020: 22). There were not nearly as many political jokes on the late-night programs during the 1990s, but even so the sexually tinged jokes about Clinton represented half of all the jokes told about him.

During 2017, Trump's first year as president, there were 626 jokes involving Russia, the top policy target on late night that year (Farnsworth and Lichter 2020: 91). Many of those jokes addressed Russian President Putin's possible efforts to help Trump win the 2016 election or allegations of a close personal relationship between the two men. Sexual matters ranked second in 2017, the subject of 235 jokes on late night, and many of those jokes were also related to Trump's own questionable behavior in that realm (Farnsworth and Lichter 2020: 91).

The late-night comics may have focused on Trump, but he was clearly not their only major target during early 2021. Taken together, Republicans faced harsh treatment on all the late-night shows. As shown in Table 4.4, Republicans as a group dominated the political content of the late-night

Late-Night Political Humor and the Two Presidents of Early 2021 **115**

TABLE 4.4 Percentage of Jokes by Show and Political Party of Target, Early 2021

Party Labels	Jimmy Kimmel Live!	The Daily Show with Trevor Noah	The Late Show with Stephen Colbert	The Tonight Show Starring Jimmy Fallon	Grand Total
D	140	430	89	109	768
No party	0	1	39	22	62
R	1,945	880	569	199	3,593
Total	2,085 (47%)	1,311 (30%)	697 (16%)	330 (7%)	4,423

Totals include late-night jokes aired during January 18–April 30, 2021, on *Jimmy Kimmel Live*, *The Daily Show with Trevor Noah*, *The Late Show with Stephen Colbert*, and *The Tonight Show with Jimmy Fallon*.

Source: CMPA

monologues during early 2021. On Jimmy Kimmel's show, which contained the most political jokes, 1,945 out of his 2,085 jokes during that study period were directed at Republicans (Trump was the target of 934 jokes, or a bit less than half of the jokes directed at Republicans). Only 140 jokes on Kimmel's show were directed at Democratic political figures (just under seven percent of the total number of political jokes). In other words, Republicans received more than ten times the volume of jokes than did Democrats on Kimmel's show during this period.

As we have seen in other comparisons among these four hosts, Fallon was the least one-sided in the political jokes relating to partisan figures, with a ratio that is just under two-to-one targeting Republicans compared to Democrats. Noah was also close to two-to-one in his margin when he joked about Republican and Democratic political figures. Colbert's margin was seven-to-one targeting Republicans over Democrats. During early 2021, very few political jokes on these programs were directed at individuals who do not have a partisan loyalty, only 62 out of 4,423 political jokes. And of those jokes directed at people other than individuals linked to Republicans and Democrats, more than half of them (39) were directed at Russian President Putin (under our coding system, we regard Sen. Sanders as a Democrat despite his professed identity as a political independent, given that he sought the Democratic presidential nomination in both 2016 and 2020 and caucuses with the Democratic Party in the Senate).

Roughly one-third of the jokes about Trump were personal, dealing with things like his appearance and mannerisms, while roughly two-thirds were not personal, which dealt with more policy-oriented concerns. As shown in Table 4.5, both Colbert and Fallon employed a very personal-oriented approach to their discussions of Trump, a sharp contrast from the

116 Late-Night Political Humor and the Two Presidents of Early 2021

TABLE 4.5 Personal Jokes by Program, Early 2021

Jokes about Trump

	Not Personal	*Personal*	*Total Jokes*
Jimmy Kimmel Live	734	200	934
The Daily Show with Trevor Noah	279	135	414
The Late Show with Stephen Colbert	23	205	228
The Tonight Show Starring Jimmy Fallon	13	108	121
Total jokes	1,184	648	1,697
Total percentage	65%	35%	100%

Jokes not about Trump

	Not Personal	Personal	Total Jokes
Jimmy Kimmel Live	871	280	1,151
The Daily Show with Trevor Noah	794	103	897
The Late Show with Stephen Colbert	81	387	468
The Tonight Show Starring Jimmy Fallon	80	129	209
Total jokes	1,835	925	2,726
Total percentage	66%	34%	100%

Jokes about Biden

	Not Personal	Personal	Total Jokes
Jimmy Kimmel Live	58	13	71
The Daily Show with Trevor Noah	186	42	228
The Late Show with Stephen Colbert	13	47	60
The Tonight Show Starring Jimmy Fallon	24	74	98
Total jokes	281	176	457
Total percentage	61%	39%	100%

Jokes not about Biden

	Not Personal	Personal	Total Jokes
Jimmy Kimmel Live	1,547	467	2,014
The Daily Show with Trevor Noah	887	196	1,083
The Late Show with Stephen Colbert	91	546	640
The Tonight Show Starring Jimmy Fallon	69	163	232
Total jokes	2,594	1,372	3,966
Total percentage	65%	35%	100%

N = 4,423
Totals include late-night jokes aired during January 18–April 30, 2021, on *Jimmy Kimmel Live*, *The Daily Show with Trevor Noah*, *The Late Show with Stephen Colbert*, and *The Tonight Show with Jimmy Fallon*.

Source: CMPA

commentary offered by Noah and Kimmel, which were far less personal in focus.

Overall, though, the pattern of roughly one-third of the jokes being personal appeared in all the jokes analyzed during this period that were not about Trump. Once again, Colbert and Fallon offered a far more personally oriented approach to their treatment of political figures, including those that were not Donald Trump, than did the other two late-night hosts.

Although he was subject to a much smaller number of jokes, more of the Biden jokes (39 percent) were personal. Perhaps because the hosts offered less criticism of the Biden policy agenda than they did of Trump at a comparable point in his presidency (Farnsworth and Lichter 2020), the jokes about Biden mocked his high-touch style and his sometimes-awkward public mannerisms and statements. For both presidents, though, more than 60 percent of the jokes were not personal in nature.

BOX 4.1 SELECTED POLITICAL JOKES, EARLY 2021

Donald Trump

Thank you for joining me, at the end of the final full day, of the presidency, of Donald Jennifer Trump. It's the end of an error. Right now, Trump is packing up his golf clubs, Barron, and all the fake Melanias too.
(Jimmy Kimmel, January 19, 2021)

According to a source familiar with the situation, Mar-a-Lago has become a "Sad" and "Dispirited" place since the ex-president moved in, as opposed to before he moved in, when it was hailed as the number-one luxury COVID hot spot where you can enjoy room-temperature chowder while a Chinese spy loads malware on your phone. But with the ex-president back, the mood has gotten so dark that a lot of people have quit Mar-a-Lago. For Pete's sake! He's been there six days! Imagine what a Donny downer he must be for people to already throw in the towel. Okay, here he comes.
(Stephen Colbert, January 26, 2021)

[President Trump has] made us all confused and nervous. (Laughter) You're like an Uber driver who has taken our country way off the Google maps route, and at first we hoped you just knew a shortcut, but then you opened your mouth, and we realized you're insane. Now we're trapped in here with you, and we just have to hope we don't die on the way to a

118 Late-Night Political Humor and the Two Presidents of Early 2021

birthday party we didn't even want to go to. Also, you're taking us to the wrong Kansas City.

(Stephen Colbert, February 3, 2021)

But let's be real, man, this is one of the most ridiculous arguments ever. Trump committed crimes on his way out of the door. So what, the people just have to let it go? That policy doesn't exist anywhere else. If you get fired at Best Buy, they don't just let you steal a TV on the way out. They don't even let you take that blue shirt with you; you walk out of there naked.

(Trevor Noah, January 25, 2021)

Yes, the bad news for Donald Trump is that seven members of his own party said that he was guilty. Which is unprecedented. The good news for him is that it wasn't enough. So, Trump is free to go, baby! 2024, here we come, bam, bam, bam, bam. We are getting the whole crew back together. Ivanka, Jared Kushner, Mike Pence, sorry about trying to get you killed. But that's in the past now, let's do this.

(Trevor Noah, February 15, 2021)

The violent and treasonous insurrection I directed was the biggest violent and treasonous insurrection in history! And he also still wants credit for the vaccine. Trump said that someone suggested to him that the vaccine should be called the "Trumpcine." And he liked that. The Trumpcine would be a mix of Adderall, Hydroxychloroquine, and ketchup. And, of course, he still says he won the election. This is getting sadder and sadder. It's like Smashmouth at a county fair telling you their new album is #1, only billboard won't report on it.

(Jimmy Kimmel, April 12, 2021)

Joe Biden

[It is] kind of crazy that our new president is older than the forward pass, isn't that wild? Even the Vince Lombardi hologram was like, "How old is this guy?" Biden was like, "Just like every kid, I wanted to be a flanker back for the NFL's top team, the Delaware Dirt Devils Under Coach Peppy LaGraine, he had one arm and three nipples."

(Jimmy Fallon, February 8, 2021)

> Let's move on to our main story, which is once again not anything about Biden. Because let's face it, guys, Joe Biden is boring. The dude's favorite Netflix show is just the search menu, which is fine for most people.
>
> (Trevor Noah, April 8, 2021)
>
> Team Biden right now is switching up the vocabulary that comes out of the White House. The Biden White House has reinstated the phrase "climate change." Which had been eliminated from official government materials and they're removing the term "Illegal alien." The term they will now use is "Noncitizen." Which isn't entirely accurate. Everyone is a citizen of someplace. But it makes sense. "People" aren't "Illegal." And that's just part of a long list of words and phrases they have put to rest. In addition to illegal alien they will no longer use the terms – fake news. China virus. Perfect call. Lock her up. Extra crispy. Crazy Nancy. My stupid son Eric. My stupid son Don. Tell Eric I'm not here. Tell Don I died. Where's Hunter? Bigly. Frankly. Hamberders. Put Jared on it. Bring me my sharpie. Get me my hair cement. Covfefe. Tim Apple. How hot is my daughter? "One of the wettest we've seen from the standpoint of water." Very fine people. "Haters and losers." Big, beautiful wall. Bing, bong, bing, bong. Everyone is saying. And – get Lou Dobbs on the phone.
>
> (Jimmy Kimmel, February 24, 2021)
>
> And the best part is, the Biden administration is going to keep us informed about what they're doing, with regular expert-led science-based public briefings. Which will be a nice change from moron-led, Clorox-based, dexamethasone ramblings. Today, we heard from a man so dedicated to proper sterilization techniques that he's the only one to emerge from the last administration not covered in the stench of failure, Dr. Anthony Fauci.
>
> (Stephen Colbert, January 21, 2021)

Examples of the jokes the late-night comics offered regarding Biden and Trump during early 2021 are found in Box 4.1. Many of the jokes related to the themes discussed earlier in this chapter, including common narratives like the peculiarities of Trump's character and questions of Biden's focus. Some of the jokes focused on COVID and the January 6 attack on the U.S. Capitol.

As Table 4.6 demonstrates, late-night comics have been tough on Republican presidential candidates and presidents going back decades. Scandal-plagued Bill Clinton, a target-rich environment for these entertainers three decades ago, nevertheless received fewer barbs than

120 Late-Night Political Humor and the Two Presidents of Early 2021

TABLE 4.6 Jokes Targeting Presidents and Presidential Candidates, 1992–2021

(Presidential Election Years and First years in office)

Year	Candidate	Party	Jokes	Rank
1992	George H.W. Bush	R	616	1
	Bill Clinton	D	421	2
1993	Bill Clinton	D	440	1
1996	Bob Dole	R	839	1
	Bill Clinton	D	657	2
1997	Bill Clinton	D	808	1
2000	George W. Bush	R	905	1
	Al Gore	D	546	3
2001	George W. Bush	R	546	2
2004	George W. Bush	R	1,169	1
	John Kerry	D	505	2
2005	George W. Bush	D	657	1
2008	John McCain	R	1,358	1
	Barack Obama	D	768	3
2009	Barack Obama	D	936	1
2012	Mitt Romney	R	1,061	1
	Barack Obama	D	401	2
[2013	no data]			
2016*	Donald Trump	R	1,817	1 [Part-year]
	Hillary Clinton	D	506	2
2017**	Donald Trump	R	3,128	1 [Part-year]
2020***	Donald Trump R 5065 1 [Part-year]			
	Joe Biden D 152 2			
2021****	Donald Trump R 2417 1 [Part-year]			
	Joe Biden D 1005 2			

Notes: Years before 2016 cover political jokes during the entire 12-month period.
*   2016 data only through November 11.
**   2017 data include from Inauguration Day to year-end.
***   2020 data include the four late-night shows aired during January 13–April 30 and only Colbert (CBS) and Fallon (NBC) during August 24–October 28, 2020 and November 2–13, 2020.
****   2021 data include late-night jokes aired on four shows during January 18–April 30, 2021 and September 6–December 10, 2021.

Programs included:
2021: *The Tonight Show* (NBC), *The Late Show* (CBS), *Jimmy Kimmel Live!* (ABC), *The Daily Show* (Comedy Central)
2020: *The Tonight Show* (NBC), *The Late Show* (CBS), *Jimmy Kimmel Live!* (ABC) [January 13–April 30 only], *The Daily Show* (Comedy Central) [January 13–April 30 only]
2016–2017: *The Tonight Show* (NBC), *The Late Show* (CBS), *Jimmy Kimmel Live!* (ABC), *The Daily Show* (Comedy Central)
2012: *The Tonight Show* (NBC), *The Late Show* (CBS), *The Daily Show* (Comedy Central), *The Colbert Report* (Comedy Central)

Late-Night Political Humor and the Two Presidents of Early 2021 **121**

TABLE 4.6 (Continued)

2008–2009: *The Tonight Show* (NBC), *The Late Show* (CBS), *The Daily Show* (Comedy Central), *The Colbert Report* (Comedy Central), *Late Night* (NBC)
2004–2005: *The Tonight Show* (NBC), *The Late Show* (CBS), *The Daily Show* (Comedy Central), *Late Night* (NBC)
2000: *The Tonight Show* (NBC), *The Late Show* (CBS), *Politically Incorrect* (ABC), *Late Night* (NBC)
1996: *The Tonight Show* (NBC), *The Late Show* (CBS), *Politically Incorrect* (ABC), *Late Night* (NBC)
1992: *The Tonight Show* (NBC), *The Late Show* (CBS), *Arsenio* (Fox)

President George H.W. Bush during the 1992 presidential campaign (Farnsworth and Lichter 2011a). Of course, the elder Bush had some gaffes of his own, as he struggled to discuss the sputtering economy of that election year. In the last eight presidential elections, stretching back to the 1992 contest, Democratic candidates have always fared better on the further reworking programs than did Republicans. Sometimes the gap was relatively narrow, as it was between Clinton and Bush in 1992 and between Clinton and Bob Dole four years later. Other times it was much larger, including the two-to-one margin of Republican candidate jokes versus Democratic candidates in 2004 (George W. Bush versus John Kerry) and 2012 (Mitt Romney versus Barack Obama).

Trump broke the record in 2016. Not only was he the subject of more late-night jokes than any presidential candidate going back decades, but he also registered the first three-to-one margin in jokes over Hillary Clinton, the Democratic nominee that year. But the standard that late-night comedy set in its treatment of Trump in 2016 was a record soon to fall. Four years later, in 2020, political humor focused on Trump over Joe Biden by an astonishing 33-to-1 margin. As the data here demonstrate, Trump remained a focus of the comedy monologues as an ex-president in early 2021, finishing ahead of the newly inaugurated president by a nearly four-to-one margin. The sheer number of jokes directed at Trump becomes doubly important when one considers that the jokes coded for the years in the table before 2013 contained the content from the full year of these late-night shows, while these studies of political humor during 2016, 2020, and 2021 included only partial years of analysis in these calculations of total jokes directed at presidents and presidential candidates. (Table 4.6 includes data from the four nightly comedy programs during Fall 2021, a section of Biden's first year in office that will be discussed as part of Chapter 5 in the context of our discussion of *Gutfeld!*, a conservative late-night comedy program that in less than two years had an audience comparable to and sometimes larger than the more established programs).

The Weekly Humor Programs during 2021

Saturday Night Live

Saturday Night Live, the longest running weekly humor program, differs in format from the other two once-a-week shows we will be discussing, *Full Frontal with Samantha Bee* and *Last Week Tonight with John Oliver*. The two more recently developed programs do not use *SNL*'s skit format, which features a large cast, changing hosts, guest stars, and musical guests. Jokes on *SNL* generally involve mockery and situational humor. The sections of the show which tend to focus the most on political humor are the "Cold Open," the start to the show, and the "Weekend Update," a mock news broadcast near the midpoint of the episodes. Even so, when political happenings are covered intensely in the news, many of their other skits contain political humor as well. Overall, there was a diminishing number of presidential jokes the further into 2021 the broadcast was from the 2020 election. Their general tone toward Trump and Biden remained consistent for each, but as the year progressed, Trump was not featured as a character in as many of the skits. The Trump conversation as the year progressed increasingly focused on his supporters inside and outside of Congress. Biden, on the other hand, was featured as a character during the segments relating to him, and his supporters were rarely mentioned. As Biden's first year in office proceeded, the jokes about him became more frequent and *SNL* began to focus on his bigger policy decisions.

The show's original indifference toward Biden at the beginning of his first year as president was revealed in the lack of mentions and harsh humor directed his way at the outset. Starting off on January 30, 2021, the opening sketch did not directly feature a political event, but instead framed itself as a mock talk show entitled, "What Still Works in America" (*SNL* 2021a). The "host" of the show opens saying that something should work with the new president, but we will have to see (*SNL* 2021a). This segment did not say anything specific about Biden's policies, appearance, or mannerisms, it simply shows nervousness surrounding the whole system itself. Then in "Weekend Update," this notion was reinforced by saying "the inauguration was good" and not saying anything else surrounding Biden (*SNL* 2021b).

SNL mocked Biden's mannerisms in the "Weekend Update" segment but did so in the context of his policy decisions. "Biden is moving ahead with a $1.9 trillion stimulus bill without Republican support – the economy needs a massage and Joe isn't waiting for permission" (*SNL* 2021d). While the comment reflected a "creepy old man" image of Biden, it also indicated that the economy needed help, and perhaps even offered support for his approach. The program became less supportive as Biden made more policy decisions. "Biden told the U.S. to 'take off your mask and smile' – 'take it off and smile' is the first example in every workplace harassment seminar" (*SNL* 2021h).

While joking that Biden is harassing America, *SNL* also expressed more confusion with Biden's COVID policies than support for them. This policy equivocation at *SNL* also extended into the program's commentary on foreign affairs: "Biden is using a light touch with Israel, everything Biden does involves some kind of touch" (*SNL* 2021h). The pairing of his creepy mannerisms and policy preference in this instance focused more on who Biden is, rather than criticizing what he was doing in terms of policy.

SNL frequently returned to jokes about Biden's age and mental capacity across his first year in office. " 'Chief' is what he calls his friends when he forgets their names" (*SNL* 2021d) and "his cheat sheet for the press conference said 'you = Biden' " (*SNL* 2021f). They are calling him past his prime, albeit in a somewhat gentle way: "Sure, Biden means well, but that is such an old white guy idea" when Biden plans to distribute vaccines in churches to appeal to black Americans (*SNL* 2021e) and "Thank you to Fixodent," for allowing Biden to do an over an hour press conference (*SNL* 2021f). These age and mental capacity jokes are not particularly harsh and often were accompanied with the "he means well" caveat that followed some expressions of general support for his policy decisions. The program also connected him to eccentric characters who generally command affection from the public. The show recalled Dr. Emmett "Doc" Brown from the *Back to the Future* films in its discussion of Biden driving the new all-electric F-150 Ford truck (*SNL* 2021h).

In the fall of 2021, James Austin Johnson began doing caricatures of Biden on *SNL*. In an October 2, 2021 episode, the scene was set as a press conference discussing the recent drone strike and issues with the Taliban. While this caricature humored Biden's preference to stay in the shadows, "like an oil change, don't think about me until you have to" (*SNL* 2021i) and mocked his accent, it did not make fun of his appearance. It also provided something of a justification for his failures. Despite poking fun at Biden's decisions in Afghanistan by having him say "my summer was bad … win some, lose some" (*SNL* 2021i), *SNL* still showed support for him by noting that he is trying to bring the Democratic Party together.

They continued this caricature with the "ghost of Biden past." They did not make this Biden younger in appearance, just less serious (SNL 2021g). *SNL* continued to mock his mannerisms in this segment having the past Biden rub current Biden's shoulders, smell him, and tell him to smile more (*SNL* 2021j). Another effort to make Biden appear creepy was saying that he likes the "playboy mansion over Joe Manchin" (*SNL* 2021j). The segment concluded with a joke about his appearance, where the Biden character bragged his teeth are 100 percent real. While *SNL* called him odd and old, they paired the comments with supportive remarks regarding his policy choices.

Meanwhile, *SNL* did not express any support for Trump and harshly critiqued his supporters. Within Congress, the show regularly mocked Rep. Marjorie Taylor Greene (R-GA) for her views that align with Trump's. The show described her beliefs as absurd, calling her a "conspiracy theorist" and asking in disbelief: "you are a real member of the United States Government?" (*SNL* 2021a). While such comments were not directly pointed at former President Trump, Rep. Greene is an avid supporter of the former president and is a vocal proponent of election fraud claims before and after the attack on Congress on January 6, 2021. The show repeated these same themes within the "Weekend Update" segments about Rep. Greene, including one where the hosts said she will single-handily crash the Republican Party and another where the hosts offered straight disbelief and shock at her statement that 9/11 was a hoax (*SNL* 2021b). The program showed no support for her and mocked her appearance as well, saying she looks like a mugshot of a former child star (*SNL* 2021e).

The program continued the notion of Trump supporters' absurdity through a skit called the "Warren Street COVID bubble" (*SNL* 2021c). In this skit, the members of the bubble started out saying the insurrection was crazy and reckless, but then slowly one by one the characters in the segment were arrested for participation in the attack on the Capitol. While a character noted that it is "good to have a pod you can trust," subsequent developments demonstrated they should not be trusting each other. The performers continued their tones of untrustworthiness by saying that now the terrorist watchlist includes white people due to the insurrection, which the show implied is a good thing (*SNL* 2021b). Once more, these jokes did not directly mention Trump but reveal negative views of him through mockery of his supporters.

SNL did two caricatures of Trump in the same context, during a Fox Channel show with Judge Jeanine Pirro (*SNL* 2021k, 2021l). In both of these cases, the Trump character followed the same pattern. A list appeared beside him with unassociated words starting with a news topic. He then goes down random paths to illustrate that Trump's thought process was unclear and idiotic. They retained his puckered lip and orange skin appearance but now employed James Austin Johnson, one of a series of performers also tasked with imitating Biden. Using the same actor to portray both men helped draw attention to the similarities in the two Presidents' age and apparent level of senility. This portrayal of Trump directly made fun of his intelligence and also joked about Republican Party members trying to disassociate from him. A caricature of Glenn Youngkin, a Republican who was elected governor of Virginia in November 2021, did not want to be associated with the former president at all, while Trump insisted that he had everything to do with the Youngkin victory: "we did it together," the Trump character bragged (*SNL* 2021k).

SNL generally offered jokes at both Biden's and Trump's expense, but the intensity and focus were different. Biden jokes were focused on his age, mental capacity, and policy decisions and generally expressed a modest "laugh at yourself" type of humor. While Trump was portrayed as idiotic, the focus was more on his supporters' outrageous actions and beliefs, which are framed to be fueled by his actions. *SNL* harshly critiqued them with jokes aimed at the absurdity of the movement surrounding the ex-president.

Full Frontal

Full Frontal with Samantha Bee is known for its news style format with a green screen, frequent news mentions, and her sometimes crude tone. During her 2021 segments, she expressed her support of candidates and social movements openly (as she had done in the past). During these COVID-era broadcasts, she often stood before a camera alone and discussed the hot news topics of the week, interjecting personal observations throughout.

In early 2021, Bee's liberal humor was in full force as she discussed the insurrection and the second impeachment of Donald Trump. But her on-air anger seemed to taper off the longer Biden was in office. Contrary to *SNL* and John Oliver, the two other once-a-week programs examined here, Bee offered little criticism of Biden's personal behavior or jokes about his appearance or age. Like *SNL*, her humor surrounding the insurrection was focused on Trump supporters, but she also directly mentioned Trump in those critiques.

Bee started her January 2021 broadcasts with a two-part episode on the insurrection. She shows her anger and dislike for the Republican Party from the start calling the insurrection the "ugliest moment at the floor of the Hill since about one hour before that" and then showing a picture of Ted Cruz's appearance (*FF* 2021a). She then strongly condemned the lack of preparation because she claims the Trump administration knew that attack was going to happen, referencing Trump's tweets in a serious tone, and then showing the preprinted insurrection t-shirts worn by some Trump supporters during the assault on Capitol Hill (*FF* 2021a). She directly stated her belief, without any humor included, that Trump and the 147 House Republicans who voted to challenge the 2020 election results should be held accountable,. The dichotomy of the seriousness of the matter with jokes about his supporters' appearances shows her direct desire for action.

126 Late-Night Political Humor and the Two Presidents of Early 2021

She furthers this condemnation by calling Trump the "ringleader" and the members who supported him "assholes" (*FF* 2021b). While her statements continued her harsh tone, there was more seriousness than humor to her show than in episodes that did not focus on the insurrection. Her humor arose when discussing those who are trying to brush it aside stating they are acting as if it was just "Nazis stealing office muffins" (*FF* 2021a). Her jokes directly about Trump and his 2021 impeachment offered a more serious tone as well, but discussed the process as rigged, showing her lack of trust in Republicans who allowed the attack on the Capitol to occur and then hesitated to blame Trump for his role in that day (*FF* 2021d).

The longer Trump was out of office, the more Bee focused on his supporters who remained in public office. Across her 2021 broadcasts, she criticized elected Republicans for repeating Trump's views on issues such as transgender participation in sports and voting for Trump policy initiatives (*FF* 2021j). She called Trump's allies fearmongers and hypocrites (*FF* 2021j, 2021l). She showed her overall distaste for the Republican Party by stating "Republicans will never do bipartisan legislation" (*FF* 2021k) and framed them as uncaring with situational humor, stating that Republicans are more concerned with the withdrawal from Afghanistan's impact on domestic political matters rather than on the many Afghan people impacted (*FF* 2021l).

When it comes to Biden, Bee did not joke about him and showed support for his decisions generally, up until the withdrawal from Afghanistan. On the day of his inauguration, she posted a short video entitled "We Made it to Biden/Harris Inauguration Day!" (*FF* 2021c). In this video she sends a cardboard cutout of herself to do the "blue" wave with fellow famous Biden supporters. This shows her direct support of Biden and dislike of Trump. Bee also shows support for his policy decisions. When discussing Biden's goal to increase the minimum wage, she says that Biden's COVID package would save millions of dollars because of the raise in minimum wage to $15, and jokes that "it will also get you a lifetime subscription to Joe's 'Only Trains'" (*FF* 2021d). Poking fun at Biden's love of trains, Bee portrays him as a potential hero and lovable guy for his actions and interests. Thus, Bee did not hold back in sharing her view of him, treating Biden more favorably than Trump.

Bee's episodes later in 2021 focused more on the history of social issues that are generally described as liberal, including Black Lives Matter (*FF* 2021h), Anti-Asian Hate (*FF* 2021i), and The Racist Past of Greek Life (*FF* 2021e). She also did a two-part segment on QAnon and its influence on white women. In this segment she discussed how the conspiracy group taps into women's desires to protect children and leads them into a rabbit hole of "crazy bitch shit" (*FF* 2021f). While this group contains many

Trump supporters, she joked about them in a gullible way – as if they were women with good hearts who fell into a pit of false information. This somewhat sympathetic framing is furthered with the display of real interviews with women who realized the truth and left QAnon (FF 2021g). While she still uses vulgar humor in this segment, she was less harsh and more pitiful of these Trump supporters, which differs greatly from her previously mentioned humor.

Bee mixed both positive and negative comments about Biden as he made his way through his first year in office. She expressed support for his order to protect transgender rights (*FF 2021j*) but objected to Biden's withdrawal from Afghanistan. Bee started one segment with her classic vulgar humor about the system stating that we were reminded how badly the U.S. Government can "f*ck up abroad" (*FF 2021l*). She admitted Biden deserves blame for the chaotic U.S. departure, using the classic saying, "Irish goodbye," to describe that exit (*FF 2021l*). She then shifted the focus to the longevity of time the U.S. military spent in Afghanistan. She found it hypocritical to critique Biden and said that the past four presidents and present Republican office members deserve blame for involvement through decades of poor decisions regarding U.S. policy there (*FF 2021l*). Thus, while she provided critiques of Biden, these generally were not harsh and were almost more sympathetic. She returned to her supportive humor when Biden's infrastructure bill passed into law, exclaiming she "drank booze alone under a bridge to celebrate" (*FF 2021m*).

Overall, Samantha Bee expressed outright support for Biden and dislike for Trump frequently in her early episodes, then tapered off into more policy-oriented content. She then returned to supporting Biden's policy decisions as his first year went on. Her Trump jokes were often focused on his supporters, rather than the former president himself.

Last Week Tonight

Last Week Tonight with John Oliver routinely offers a digital display next to the host that provides the sources and information to support the claims being made. Unlike the other two shows, *LWT* did not start its 2021 programming until February and instead had a "premiere trailer" in January (*LWT 2021a*). In a pattern like that seen in the other shows, Oliver criticized both presidents. In a now-familiar pattern, *LWT* started out with more negative commentary on Trump and then started to critique Biden more as his first year as president took shape. Oliver's humor was blunt and factual, and occasionally he did reveal his personal opinions within his humor (*LWT 2021b*, *LWT 2021c*).

128 Late-Night Political Humor and the Two Presidents of Early 2021

When it came to Trump, Oliver primarily critiqued his actions and his supporters for the insurrection, particularly around the time of the former president's second impeachment trial shortly after he left office (*LWT* 2021c). Oliver expressed disappointment in the system for its predetermined polarized nature, citing a statement by Sen. Ted Cruz that Trump's lawyers did not have to try to be persuasive, given the partisan divisions in Washington (*LWT* 2021c). He went on to describe the evidence pointing to Trump fueling the insurrection, specifically on Twitter, and saying the quotes to fight the election results in Arizona were from the "worst Rambo movie" (*LWT* 2021c). By connecting Trump's supporters with that low-brow film franchise, Oliver suggested the Trump supporters have bad taste and are not the brightest. Oliver further expressed his disgust at Trump supporters in a segment entirely on Fox News host Tucker Carlson (*LWT* 2021d), whom he called a "wedge salad." He discussed Carlson's anger at the maternity flight suit and then points out that that was Trump's idea. Oliver expressed confusion as to why Carlson thinks pregnancy-friendly clothing was feminizing the military as a whole (*LWT* 2021d). Oliver's discussion made it seem as though Carlson was not all that smart and did not properly provide information to Fox News viewers. It furthered Oliver's recurrent observation that some Trump supporters, including those at Fox News, are not intelligent and are misguided.

Oliver was also critical of Biden but did not involve his supporters in the condemnations. In an episode focused on immigration, he first said "this f*cking guy" (Trump) slashed the admissions cap down to a historic low and Biden promised to raise it back up (*LWT* 2021e). He then played a clip of Biden's promise and observed, "underneath the patriotic word salad, he is making a good point" (*LWT* 2021e). This statement's focus on a clip where Biden was inarticulate questions, at least to some degree, Biden's mental capacity and speaking capabilities. Oliver then went on to state that Biden has yet to complete his promise and his secretary is waving away concerns about refugees like a cavalier Spirit Airlines gate agent dismissing the concerns of the flying public (*LWT* 2021e). This critique of Biden's inaction on this issue, paired with a reference to the famously low-cost and low-service airline, provided a feeling of dismissal and poor conduct ethics on the part of the new president. Oliver also noted that he was infuriated , particularly since Biden's supporters voted for him to help refugees (*LWT* 2021e). His critical disappointment and anger were unprecedented in his treatment of the new president. In this case, Oliver did not frame Biden as a well-meaning old man, but a dishonest one.

John Oliver focused more on Biden over the course of 2021 and as the new president began making policy decisions, as the other two once-a-week shows examined here had done. Oliver was the most aggressively critical of the three hosts regarding Biden's withdrawal from Afghanistan. He mentioned that Biden walked into Trump's poorly made withdrawal plan, which excluded the Afghan Government from the key negotiations, and then proceeded to critique Biden's exit from the war-torn nation. He called Biden a "child ensemble member of Matilda," referring to the clip of Biden making a zero with his fingers when asked about U.S. responsibility for the Afghan people (*LWT* 2021f). Oliver used these similes to mock what he considered Biden's heartless attitude toward those suffering in Afghanistan.

Oliver also criticized Biden's lack of action when it came to trying to end the Senate filibuster (*LWT* 2021g) and the struggle to pass Biden's first spending bill (*LWT* 2021h). Oliver cited news reports on Biden's statements that voters simply need to turn out and then states, "Sure Joe, maybe they'll show up and then get turned away" (*LWT* 2021g). Oliver expressed this thought in a mocking tone that suggested the president was not smart enough to think of that. Oliver's humor around this subject was more pointed when directed at other Democrats, such as Joe Manchin, for their lack of justification for opposing the Biden legislation.

John Oliver's show decreased its mentions of the two presidents of early 2021 as the year progressed but, at times, he criticized both with tones of anger. The jokes surrounding Trump were focused on his supporters and his rallies leading up to the insurrection. The Biden jokes, on the other hand, were focused on his mental capacity and lack of action on his immigration promises, missteps in Afghanistan, problems with the Senate filibuster, and the struggle to pass Biden's Build Back Better Act. Therefore, while the emphases were different, there was less one-sided treatment of the two presidents throughout many of the Oliver episodes of 2021.

Though different in format and not systematically analyzed, the three shows all revealed pervasive anti-Trump sentiment, but it was mainly directed toward his supporters and their beliefs. *SNL* and *LWT* both provided criticism of Biden and focused on Biden's age and mental capacity, but *SNL* offered a more supportive and "laugh at yourself" tone, while *LWT* was directly critical of Biden's policies. Meanwhile, *FF* offered support of Biden purely and only critiqued his withdrawal from Afghanistan. The longer Biden was in office, the more the shows reduced their humor surrounding the presidents in general and focused more on social issues and events. All three of the shows keyed in negatively on one major event in Biden's first year, Afghanistan, calling it a "stain on his presidency" (*LWT* 2021f), "world's worst Irish goodbye" (*FF* 2021l), and "a bad summer" (*SNL* 2021i). Despite this one major event, the three shows remained overall positive surrounding Biden's presidency and

130 Late-Night Political Humor and the Two Presidents of Early 2021

mainly varied in reaction to his policy decisions. *LWT*, though, was the least positive of the three.

Conclusion

Our study of the attention late-night comics paid to politicians during the start of the Biden presidency confirms the previous findings that Donald Trump stood in a class by himself as a target of the late-night comics during his years in politics. Even as an ex-president, Trump continued to set the political humor agenda. Of course, the political environment of 2021 did contain some distinct features that made Trump more than an ordinary former president: There was the January 6 insurrection, of course, as well as the second congressional effort to impeach Trump and his subsequent Senate acquittal. Then there were Trump's frequent campaign appearances as a former president, where he continued to argue without evidence that the 2020 presidential election was stolen. Indeed, given all that was going on at the time, it would have been odd if Trump had not been the focus of considerable late-night attention during these months. But the distance between the comedic attention paid to Trump and to his Democratic successor as president was vast indeed.

Both the nightly comedy shows, and the weekly programs, found Trump an appealing target, even out of office. When the nightly humorists turned to his Democratic successor, they had comparably little to say. The once-a-week humorists focused a bit more on the new president, but in both formats the comedians struggled to make the early 2021 version of Biden all that funny, particularly when compared to the high-energy counterpoint of his predecessor in the Oval Office.

Throughout this book, we have remarked repeatedly on the very liberal orientation of the content of late-night comedy in recent decades. Our data show that Republicans have been at a disadvantage since the days of George H.W. Bush's presidency. While there have been some conservative voices appearing on late-night comedy programming, they generally did not generate substantial audiences and did not last long on the air. Only during the Biden presidency have we seen a commercially successful conservative late-night comedy program with staying power.

That Fox News program, *Gutfeld!*, is the subject of Chapter 5.

5

THE CHALLENGE OF CREATING CONSERVATIVE COMEDY

From its earliest days, political humor frequently has offered an anti-authority message. The mocking of those with influence if not control over one's life can provide a cathartic release, a means of accepting one's own relative weakness within a given political or economic system. A worker bee is a worker bee, regardless of whether the leader is a Roman Emperor, a medieval monarch, or a modern president. Across time, many humans have chafed or at least sometimes have been frustrated with the existing hierarchy in the workplace or in the larger society. If one must submit to the dictates from above, one at least can make this business of sometimes grudging submission more tolerable by making a crack about those elites.

From court jesters to satirical writers to the comics working in the early days of film, the targets often were those in power, regardless of their ideological or partisan identities. A political humor that provides equal opportunity mockery fueled popular writers like Mark Twain, radio superstars like Will Rogers, and early filmmakers like Charlie Chaplin. That same bipartisan mockery helped spur the rise of political humor on television, where it flourished like never before.

In this chapter, we examine the rise of explicitly conservative political humor, developed in response to the growing leftward tilt in recent years of mainstream political humor offered by late-night television comics like Stephen Colbert, Trevor Noah, and others. Our focus here will be on the commercially successful *Gutfeld!*, which first aired as a nightly humor show in April 2021 on Fox News. The program has rapidly become a top-rated competitor to the more established programs and the first genuinely successful late-night comedy program by and for conservatives. Before

DOI: 10.4324/9781003283041-5

132 The Challenge of Creating Conservative Comedy

we get into a detailed analysis of the political humor of that program, though, we chart the movement from political humor that offered material to satisfy liberals and conservatives, and the subsequent trend toward more liberally focused content on late night over the past few decades. In addition, this chapter also compares the content of *Gutfeld!* jokes during late 2021 with those of the four nightly humor shows that have formed the shape of this project.

Political Humor for All, and Then Mainly for Some

While many entertainers have eschewed political content, particularly those employing early- and mid-20th-century communication technologies that placed a premium on widespread public appeal, those entertainers who did offer political humor often mixed liberal and conservative messages in nearly the same breath. By doing so, they could potentially expand their mass audience beyond those who would favor a consistently monochromatic message. (In addition, ideologically mixed messages might also keep the media censors off-balance).

Consider, for example, the case of Chaplin, a pioneering early comedic filmmaker whose work often contained more political messages than the work of many of his contemporaries. In film after film of his during the first third of the 20th century, "The Tramp" delighted (along with his audience) in giving figures of power, like a narrow-minded police officer, a kick to the backside when one could get away with it (Robinson 1986). Chaplin's films, particularly those created during the Great Depression, often portrayed the decency of working-class characters, confronting as best they could a highly challenging political and cultural environment that often ended up treating them poorly (Chaplin 1964). In his films, these financially precarious characters struggle mightily to avert disasters: to keep orphans out of government workhouses, to keep themselves gainfully employed, and to avoid becoming homeless (Robinson 1986).

Even so, Chaplin's body of filmmaking is not a communist manifesto. In *Modern Times* (1936), arguably his most important work, the greatly put-upon Chaplin character dreams above all of living in a stable middle-class community where he can enjoy a hot breakfast from a kitchen equipped with the very latest appliances, like gleaming white electric stoves and refrigerators (Chaplin 1936).

For his Depression-weary audience, the Chaplin character in *Modern Times* offered political humor that was hardly a partisan or an ideological call to arms; rather it was a narrative that argued that authorities can be unfeeling, clueless, and not particularly helpful (Ryan and Kellner 1988). As a result, Chaplin indicates, one must look out for oneself rather than relying on a revolution.

The same absence of monochromatic partisan humor also marked Chaplin's most explicitly political film, *The Great Dictator* (1940), which offers a harsh mockery of a Hitler-like authoritarian leader. Once again, the political humor transcended partisan labels, offering an intense anti-Nazi message that was nearly universally held while western democracies battled Germany in World War II (Chaplin 1940). Indeed, this commercially successful film was widely praised for its political content across the ideological spectrum, adored by conservative fans like U.K. Prime Minister Winston Churchill and liberals like U.S. President Franklin Delano Roosevelt (Robinson 1986).

This traditional view of political humor, espoused by Chaplin and so many others, concentrated on mocking whoever is in power – regardless of their partisanship. This flexibility offered considerable opportunity for political humor from a range of perspectives over time, and even within a single film or program. Liberal leaders and conservative leaders could be mocked in turn as each side gained and then lost political authority. Conservative messages embedded in political humor, particularly regarding the moral failings of libertine political figures, could be offered side-by-side with liberal messages mocking the arrogance and the authoritarian tendencies of those in power on the right. Modern eyes and ears might object to some of the humor of the past that harshly employed stereotypes of race, class, and gender, but such content generated less hostility from the audiences of decades ago. Many of our ancestors would have laughed at things that would not be said, or written, or viewed today without a public uproar over what many today would consider offensive content (Sienkiewicz and Marx 2021).

When television came along, early comedians rarely adopted a partisan tone and mostly avoided political humor altogether. Retained the bipartisan tone that marked political humor developed in the preceding centuries. Even after television became commonplace, that pattern remained. Johnny Carson, the most famous late-night political humorist, from the 1960s onward set the standard of bipartisan mockery that his successors would struggle to emulate, particularly as the external political environment grew more combative and more partisan (Farnsworth and Lichter 2020). Indeed, many of Carson's late-night successors deliberately departed from his even-handed style and sought instead to reflect the more combative public preferences of the post-Carson era (Farnsworth and Lichter 2020). As the results presented in previous chapters have demonstrated, since the 1990s little opportunity has remained for Carson-style bipartisan political mockery on the traditional late-night venue where that style once reigned supreme.

134 The Challenge of Creating Conservative Comedy

As political humorists and their audiences leaned in on liberal values during recent decades, even the concept of conservative politics itself became a joke to some of these humorists. Before he took over as the leading late-night host on CBS, *The Daily Show* alumni Stephen Colbert demonstrated for nearly a decade on the spin-off *Colbert Report* that an entire half-hour program that airs four days a week can succeed as a parody of conservative politics. But Colbert's faux conservatism did little to satisfy those right-of-center viewers yearning for political humor that spoke to their values and their perspectives. Particularly in the wake of the rise of Fox News, a reliable and consistent source of conservative messaging from the 1990s onward, viewers started to ask the question: Where is the political humor produced by and for conservatives?

Creating Stand-Alone Conservative Political Comedy

As we have noted, the nearly complete absence of conservative political humor in conventional channels is a relatively recent development. Until recent decades, conservative political comedy struggled to shared the stage with jokes that were more liberal in orientation. But as political humor started to become more one-sided, a trend that started with *Saturday Night Live* and blossomed during the 1990s with a new generation of nightly late-night hosts offering increasingly liberal content, conservatives started to dream of a mirror version of *The Daily Show* designed for themselves.

At first these efforts did not generate commercial success. One problem that conservative comedy has faced when it stood alone was that the outrage that works so well on Fox News programming did not seem to translate well into jokes. (Liberals, one might note, have struggled to make talk radio formats work effectively for their side). Anger, a dominant narrative of conservative media in recent decades, can be more scary than funny, except when someone is making fun of it. Indeed, as Colbert notes, laughter is about relieving tension and fear, not reflecting those feelings.

> I don't know what the next day is like for anybody. If the show goes well, maybe the audience sleeps a bit better. And maybe that's all the show should be. I have said this before, but I know that when you're laughing, you're not afraid.
>
> [Question: Is that true, though? Isn't nervous laughter a laughter that comes from fear?] Nervous laughter is not the same thing as laughing, in my opinion. I would say nervous laughter is evidence that I'm right, because that is your body autonomically trying to relieve tension. If someone can do that for you from the outside, it relieves that tension

and fear, and you are momentarily not afraid. If you're not afraid, you can think, and we have to think our way out of this one.

(Colbert, quoted in Marchese 2019)

One early conservative attempt to recreate a *Daily Show* for the right – *The 1/2 Hour News Hour* – briefly aired on Fox News in 2007. The show generated poor ratings and was pulled off the air that same year, as critics claimed it was more political than humorous (Morrison 2015) and that its attempts at humor were sometimes juvenile and borderline offensive (Baym 2012). For whatever reason, even viewers weaned on the conservative content of Fox News had little interest in the show. Given that program's failure, it was several years before Fox News was again willing to make a substantial investment in nightly conservative political humor.

Some scholars believe that psychological factors are particularly important for explaining the problems of creating a successful conservative political humor show during these years. Perhaps conservatives possess greater fear of uncertainty and therefore possess less appreciation of the irony or ambiguity that can exist at the heart of political humor (Young 2020; Young et al. 2019). These differences may also reduce the number of conservatives who choose to make a career of comedy, reducing the number of potential hosts with right-of-center views (Morrison 2015). Research shows that conservatives enjoy humor as much as liberals do. But certain forms of humor, like satire – the attacking of political institutions – can be problematic for conservatives, who often are more supportive than liberals of traditions, authority, and existing political institutions (Hesse 2013).

> Every attempt at delivering such a program ends up being viewed even by conservatives as mostly unwatchable. (Despite featuring appearances by Ann Coulter and Rush Limbaugh, *The Half-Hour News Hour* was cancelled after only 13 episodes.) It's possible that the reason for this can be found in the way every single one of these short-lived programs is described, even by the creators themselves, as a "conservative version of The *Daily Show* or 'Weekend Update.'" Similar to alcohol-free beer or soy burgers, the attempt to brand yourself as a polar alternative to the product you're ideologically opposed to is rarely accepted in America.
>
> *(Hesse 2013)*

Another potential problem for conservative political humor is the issue raised earlier in this work: the truism that good comedy punches up and bad comedy punches down (McClennen 2018). Where was the conservative comedy that punches up? Many favorite targets of conservative news commentators, such as struggling immigrants and indigent welfare recipients, are not politically powerful and therefore do not lend themselves to effective comedic mockery. There is also the risk of crossing lines of acceptable racial or ethnic discourse (known on the right as political correctness), if one were to attack such vulnerable groups via humor (Morrison 2015).

Some political targets of the right are well-heeled or influential, like Hollywood celebrities and liberal philanthropists. But these targets may be too narrowly defined (or too unfamiliar) to offer sufficient material for a regular late-night comedy program tilted in a conservative direction. One also might wonder whether some of the political humor efforts against Hollywood, for example, might stick. Film stars play a range of characters across their careers, and therefore may have a broader appeal that extends beyond liberals. Conservatives go to blockbuster films, just as liberals do.

> There are, of course, high-profile conservative comedians in America, such as the members of the Blue Collar Comedy Tour. But these performers, who include Jeff Foxworthy and Larry the Cable Guy, tend carefully to avoid politicized topics, mocking so-called "rednecks" in the same spirit as Borscht Belt acts mocked Jewish culture.
>
> When it comes to actual political satire, one of the most well-known figures nationally is Dennis Miller, a former *Saturday Night Live* cast member who had a weekly segment on Fox News' *O'Reilly Factor*. On a show, O'Reilly brought up the Democrats' election losses, and Miller took the bait. "I think liberalism is like a nude beach," Miller said. "It's better off in your mind than actually going there." His jokes are sometimes amusing, but they tend to be grounded in vague ideologies, not the attentive criticism to the news of the day that has given liberal satires plenty of fodder five days a week. The real problem, Frank Rich wrote about Miller, "is that his tone has become preachy. He too often seems a pundit first and a comic second."
>
> *(Morrison 2015)*

To the extent that Fox News hosts in recent years followed Trump's rhetorical lead and increased public anxieties, they pushed their audiences away from being receptive to the cathartic release of comedy, even though conservatives – like anyone – could use a good laugh now and then. While conservatives can and do mimic the format of more established political humor programming, efforts on conservative programs to attack or criticize already marginalized groups may lead liberals to underestimate the appeal and reach of such programs (Sienkiewicz and Marx 2021).

While liberals may comfort themselves in the belief that conservatives cannot do comedy effectively, given a supposed reliance on the unappealing approach of punching down as a comedy strategy, conservative humor has become effective in helping build commercial audiences via such venues as talk radio, cable channels, sitcoms, and social media (Sienkiewicz and Marx 2022). Conservative political humor may not be the focus of programming on the right, analysts note, and while it may not yet be mainstream, it at least has become economically sustainable and influential within the environment of conservative political discourse (Sienkiewicz and Marx 2022). Recently the Fox News political humor show *Gutfeld!*, which we discuss throughout this chapter, has generated audiences comparable in size to the more established late-night comedy shows (Grady 2022).

While *Gutfeld!* has become most visible platform for conservative humor during the Biden presidency, there are many other humor sources available online for those favoring anti-left jokes, including the *Babylon Bee*, a conservative online news satire version of *The Onion* that contains a religious dimension (Goldberg 2020). As editor in chief Kyle Mann observed:

> When people find the *Babylon Bee* they go, "Hey this comedy makes fun of everybody, but it's a little harder on the left, and when it makes fun of the right it's not hateful." People can tell it's loving humor.
>
> *(quoted in Goldberg 2020)*

Although it previously mocked presidential candidate Donald Trump in 2016 for his hypocrisy on religious matters, The *Babylon Bee* went on to find common cause with President Trump by joining him in attacking enemies of conservatives, including the mass media, liberal protestors, Hollywood leftists, and Democratic politicians like Joe Biden (Goldberg 2020). By attacking those critics of conservatives, long presented by right-of-center media outlets as voices of privilege, conservative political humor try to avoid the "punching down" problem discussed earlier. Even if conservatives may control the White House and the Congress and the Supreme Court, as they did between Donald Trump's inauguration in 2017 and the 2018 midterm elections, conservatives still presented themselves as underdogs in the cultural realm. Much of conservative politics in the age of Trump took the shape of grievance politics, after all. In this formulation, Trump presents himself as the savior of working-class whites who have lost ground politically and lost relevance culturally during recent decades (Farnsworth 2018).

As Anthony Nadler, a Ursinus College professor who studies political humor noted: "Conservatives see liberal culture as the source of power. They see liberals as setting norms in popular culture, television, and film, and they present themselves as rebels against that" (quoted in Goldberg

138 The Challenge of Creating Conservative Comedy

2020). The same conservative critique is applied to other liberal elites like the mainstream news media, censorious left-wing college professors, and busybodies in self-ordained "public interest" groups.

Of course, conservatives have been impacted by decisions made by social media content moderators, which can buttress concerns of those on the right that they are being treated unfairly. The *Babylon Bee* ran afoul of the leadership of Twitter in early 2022 and was banned from the site after refusing to delete a tweet referring to a transgender woman as a "Man of the Year." The comment violated Twitter standards in place at the time that prohibited identifying transgender individuals by the name or gender used before transitioning (Zakrzewski et al. 2022). Once Elon Musk acquired Twitter in the fall of 2022 and promised to loosen content moderation standards, the *Babylon Bee* returned to the social media site (Zakrzewski et al. 2022).

The range of conservative political humor includes more than just the comedy stylings of The *Babylon Bee* and *Gutfeld!* Also prominent among the voices of conservative political humor are libertarian comedy podcasts, most notably *The Joe Rogan Experience*, which exposes its audience to a variety of conservative voices, as well as more extreme voices like those of white supremacists (Sienkiewicz and Marx 2022). But *Gutfeld!* has become the main televised source of political humor for conservatives during the Biden years.

Gutfeld! Rises

Fox News' long-running efforts to create a successful conservative political humor program have long involved Greg Gutfeld. Gutfeld began hosting *Red Eye*, a Fox comedy show that aired during the graveyard shift of 3 a.m., in 2007. The host later graduated to a weekends-only program, *The Greg Gutfeld Show* in 2015, and then to an 11 p.m. weeknight show that debuted in April 2021 with the provocative tagline "Cancel culture just got canceled" (Grady 2022). In little more than a year after it became a nightly show, *Gutfeld!* became a top-rated late-night humor offering, drawing in two million viewers a night (Parker 2022).

From the start, the program was designed to retain significant parts of the Fox News evening audience by appealing to the conservative sense of being under siege and outnumbered in the media sphere. Gutfeld's first monologue laid down his combative vision for the program, one that plays familiar ideological tunes to those those watch Fox News during the hours before *Gutfeld!* airs. In a comment that suggested a bit of defensiveness regarding conservative humor, Gutfeld implied that what the show *is not* can be as important as what the show *is*.

As for those late-night shows we're supposed to compete against – why bother? Who do they offend? The only time Stephen Colbert ruffles feathers is in a pillow fight. The definition of risk for Kimmel is dehydration from crying too much. Fallon? That guy fawns more than a herd of deer. And I heard Seth Meyers and Trevor Noah have run off to be obscure together.

(quoted in Grady 2022)

Outsiders are divided in their assessments of this successful program. The commercial success of *Gutfeld!*, some analysts argue, is a result of a successful merging of two things: applying the mockery of traditional late-night comedy to a conservative program and the familiarity of traditional white male conservative comedy personified by voices like Tim Allen and Dennis Miller, what Sienkiewicz and Marx (2022) describe dismissively as "paleocomedy."

Whereas before conservative viewers may have scoffed at Gutfeld's bombast, irreverence, and utter disregard for intellectual or ideological consistency, Donald Trump has primed viewers to accept these as well as a number of far uglier traits. The rise of Trump and Trumpism in the 2010s offered a transitional moment for existing Fox News viewers to reconsider Gutfeld's style. Embracing Trump's eccentricity while de-emphasizing much of the brazen racism and misogyny of Watters' show *Watters' World*, Gutfeld promised Fox News leadership a chance to appeal to a younger audience hungry for comedic content.

(Marx and Sienkiewicz 2022)

As communication scholar Dannagal Young observed, the *Gutfeld!* approach to political humor does not require the political knowledge that is a prerequisite for some of the more policy-focused jokes to work on more wonkish humor programs like *Last Week Tonight*. "What they're doing [on *Gutfeld!*] is exaggeration-based humor. It's insult humor. It doesn't take a lot of unpacking. But for that audience, it scratches an itch" (quoted in Grady 2022). Research has shown that conservatives are drawn to jokes with clear resolutions (Wilson 1990; Young 2020), like those that air on *Gutfeld!*

One common assessment of the show's success draws from its broad range of targets, many of them not connected to politics. While the show is designed to appeal to Fox News viewers, it tries to offer a range of content that reaches beyond the audiences of Sean Hannity and Tucker Carlson. As Marx and Sienkiewicz (2022) note, Gutfeld's humor can be "equal parts Trump boosterism and scattershot pop

140 The Challenge of Creating Conservative Comedy

culture references, offering a touchpoint of engagement for viewers who might not be as securely anchored in red-state politics as the rest of Fox News' viewership." The anger of the earlier evening hours gives way, at 11 p.m., to generally lighter fare. But the political humor on Fox News still attacks familiar targets on the left. In other words, *Gutfeld!* offers Jon Stewart-style ironic detachment with a conservative face (Marx and Sienkiewicz 2022).

> Whereas most Fox News programming is fueled by anger and fearmongering, Gutfeld's comedic double act celebrates the right's self-realization that unseriousness can be wielded by and attractive to a wide array of demographic groups within its ideological coalition.
>
> *(Marx and Sienkiewicz 2022)*

Keys to his success involve his efforts at self-deprecation, a key strategy for winning over the public, as Lincoln, Roosevelt, and Reagan, among others, have demonstrated. Indeed, Trump might have been better received beyond his base if he had been willing to laugh at himself now and then (Deen 2018). Gutfeld also appears to be enjoying himself on-air, particularly in the post-monologue conversations with show regulars and other guests. In his assessment of the success of *Gutfeld!* that appeared in *The Atlantic*, James Parker (2022) took note of the host's very effective strategy to appear not to take himself too seriously on the way to attacking liberal and Democratic targets.

> He's crass and hacky-on-purpose, with a deplorable private life. That's the conceit, at any rate. Now he's steaming into his monologue, castigating Joe Biden for his confused/confusing statements about Vladimir Putin. "For us," booms Gutfeld in his beefed-up, semi-ironic *WrestleMania* voice, "toppling regimes has worked out about as well as dating a stripper. At least for the people I dated when I was stripping."
>
> *(Parker 2022)*

At the same time, though, some of the nastier writing on the program continues to offer some of the "punching down" content that makes conservative political humor somewhat limited in its appeal beyond regular Fox News viewers. Reviewers have also noted the very harsh treatment of presidential son Hunter Biden on the show, arguing that *Gutfeld!* also presents the mean streak of Fox News content earlier in the evening.

The Challenge of Creating Conservative Comedy **141**

But watching Gutfeld sneer at an addict in recovery – in the opioid era, as addiction is among the defining threads of American life – and to repeatedly use his personal struggle as the only available cudgel against his father, felt unworthy of even of a network that has showcased advocates of the Obama birther conspiracy, specious anti-climate change experts and baseless voter election fraud claims, among other outrages.

(D'Addario 2021)

Or one can consider a Gutfeld commentary on homeless people in urban areas run by Democratic mayors:

When I was a kid, I had a dog named Chipper … and whenever the dog got out, you'd think it would run to the park to pee or poop – you know, like vagrants in Democrat-run cities. But no, it always ran up the street towards the traffic.

(Gutfeld, quoted in Parker 2022)

While this one-liner was far from the funniest thing on the program, the joke demonstrates the challenge of trying to offer conservative content aimed at favorite targets who nevertheless are living in desperate circumstances. One cannot imagine most comics finding anything funny in mocking homeless people needing to go to the bathroom, which seems like one of the clearest examples of "punching down" that one can imagine. But part of the appeal of *Gutfeld!* is that the show (at least part of the time) is not like the other comedy programs.

Another advantage that the show has when compared to its competitors is the same general advantage that Fox News itself has – that of a deliberate marketing strategy of product differentiation. By being very different from its competitors, those viewers seeking something different from conventional television content will be drawn to Fox News, and to *Gutfeld!* – both of which often proclaim how different they are from more mainstream media offerings. "The boring, dull, uninteresting comedians on late-night TV were and continue to be obsessed with Donald Trump, and that's what actually destroyed their shows," noted *New York Post* writer Karol Markowicz (2022).

As the only non-liberal late-night comedy show, "Gutfeld!" has automatic wider appeal than the same-same-same Jimmy-Jimmy-Stephen shows on network TV. It averaged 2.19 million viewers in August. Gutfeld also happens to be actually funny, and his co-hosts Kat Timpf and Tyrus are hilarious too. They aren't making lame jokes about

142 The Challenge of Creating Conservative Comedy

Trump or the guy who is president right now. They aren't predictable like the rest of the late-night lineup.

(Markowicz 2022)

With this overview in mind, the chapter now turns to a content analysis of the jokes offered by Gutfeld during the fall of 2021, the final months of Biden's first year as president. In this next section, we also compare the content of Gutfeld's jokes with those of the four nightly comics who have formed the core of the analysis throughout this book.

Analyzing the Jokes of *Gutfeld!*

Our analysis of the jokes of *Gutfeld!* does not start when the show debuted in April 2021. Rather we wished to give the new nightly program a few months to establish itself and to develop its own voice during what, for any new program, would be a rocky stretch as it sought to find its footing. As a result, our analysis considers the jokes on the new nightly humor program between September 6 and December 12, 2021, roughly the period between Labor Day and the Christmas season. As has been the case throughout this project, the content analysis considers the opening monologue of the show, not jokes told across the entire program, the bulk of which includes interviews with guests. The Fall 2021 period of analysis includes the aftermath of the chaotic U.S. military withdrawal from Afghanistan during August 2021 and the election of Republican Glenn Youngkin as governor of Virginia in November 2021. Youngkin's victory was seen by some political observers as an early political indicator of potential political problems for Biden, who had been elected president a year earlier (Crowley and Barnes 2021; Lerer 2021).

Table 5.1 provides the focus of jokes told by Greg Gutfeld on his show between September 6 and December 12, 2021. The data demonstrate that the contrast with the comedians we have considered so far in this project is immense. Political humor, as one would expect, was very different on this Fox News program.

Donald Trump, the former president, who had been an overwhelming force on late-night comedy year after year, was the subject of only 11 jokes during this roughly three-month period, less than one per week. Of the ten individuals who were the subject of at least 10 jokes during the period on *Gutfeld!*, Trump was the only Republican. President Biden was the subject of more than half the jokes – 334 out of 613 – told on this comedy show during this period.

In second place was presidential son Hunter Biden, whose personal scandals have drawn considerable attention from conservatives and conservative

The Challenge of Creating Conservative Comedy **143**

TABLE 5.1 Leading Targets of *Gutfeld!*, Fall 2021

Joe Biden	*334*
Hunter Biden	53
Kamala Harris	36
Alexandria Ocasio-Cortez	36
Andrew Cuomo	19
Bill de Blasio	15
Kyrsten Sinema	13
Pete Buttigieg	12
Donald Trump	11
Jen Psaki	10

Total N = 613.
Note: Only individuals and institutions that were the subject of at least ten jokes are included here.
Totals include late-night jokes aired during September 6–December 12, 2021, on *Gutfeld!*

Source: CMPA

comics over the past several years (Baker 2020). Hunter Biden, the subject of 53 jokes during the period, is not part of his father's administration, unlike presidential daughter Ivanka Trump, a top aide to her father through his four years in office. The joke total for Hunter Biden exceeded that of Vice President Kamala Harris and highly visible Congresswoman Alexandria Ocasio-Cortez (D-NY), both of whom were the subject of 36 jokes during the study period and are frequent targets of commentators on Fox News. New York Gov. Andrew Cuomo (D), who resigned in 2021 following allegations of mistreatment of women in state government, ranked fifth with 19 jokes, followed by New York City Mayor (and unsuccessful Democratic 2020 presidential candidate) Bill de Blasio, with 15 jokes.

The show, compared to its counterparts, had an unusual New York City-focused rundown of the leading targets of humor, as three of the top six targets were or are elected officials in New York. Normally shows aiming for a national audience would be careful not to make the show too much about New York (both the city and the state), but perhaps both New York City and New York State are places that middle America enjoys seeing mocked. During his time as president, Donald Trump (who grew up in and made his fortune in the New York City region) nevertheless often criticized his birthplace. His attacks on the region were most aggressive during the early days of COVID, when city and state governments engaged in aggressive health protection policies that conflicted with Trump's early desires to downplay the severity of the pandemic (Cillizza 2020).

Not all Democratic leaders were appealing targets on this program. Although they did not make the Top Ten, former president Barack Obama

144 The Challenge of Creating Conservative Comedy

TABLE 5.2 Leading Targets of *Gutfeld!* by Month, 2021

September		October		November		December	
Joe Biden	19	Joe Biden	62	Joe Biden	72	Joe Biden	9
Hunter Biden	34	Bill de Blasio	14	Kamala Harris	12	Donald Trump	2
Alexandria Ocasio-Cortez	28	Hunter Biden	13	Andrew Cuomo	8	Devin Nunes	2
Kamala Harris	9	Kamala Harris	13	Alexandria Ocasio-Cortez	7	Hunter Biden	1
Andrew Cuomo	9	Kyrsten Sinema	13	Terry McAuliffe	7	Jill Biden	1
Total	306		139		150		15

Total N = 613.
Note: The total numbers include many targets not listed here.
Totals include late-night jokes aired during September 6–December 12, 2021, on *Gutfeld!*

Source: CMPA

(D) was the subject of four jokes on the show during the period we examined, and Democratic House Speaker Nancy Pelosi was the subject of three jokes.

Table 5.2 breaks the *Gutfeld!* jokes into monthly rankings. As expected, President Biden ranked first in every time period in this study, always by a margin of two-to-one or more. Hunter Biden ranked second in September and third in October, while New York City Mayor Bill DeBlasio ranked second in October and Vice President Harris ranked second in November. She also ranked fourth in September and October. Former Virginia Gov. Terry McAuliffe, who lost a bid for a second term in November 2021 to Youngkin, ranked fifth as a joke target on the show that month.

The focus of jokes told on *Gutfeld!* could hardly be more different from the political humor perspectives of the four nightly comics we have been examining throughout this book. As shown in Table 5.3, Donald Trump continued to dominate the attention of the longer-running late-night comics, though the gap between the number of jokes about Trump and Biden narrowed considerably when compared to Biden's first months as president in early 2021 (the period we examined in Chapter 4). Trump was the subject of 720 jokes for the four veteran late-night host during the fall analysis period, as compared to 548 jokes for Biden, who finished second. Rep Paul Gosar (R-AZ), the third-place finisher and one of the more combative supporters of former President Trump, was far behind those two figures, with 104 jokes. Gosar was censured by Congress, the first member so sanctioned in more than a decade, after posting an anime version of himself doing battle with figures altered to represent Biden and Rep. Ocasio-Cortez (Grayer and Foran 2021).

For these long-running hosts, Republicans as a group ranked fourth with 97 jokes, while Democrats as a group ranked fifth with 77 jokes.

The Challenge of Creating Conservative Comedy **145**

TABLE 5.3 Late-Night Humor Targets on Four Long-Running Shows, Fall 2021

Donald Trump	720
Joe Biden	548
Paul Gosar	104
Republicans*	97
Democrats*	77
Michael Flynn	72
Lauren Boebert	70
Mike Pence	62
Biden Administration*	62
Bernie Sanders	55
Congress*	53
Josh Hawley	46
Rudy Giuliani	43
Eric Trump	41
Kyrsten Sinema	41
Donald Trump Jr.	34
Ted Cruz	33
Senators*	31
Mitch McConnell	30
Hillary Clinton	29
Joe Manchin	29
Lindsey Graham	27
Larry Elder	25
Dr. Oz	24
Gavin Newsom	24
House*	23
Bill de Blasio	23
Barrack Obama	21
Marjorie Taylor Greene	20
Terry McAuliffe	19
Glenn Youngkin	18
Ron Johnson	17
Melania Trump	16
Kamala Harris	16
Vito Fossella	16
Steve Bannon	15
Ken Weyler	14
Janice McGeachin	12

(Continued)

146 The Challenge of Creating Conservative Comedy

TABLE 5.3 (Continued)

Devin Nunes	12
Mark Meadows	12
Eric Adams	12
Alex Jones	12
Dick Durbin	10

Total N = 3,013.
Note: Only individuals and institutions that were the subject of at least ten jokes are included here.
* General categories are used for jokes that focus on the institution or a group rather than a specific individual. Jokes that name individuals are coded as jokes directed at that individual.

Totals include late-night jokes aired during September 6–December 10, 2021, on *Jimmy Kimmel Live*, *The Daily Show with Trevor Noah*, *The Late Show with Stephen Colbert*, and *The Tonight Show with Jimmy Fallon*.

Source: CMPA

Further back in the rankings were former Gen. Michael Flynn and Lauren Boebert (R-CO), highly visible conservative backers of Trump, who were the subject of 72 and 70 jokes, respectively. Former Vice President Pence tied with the Biden administration for eighth place with 62 jokes each, while Sen. Bernie Sanders (I-VT) placed tenth with 55 jokes.

Before moving on, one might also note that Gutfeld tends to tell fewer jokes than the hosts of the other late-night comedy programs. His total of 613 jokes during the study period is fewer than one-quarter of the 3,013 jokes told by the other four comics. .

When examining the four individual hosts, one sees that not one of them offers a menu of mockery comparable to that of Gutfeld. As shown in Table 5.4, only one of the hosts – Jimmy Fallon – told notably more jokes about Biden than Trump (193 jokes versus 70 jokes, respectively). But once you get beyond the two presidents, the humor diverges. Gutfeld's Democratic non-presidential targets, including Vice President Harris, Hunter Biden, and other prominent Washington politicians that Gutfeld skewered did not qualify as major targets of humor for the more senior late-night comics.

Fallon once again was an outlier when compared to his fellow long-running late-night hosts. During the fall of 2021, none of the others were so focused on Biden and so willing to move past Trump. While Stephen Colbert told roughly as many Biden and Trump jokes (254 jokes versus 250 jokes, respectively) during the study period, both Jimmy Kimmel and Trevor Noah told far more jokes about Trump than Biden. For all four hosts, as for Gutfeld, Biden and Trump ranked first and second as the targets of humor, but the proportion of mirth directed at the two men varied a great deal depending on who was telling the jokes.

The Challenge of Creating Conservative Comedy **147**

TABLE 5.4 Leading Target Frequency on Four Long-Running Shows, Fall 2021

	Kimmel	Noah	Colbert	Fallon	Total
Donald Trump	202	198	250	70	720
[Percentages]	[28%]	[27%]	[35%]	[10%]	
Joe Biden	35	66	254	193	548
Paul Gosar	2	102	0	0	104
Republicans*	5	71	16	5	97
Democrats *	4	56	17	0	77
Michael Flynn	0	0	72	0	72
Lauren Boebert	8	45	17	0	70
Mike Pence	12	2	48	6	68
Biden Administration*	0	29	16	17	62
Bernie Sanders	0	7	48	0	55
Congress*	0	27	10	16	53
Josh Hawley	0	32	14	0	46
Rudy Giuliani	1	12	23	7	43
Eric Trump	0	0	41	0	41
London Breed	0	0	40	0	40
Ted Cruz	26	0	6	7	39
Donald Trump Jr.	24	1	9	0	34
Senators*	0	9	12	10	31
Total	**421**	**813**	**1,320**	**459**	**3,031**

Total N = 3,013.

* General categories are used for jokes that focus on the institution or a group rather than a specific individual. Jokes that name individuals are coded as jokes directed at that individual.

Totals include late-night jokes aired during September 6–December 10, 2021, on *Jimmy Kimmel Live*, *The Daily Show with Trevor Noah*, *The Late Show with Stephen Colbert*, and *The Tonight Show with Jimmy Fallon*.

Source: CMPA

Beyond the presidents, and beyond the different focus all four of these established comics had when compared to Gutfeld, one notices other important differences within the group's treatment of current events in late 2021. Several of the hosts continued to attack targets who were key figures in attempts to block the ratification of Joe Biden's election by Congress on January 6, 2021. Colbert focused a great deal on retired General Michael Flynn, a former Trump National Security Advisor turned "stop-the-steal" ally (Colbert told all 72 jokes the four comics offered about Flynn). Colbert also focused on former Vice President Mike Pence (48 jokes), Bernie Sanders (48 jokes), and Eric Trump, the former president's second son. Noah focused

148 The Challenge of Creating Conservative Comedy

on Rep. Boebert (45 jokes) and devoted 32 jokes to Sen. Josh Hawley (R-MO), who famously waved a fist in support of the January 6 rally outside the Capitol (and a few hours later was captured on video sprinting to safety when those same demonstrators overran the Capitol and started searching for elected officials). Kimmel was more interested in mocking Sen. Ted Cruz (R-TX), another vigorous supporter of Trump's unsupported claim that the 2020 election was stolen (26 jokes), and presidential son Donald Trump Jr. (24 jokes). Fallon, who routinely tells fewer political jokes than other three long-time late-night hosts, often chooses not to joke about political figures: He told 17 jokes about the Biden administration, 16 about Congress generally, and 10 about senators generally.

Few Democrats beyond Biden were all that high in the ranking of these four comics not working at Fox News. Democrats generally were the subject of 56 jokes on *The Daily Show* (out of a total of 77 jokes offered by the four comics. Republicans generally were the subject of 97 jokes, with 71 of them on *The Daily Show*. Aside from Biden, and Sanders, who ranked tenth overall among those four comics, San Francisco Mayor London Breed, a controversial figure who generated 40 jokes from Colbert and none from the other three establishment late-night hosts, was the only Democrat at or near the top of the rankings.

Taken together, we can see the sharp differences between the partisan focus of the jokes told by Gutfeld and those told by the four longer-running nightly comics. Democratic figures are the targets of 96 percent of the jokes offered by Gutfeld, as compared to 59 percent of the jokes by Fallon, 37 percent of the jokes by Colbert, 31 percent of the jokes by Noah, and 15 percent of the jokes from Kimmel. These analyses also reveal that Gutfeld was more focused on Democratic targets in late 2021 than the other comics were focused on Republicans during Biden's first year in office. Gutfeld was also more focused on first-year president Joe Biden during this study period than the other comics were when they focused on Trump during his first year in office. During 2017, for example, 76 percent of the jokes focused on Republicans on those four long-running comedy programs (Farnsworth and Lichter 2020: 84–85). Gutfeld's 96 percent focus on Democratic figures in late 2021, though, is comparable to the Trump-focused narratives of the other leading late-night television comedy hosts during the 2020 presidential campaign. One might note, though, that Trump was both an incumbent president and a candidate for reelection during that year (see Table 4.6 in Chapter 4 for data on this comparison).

In Table 5.5, we examine the tendency of the five comics compared in this chapter to emphasize (or not) personal matters in their jokes mocking political figures. As we have done in our previous content analyses of political humor, we define personal jokes as those that focus on individual attributes, such things as a political figure's temperament, demeanor, or personal

The Challenge of Creating Conservative Comedy **149**

TABLE 5.5 Personal Jokes by Program, Fall 2021

Jokes about Trump

	Not Personal	*Personal*	*Total Jokes*
Jimmy Kimmel Live	5	197	202
The Daily Show with Trevor Noah	126	72	198
The Late Show with Stephen Colbert	90	160	250
The Tonight Show Starring Jimmy Fallon	39	31	70
Gutfeld!	6	5	11
Total jokes	266	465	731
Total percentage	36%	64%	100%

Jokes Not about Trump

	Not Personal	*Personal*	*Total Jokes*
Jimmy Kimmel Live	31	188	219
The Daily Show with Trevor Noah	525	92	615
The Late Show with Stephen Colbert	669	401	1070
The Tonight Show Starring Jimmy Fallon	262	127	389
Gutfeld!	346	256	602
Total jokes	1,831	1,064	2,895
Total percentage	63%	37%	100%

Jokes about Biden

	Not Personal	*Personal*	*Total Jokes*
Jimmy Kimmel Live	6	29	35
The Daily Show with Trevor Noah	31	35	66
The Late Show with Stephen Colbert	183	71	254
The Tonight Show Starring Jimmy Fallon	159	34	193
Gutfeld!	204	130	334
Total jokes	583	299	882
Total percentage	66%	34%	100%

Jokes Not about Biden

(Continued)

150 The Challenge of Creating Conservative Comedy

TABLE 5.5 (Continued)

Jokes about Trump

	Not Personal	Personal	Total Jokes
Jimmy Kimmel Live	30	356	386
The Daily Show with Trevor Noah	618	129	747
The Late Show with Stephen Colbert	575	490	1,065
The Tonight Show Starring Jimmy Fallon	142	124	266
Gutfeld!	148	131	279
Total jokes	1,513	1,230	2,743
Total percentage	55%	45%	100%

Total N = 3,626

Totals include late-night jokes aired during September 6–December 10, 2021, on *Jimmy Kimmel Live*, *The Daily Show with Trevor Noah*, *The Late Show with Stephen Colbert*, *The Tonight Show with Jimmy Fallon*, and *Gutfeld!*

Source: CMPA

qualities, such as allegedly being feeble or not all that smart. Jokes that are not personal could focus on some humorous aspect of the president's policy preferences or political interactions with others in government, for example.

As one would expect given his own larger-than-life public presence, and the fact that he as an ex-president was no longer making policy, the jokes that focused on former president Trump during the fall of 2021 were largely about personal matters. Such jokes represented nearly two-thirds (64 percent) of all the jokes the comics offered regarding him during the study period. That pattern of humor for the former president is in sharp contrast to the jokes the comics offered about everyone else, which emphasized personal matters only 37 percent of the time.

With respect to the jokes about Trump, one notes very distinct patterns of humor for the individual comics. For Jimmy Kimmel, the jokes about Trump were overwhelmingly personal in nature (197 of the 202 Trump he told related to personal themes). Stephen Colbert also told more personal jokes than jokes not focused on personal matters (160 of 250 jokes of his Trump jokes during the study period were personal in nature). Jimmy Fallon told far fewer jokes about Trump in late 2021 than did three of his late-night colleagues (Fallon offered a total of 70 barbs aimed at Trump during the study period). But Fallon's total still represented far more targeting of Trump than one saw on *Gutfeld!*, which offered only 11 jokes about Trump. For Fallon, 39 of his 70 jokes about Trump were not about personal matters,

The Challenge of Creating Conservative Comedy   **151**

while Gutfeld offered a nearly even split during his monologues: six Trump jokes were not about personal matters and five were.

Stephen Colbert told the most political jokes of the five hosts during the survey period and ranked first in the number of jokes about Trump (250 jokes versus 202 Trump jokes from Kimmel, who ranked second in that category). Colbert also told the most political jokes about figures other than Trump, with 1,070 non-Trump political jokes, followed by 615 non-Trump political jokes from Noah and 602 non-Trump political jokes by Gutfeld. Kimmel, who ranked second among the five comics in the number of jokes about Trump, told the smallest number of political jokes about people who were not Donald Trump.

For political jokes during this period that were not focused on Trump, only Kimmel retained his intense focus on personal matters in his humor, with 188 of 219 non-Trump jokes focused on personal matters. Even Fallon, who tends to offer the least political humor overall, told more non-Trump jokes than did Kimmel (389 jokes, compared to 219 jokes, respectively).

For the other four humorists beyond Kimmel, nonpersonal matters dominated the political humor. Among the five hosts, Trevor Noah was the least interested in personal-oriented humor in his jokes about people other than Trump (523 of his 615 political jokes were about nonpersonal matters relating to his targets other than the former president). Among the five hosts, Gutfeld was the most inclined to balance his humor between political and nonpolitical jokes aimed at individuals other than Trump (346 out of his 602 not-Donald Trump jokes were nonpolitical).

Turning now to the 882 jokes the five humorists offered regarding Biden during the study period, one can note once again the sharp contrasts in their approaches. Gutfeld, who told the most jokes about the president (334), continued to de-emphasize personal humor. Gutfeld told 130 jokes about Biden that focused on personal matters, as compared to 204 that did not. Colbert, who ranked second in the number of jokes that focused on Biden (254), also emphasized jokes that did not concentrate on personal matters (183 jokes of his jokes were not focused on personal matters, as compared to 71 that were). Fallon likewise de-emphasized personal matters in his jokes about Biden, with only 34 of 193 jokes taking aim at some personal aspect of the president.

Only two of the five hosts told more personal-oriented jokes about Biden than not, and both hosts – Noah and Kimmel – told far fewer jokes about the president than the other three hosts. For Noah, the split was close to even, with 35 of 66 Biden jokes emphasizing personal matters. For Kimmel, the focus was overwhelmingly toward personal humor, with 29 of 35 jokes focused on personal matters. Of course, Kimmel's jokes about political figures other than Biden were likewise very oriented toward personal matters (only 30 of the 386 jokes he told during the Fall 2021 study period were not personal in nature).

152 The Challenge of Creating Conservative Comedy

BOX 5.1 SELECTED POLITICAL JOKES ON *GUTFELD!*, FALL 2021

Biden

These idiots are wrong more often than Biden trying to button up his shirt.
(*Gutfeld!* – September 7, 2021)

As vice president Joe went to funerals. As president he causes them. It's amazing this joker has been in politics forever. In the moment he's put in charge I would not trust him with the keys to a Rascal Scooter.
(*Gutfeld!* – October 8, 2021)

The chain that supplies lying is flowing more smoothly than the flatulence out of Biden's butt. I should stop making those job jokes, but I won't.
Gutfeld! – November 15, 2021

Sleepy Joe might owe 500 large. Who knew that falling asleep in your soup, forgetting the name of foreign heads of state, smelling the hair of Oval Office visitors, were all tax deductible. Turns out he might owe $500,000. Smelling the hair of Oval Office visitors wasn't ideal. A new court ruling shows he improperly avoided paying Medicare taxes of a half million dollars. He can order some fresh new hair plugs and plant them on his head.
(*Gutfeld!* – September 24, 2021)

Hunter Biden

Politico just published quite the bomb shell. The e-mails from Hunter Biden's laptop were authenticated. Imagine that. Authenticating things we already knew to be true. So, what are you gonna tell us next? Hunter needs blow and hookers? (pause) Who doesn't, though?
(*Gutfeld!* – September 22, 2021)

But the most affluent places in America are Arlington, Fairfax, and Loudoun counties. Their people make six or even seven figures. The type of folks who can afford Hunter Biden's artwork and drug habit. And they vote Democrat overwhelmingly, knowing that it only leads to paying much higher taxes.
(*Gutfeld!* – November 4, 2021)

Trump

So, it is late night getting together but they refused to invite the battle of the bulge, me, Snow White. They make sure to send invitations to all of the seven dorks. Including CBS's Stephen Colbert, and who knows more about harmful carbon emissions then this windbag? ABC's Jimmy Kimmel, who will no doubt cry and then claim his tears are made of acid rain. James Gordon, whoever that is. Maybe he will do a karaoke version of here comes the rain and – for Jimmy Fallon. Will pretend to laugh at the rest of everything and everyone else will say they will still hate him. And then there is this guy, Seth, I don't know his last name. His sole purpose of being there is to make the rest of them seem funny. Then blame the receding ice caps on Trump hair spray. You can have that joke.

(*Gutfeld!* – September 16, 2021)

Cultural Politics Jokes

We saw this coming. Remember everyone is politically deputized by the Democrats now. Get into your face. Science doesn't even matter, or in this case biology. Last week we were told the CDC has gotten rid of the term "Woman" when discussing pregnancy. That's both sexist and misogynist and boy have the broads been complaining. [Scattered laughter] The *Washington Post* joined in, saying that reporters will now be expected to write pregnant individuals, because not all pregnant people are women. The complete phrase "Pregnant women and other pregnant individuals," meaning, I suppose, man. But once again, a reminder to all you narrow-minded types, yes, men can get pregnant. I refer to the men who have ovaries and wombs and can fertilize an egg and bring a baby to term – oh wait, men don't have that stuff. Good luck trying.

(*Gutfeld!* – October 4, 2021)

Here is another lefty with stage IV cancer of the funny bone. These people can't spell funny if you gave them the F you. That guy is columnist for the *Washington Post*, you couldn't tell the difference between parody and reality when lefties spend all their time around other lefties they don't need to. They just agree with their own feverish fantasies, and no one is there to apply the brakes.

(*Gutfeld!* – December 3, 2021)

So, it turns out there are only two sexual orientations, leftists, and everyone else. It is true. According to a new poll, 71% of Democrats,

> college students, say they wouldn't go on a date with someone with opposing views. Versus only 31% of Republicans ... Apparently the newly woke prefer to judge you as good or evil based on political affiliation.
>
> *(Gutfeld! – December 8, 2021)*

In Box 5.1 we offer some of Gutfeld's political jokes, selecting some key one-liners that relate to the two presidents, presidential son Hunter Biden, a key topic of conservative humor and media attention, and to matters of cultural politics, another area of emphasis for conservative humor and conservative news. (Since we have discussed the other four comics at length across the other chapters of this book, we want to leave this comparative discussion and return our focus to Gutfeld during the remaining part of the chapter).

As the selected Gutfeld jokes demonstrate, the idea that President Biden may be too old to be an effective president is a theme for humor on the Fox News comedy program. We saw similar dynamics in the jokes of other comedy programs considering the new president in our discussion in Chapter 4. Gutfeld's invocation of a Rascal Scooter, a motorized mobility device employed by some seniors who find walking difficult, may not have much actual resonance for Biden, a relatively fit senior citizen known to enjoy bicycling. But the reference draws attention to how feeble some elderly citizens can become and tries to link that image to Biden. Suggesting in another joke that Biden struggles to button his shirt, a rather basic task of daily personal independence, likewise raises the question of whether Biden retains the cognitive capacity to be president.

The selected jokes from Gutfeld also raise policy questions, like the reference to Biden's responsibility for causing deaths, which was made shortly after the U.S. military left Afghanistan in a chaotic exodus marked by the death of more than a dozen U.S. service members who were killed by suicide bombers as the military prepared to depart (Aikins et al. 2021).

When Gutfeld turned attention to Hunter Biden, the mockery often turned to key themes that have energized prominent conservatives beyond the comedy program about the presidential son – the questions of potentially incriminating information contained on Hunter Biden's laptop and the younger Biden's use of drugs (Goldman 2020; Goldman et al. 2020; Vogel and Schmidt 2022). One selected Gutfeld joke about Hunter Biden also served double-duty by mocking both Hunter Biden and the affluent northern Virginia suburbs, home to many affluent Washington area workers who often vote Democratic.

One particularly interesting dynamic seen in Gutfeld's humor is a sort of self-mockery employed while he makes fun of others. As we have discussed previously, presidents who were able and willing to make jokes at their own expense often endeared themselves to their audiences. When Gutfeld makes even veiled references to his own connections to the world of personal misconduct, he can connect with viewers. When Gutfeld asks his audience who doesn't need "blow and hookers," he implies that he is at least somewhat conversant with such matters of personal misconduct. But he stops short here, and elsewhere, of admitting to anything specific that might offend the many Christian conservatives who rely on Fox News programming. His comments about prostitution and illegal drug use may just be part of the act, one might note. Leveling a rhetorical attack on Hunter Biden seems less harsh when there is a little self-deprecation by the comic along the way. Gutfeld's less than earnest approach also reinforces a "sense of play" that is crucial to effective political humor – and he can always say he was only kidding if someone seeks to follow up the joking "admission" of misconduct.

Box 5.1 includes an example from the relatively tiny number of jokes from Gutfeld that referenced former president Trump during the study period. What's particularly interesting about this example is how the joke is primarily about his fellow late-night hosts and what they would say about Trump, rather than what Gutfeld had to say about Trump. The clip drips with resentment for those more established late-night comics, a serving of hostility toward Colbert et al. that would be very well-received by a Fox News audience primed by Trump, Hannity, Carlson, Ingraham, and others to think the worst of the late-night hosts appearing on places other than Fox News.

Conservatives delight in making fun of liberal pieties, and few targets are more appealing than the mass media. Some of Gutfeld's jokes in the realm of cultural politics ridicule the language choices of the *Washington Post*, while others take aim at "woke" narratives relating to sexual identities. In a commentary that may appeal to some of Gutfeld's young adult male viewers, the host laments the extent to which Democrats say they refuse to date Republicans.

Jokes like those in Box 5.1 serve to underscore the iconoclastic nature of conservative humor, a humor not aimed at respecting authority, as traditional conservativism often encouraged. But the attacks are directed at very specific elites: the celebrities of late night, Democratic politicians, and Democratic activists. By making liberals the rulers and conservatives the victims, Gutfeld flips the script of those other, more liberal, late-night voices who lamented the power of Donald Trump over the country during

156 The Challenge of Creating Conservative Comedy

the past several years. Gutfeld's approach represents a way to punch up – and does so by nodding to existing conservative grievances, particularly regarding cultural politics. His comedy, in other words, very much resembles the narrative of a combative former president who, despite all the power that comes with being the nation's chief executive, nursed his perceived offenses like few people in power in this country ever have.

Conclusion

As a candidate, as a president, and as a former president, Donald Trump has dismissed presidential norms. His great interest in employing personal attacks on his critics made him popular with his base (Schier and Eberly 2017). But the aggressive fact-checking about the president and his very public presidency – and very public ex-presidency – have also made him once again an immensely popular target for most of the humorists of late-night talk shows. Everything about Donald Trump that seems larger than life – his gilded lifestyle, his private resorts and golf courses, his abandonment of policy consistency in favor of being able to declare momentary victories, and his aggressive plotting to regain power – all allow most of the humorists we have discussed in this book to have a field day regardless of whether he is a presidential candidate, a president, or a former president. Particularly when compared to his predecessor, the calm, cool, self-controlled introvert Barack Obama, Trump was a comedic dream come true. Indeed, joke writers who might like to exaggerate for humorous effect might find the need to do little more than read the headlines to poke fun at this inconsistent, angry man of immense appetites who loves to see the spotlight turned toward himself.

But one new late-night voice found little interest in farming the fields of humor told at Trump's expense. Even though mocking Trump had offered a huge payoff for most of these comics, Greg Gutfeld rejected the temptation that so many other late-night hosts have succumbed to for eight years now: tearing into Trump from a multitude of directions. He did not join them in making fun of the former president's physical appearance, his clothing style, his chaotic administration, his policy ignorance, inconsistency in his statements, his neediness, his narcissism, and his volatile temperament. In fact, he barely mentioned Trump at all.

Gutfeld has sought to chart a different course, one more familiar to the Fox News audience. While he does make some jokes about Trump, it is clear that he directs the humor toward Democratic targets about as much as the other late-night hosts have focused on Republicans. While Joe Biden, or at least the version of Joe Biden in the public arena in 2020 and the years that followed, may not offer the same range of humor that

Trump provided, Gutfeld still finds plenty of jokes to be told relating to the president's age, and particularly his son Hunter Biden, the latest in a long-tradition of scandal-plagued presidential family members, apples that have fallen some distance from a more noble family tree.

The different product that Gutfeld offers makes sense, both for the Fox News audience and when one considers the larger political humor landscape. As early as 2016 there was some indication that the market for conventional political humor may have become saturated. A few months before Trump's election, Comedy Central cancelled Larry Wilmore's *The Nightly Show*, a successor program in the coveted time slot after *The Daily Show* that was once occupied by Stephen Colbert. The network said Wilmore's show failed to attract a sufficiently large audience (Butler 2016). The mixture of experimentation with new formats and new Fox News audience-friendly areas of emphasis that marked the first two years of *Gutfeld!* suggests that this program is likely to continue to be a valuable part of the Fox News lineup in the years to come.

This chapter, and Chapter 4, offered information on what the nation's most prominent comics said about the last two presidential campaigns and the last two presidents. The next question to consider is the impact of this humor on the late-night audience. In Chapter 6, we consider who watches late-night comedy and whether these programs have an influence regarding political interest, political knowledge, and political action.

6

POLITICAL CONSEQUENCES OF LATE-NIGHT HUMOR

Learning about Politics via Political Comedy

Political humor has become an increasingly important part of U.S. political communication, particularly regarding presidents and presidential elections. This chapter focuses on public opinion relating to learning about politics via late-night political comedy, and it reveals that younger voters, liberal voters, Democratic identifiers, and Biden voters all were more likely to report having learned from political humor programs than did respondents who were older, more conservative, Republican identifiers, and Trump voters. In a sharp contrast with previous research that found linkages between consuming late-night comedy and increases in viewers' cynicism and political negativity, this chapter examines the findings that those most inclined to trust the national government in 2021 were also most likely to have reported learning about something about the 2020 presidential election via the late-night shows.

For the past few decades, late-night comedians have been getting more attention from candidates and presidents as well as from journalists who cover politics and political campaigns. Even as traditional news formats like print newspapers and network television newscasts have lost significant shares of their audiences, the late-night talk shows continue to command substantial attention, as viewers turn to those shows at the traditional late evening hours or, increasingly, whenever they wish via online media sharing of late-night content now available 24/7.

For many years now, all the prominent late-night comics had their own YouTube channels to allow for the replaying of late-night content. Some, including Jimmy Fallon's *The Tonight Show*, ranked in the top 100 most popular channels on YouTube (Baumgartner and Becker 2018). And the

DOI: 10.4324/9781003283041-6

online presence of political humor has only increased in recent years, as even establishment information sources like the *New York Times* provide regular online summaries of the late-night shows shortly after they are broadcast.

While Donald Trump was not the first president to wish to avoid the mockery of late-night humor, the ferocity with which he criticized these humorists while he was serving as president – and his talk of using federal regulatory powers to curb their attacks on him during his time in office – drew attention to these comics in ways that previous presidents would have considered unproductive. To Trump, though, the best strategy is usually an immediate and massive response. As far as he was concerned, the stakes connected to late-night programming were too great to be ignored during his presidency. They remain so as he undertakes a 2024 campaign – and as he continues to remain a central target of late-night comedy (Farnsworth et al. 2022). Trump excels at treating his political rivals with the very same personal attacks and undermining of individual reputations that are the bread and butter of late-night humor, particularly the insult comics. Even as he employs similar tactics against his rivals, Trump seems to believe that these critical voices of late-night comedians have undermined public respect for himself and for the political system. But is that true?

This chapter examines previous scholarly research as well as a 2021 public opinion survey on late-night political humor, which was conducted by Research America Inc. (RAI 2021) and was designed to consider possible political impacts of late-night comedy. We examine who learns from political humor and the importance of various individual factors, including partisanship, ideology, and age, to that learning.

Late-Night Humor and Political Support

Long before there were late-night television comics, indeed long before there was television, there were citizen frustrations with government. The U.S. political system itself was created by revolutionaries with deep skepticism about centralized power, human nature, and even the capacity of self-government.

Even though American history includes many political, social, economic, cultural, and military successes, political figures have learned repeatedly that it is not easy to keep citizens happy, or even to succeed in securing one's preferred policy outcomes in the complicated political system devised by the Founders to minimize the risk of a too powerful government. Even with those precautions, there remains a constant public concern about political leaders becoming too distant from the people they serve and national power becoming too great. Political humor can be a way to focus,

160 Political Consequences of Late-Night Humor

codify, and perhaps even respond to the gap between what people say they would like to see from government and what the government delivers in terms of policy outcomes. Late-night comedy programming is a popular enough format to have survived decades of changes in politics and culture and is now thriving in a variety of communication channels, including many social media platforms.

This nation's bedrock commitment to free speech, with stronger constitutional protections than in many other democratic societies, permits and even encourages a great volume of critical discourse aimed at the government. Since government policy often involves trade-offs, differing opinions among policymakers and limited resources, public disappointment with outcomes is a common condition regardless of the topic at hand. Indeed, the wide range of policy concerns that citizens think government should address creates a climate where public expressions of frustrations with government are particularly intense in modern western democracies. Of course, our ancestors would be amazed at what today's citizens demand from government. The capacity of the modern democratic state to provide general satisfaction regarding the traditional and comparatively modest public expectations of a national government (i.e., to secure a healthy economy and keep the nation's enemies at bay) is far from sufficient for today's difficult-to-please citizens.

Today, people living in modern western democracies possess a variety of higher-level and harder-to-satisfy public demands dealing with quality-of-life issues like environmental regulation, health care provision, and navigating the conflicting tax and service demands of the modern welfare state (Farnsworth 2001, 2003a, 2003b; Habermas 1973; Inglehart 1990). These contemporary, harder to resolve policy challenges represent a sort of "demand overload" for government as it concentrates on areas where there is less public consensus about how to proceed – and where government itself has less experience in addressing the policy matters at issue (Inglehart 1977, 1981, 1988, 1990). Some of the harshest political battles over recent decades have been over how to deal with "post-materialist" demands regarding the government's relatively new social welfare responsibilities, including health care, housing, welfare, and the environment (Cohen 2006; Hopper 2017; Schwartz 2014; Skocpol 1997). When governments fall short on these highly challenging policy matters – and how can they not? – we can expect the late-night comics to take note.

As modern western governments descend deeper into gridlock, there is also a level of "procedural frustration," where the focus of discontent is at least as much on the procedures as the outcomes (Bond and Fleisher 2000; Campbell 2016; Mann and Ornstein 2012; Mayer and Canon 1999). At the core of this public objection is the sense that government is not responsive to public demands and should do more to provide fair access to the policy process for everyone (Tyler 1988, Tyler and Rasinski 1991). This citizen frustration was a key component of public support for the self-proclaimed outsider Donald Trump, whose election in 2016 and subsequent presidency represented a populist reaction to the sense that elites were looking out for themselves rather than ordinary Americans (Abramowitz 2017; Ceaser et al. 2017; Schier and Eberly 2017). Still others frustrated by government may turn inward; they are tuning out, or "bowling alone," in response to what some citizens feel is a society unraveling before their eyes (Putnam 2000).

These theories of citizen discontent dovetail with significant components of the late-night jokes directed at American presidents generally, and particularly with Donald Trump's time in public life. As previous chapters have shown, the late-night comedians delight in skewering the national government's dissatisfying policy outcomes, its inability to resolve policy disputes, the former president's erratic behavior, and the dubious qualifications of some Trump friends and family members that he placed in positions of great authority and influence during his four years as president.

The late-night comics regularly make use of the fact that cynicism regarding people in power seems to be part of our political DNA; they have made the cultivation of that cynicism an art form. That has its advantages, of course. Aggressive questioning or even mocking people in power is not necessarily a bad thing, to be sure, as "those who are overready to approve of government are overready to yield to it" (Sniderman 1981: 148).

Given the combativeness of today's late-night comics, though there seems little chance that the above description of faith-based support for government would apply to large numbers of their viewers. Indeed, previous research has shown that the overwhelmingly negative nature of political humor can lead to more negative evaluations of the political figures being skewered (Baumgartner and Morris 2006; Morris 2009; Young 2004). Studies that examined the impact of *The Daily Show* during the 2004 presidential campaign found that viewership led to lower evaluations of candidate John Kerry (Baumgartner and Morris 2006). A focused study of *The Daily Show*'s coverage of the 2004 national party conventions found that the show was more critical of the Republican convention and that evaluations of Bush and Vice President Dick Cheney fell more among viewers of that program than did evaluations of Kerry and Democratic vice presidential nominee John Edwards (Morris 2009). Tina Fey's treatment of 2008 vice presidential nominee Sarah Palin likewise lowered evaluations of Palin among viewers of *Saturday Night Live* (Baumgartner et al. 2012). Late-night humor directed at the news media also undermined public assessments of the journalism profession (Morris and Baumgartner 2008).

162 Political Consequences of Late-Night Humor

The process of increasingly negative evaluations of political figures seems most powerful with respect to the least informed viewers of the late-night shows. A study of the impacts of late-night humor on public perceptions of Al Gore and George W. Bush during the 2000 election found that viewers with relatively little knowledge about politics developed more negative assessments of both candidates after seeing them skewered by the late-night comics (Young 2004). Some researchers have found that critical political humor lowers public assessments of the political system generally, as well as evaluations of the candidates targeted by the hosts of these programs (Baumgartner 2013). There is a sense in some research that political humor can generate "blowback" that undermines the general social fabric at the same time it may also increase political interest (McClennen 2018).

Because political humor contains policy content, some researchers believe such political messaging is particularly effective in shaping viewer preferences because of the process described by the Elaboration Likelihood Model (ELM) of persuasion. Humorous messages are particularly effective because they are processed through the peripheral (noncognitive) route without being subject to highly critical and analytical brain pathways involved in scrutinizing the accuracy of the claims made within the jokes (Petty and Cacioppo 1986). In other words, a viewer's focus is on getting the joke rather than on evaluating the truthfulness of the comments that comprise it. This alternative persuasion path increases the chances of viewer agreement and therefore can increase the impact of the joke on a viewer's perceptions of the target of the humor (Becker 2018; Petty and Cacioppo 1986). One aggregate study of political humor content and news coverage suggested that both affect presidential evaluations over the longer term (Lichter et al. 2015), though more research on longer-term impacts is needed to refine these linkages.

Politicians Can Tell Jokes Too

Of course, candidates and elected officials do what they can to reduce the damage they may face from the tidal wave of late-night ridicule that may come their way. Politicians often try to "work the refs" of political comedy, by appearing on these shows as guests or by criticizing their content on social media as to minimize the impact of the mockery (Farnsworth 2018; Lichter et al. 2015). The operative theory here is that of "inoculation," where self-deprecating jokes by prominent political figures can deflect the more hostile humor that the hosts otherwise might aim at people who appear to be putting on airs or who just seem humorless (Compton 2018). In other words, if an elected official is willing to appear on a given program, its host may treat a current or recent guest more gently. If nothing else, it is harder to mock or insult someone who is sitting across the table.

Even if the host would not offer kinder treatment to a political figure willing to appear on a late-night talk show, at least the public would respect a politician who is willing to meet one's late-night critics face-to-face. If you do not appear, particularly after promising to do so, you run the risk of weeks of mocking as David Letterman directed at John McCain, the 2008 GOP presidential nominee (Farnsworth and Lichter 2011a, 2020).

For evidence of just how effective self-deprecating humor can be, consider Ronald Reagan's use of a humorous remark during the second presidential debate of the 1984 presidential election. Few presidents were as good at inoculation as Ronald Reagan, who during his decades in political life joked about his aversion to hard work, his age, his film career, and even the content of his speeches (Cannon 1991). His comfort in front of the camera stemmed from his years as a movie actor and as a pitchman for the General Electric Co. before entering elective politics (Cannon 1991). Despite his extensive public-oriented experience, which also included his first term as president, Reagan struggled at some points during the first presidential debate in 1984. Reagan's stumbling remarks during that debate immediately raised questions about whether the elderly president had the fortitude to take on the challenges of a second term in the White House. Reagan planned a counterattack that would demonstrate he was up to the challenge with a one-liner prepared for deployment at the second debate. When the opportunity arose, Reagan pounced, saying, "I will not make age an issue of this campaign. I am not going to exploit, for political purposes, my opponent's youth and inexperience" (quoted in Stewart et al. 2018: 123). After making that absurd quip about how he would not focus on the age of Democratic rival Walter Mondale, himself a highly experienced former vice president and senator, would it not seem unduly harsh for Democrats to offer further questions about Reagan's fitness for office and alleged mental decline? In the moments after Reagan's joke, even Mondale chuckled, and that made-for-television one-liner threw the challenger off his stride during the rest of the debate (Compton 2018; Gergen 2000).

Concerns over the aging president's mental fitness evaporated in an instant, thanks to a well-timed joke, delivered by an experienced Hollywood actor turned politician. Reagan's joke did not just undermine concerns that had arisen in the weeks before the second debate. The quip also protected the president – like an injection in a doctor's office – from subsequent threats along these same lines. The quip largely put to rest concerns that by 1984 Reagan may have lost ground physically and mentally during his first four years in office and may not retain sufficient intellectual capacity and the vigor that would be required for a second presidential term (Compton 2018).

164 Political Consequences of Late-Night Humor

As the Reagan example demonstrates, self-deprecatory humor serves a politician's purposes in trying to preempt and redirect potential critical lines of attack. Making a joke at one's own expense also serves the process of making a political figure more likeable. The explicit public discussion of one's own flaws, or at least the hinting of one's shortcomings, signals that the speaker does not take himself or herself too seriously (Stewart et al. 2018).

Self-deprecating humor is a common approach employed by many presidents, particularly during times of peril on the seas of public opinion. Consider the case of Franklin Roosevelt, whom we now know was desperately ill when he ran for an unprecedented fourth term in 1944 (Burns and Dunn 2001; Goodwin 1994). During that campaign, FDR chose to respond to a Republican attack on the use of a military destroyer to pick up the president's dog, Fala, a Scottish terrier left behind by mistake while accompanying the president on a wartime trip to Alaska. The Republican focus on this incident, which implicitly raised questions about an ailing and potentially forgetful president as well as the potentially improper use of taxpayer resources during wartime, represented a short-lived news story that could easily have been ignored until it faded from the headlines (Burns and Dunn 2001; Goodwin 1994). But FDR saw the opportunity to offer a humorous statement that would belittle his opponents by redirecting the conversation back to Fala, who FDR joked, was a dog with a short temper that was very upset about the expense and the controversy.

> Then came his rebuttal of the Fala story, his dagger lovingly fashioned and honed, delivered with a mock-serious face and in the quiet, sad tone of a man much abused. "These Republican leaders have not been content with attacks on me, on my wife, or on my sons. No, not content with that, they now include my little dog, Fala. Well of course I don't resent attacks, and my family doesn't resent attacks, but Fala–being Scottish–*does* resent them!" Some reporters saw this as the turning point of the campaign.
>
> *(Burns and Dunn 2001: 482: emphasis in original)*

Another example of self-deprecating humor was how Barack Obama responded with humor to the birth certificate dispute, raised by his opponents during the 2008 election and kept alive during his time in office by Donald Trump and others. After Obama had released the official "long form" birth certificate demanded by his critics to show the proof of his birth in Hawaii, he aired a segment from the film *The Lion King* at the 2011 White House Correspondents Dinner. He then claimed, with tongue in cheek, that the animated film clip of a newly born royal lion cub was

Political Consequences of Late-Night Humor **165**

in fact the video of his own birth (Cooper 2011). By doing so, Obama made light of both the high public expectations that surrounded his 2008 campaign and the critics (including Trump, who was in the audience), who had sought to make Obama's birth location such a long-running and absurd controversy. The humorous segment was a double play, a self-deprecating remark to endear himself to the public combined with a simultaneous skewering of his critics.

Donald Trump, of course, does not make fun of himself, at least not in public. His main star turn before his presidential campaign, the way many Americans first learned of him, was through his portrayal of a no-nonsense businessman on NBC's *The Apprentice*. Trump was the star of the show, to be sure, and presented in a deeply serious vein.

> Trump is god of "The Apprentice," its fate, its hero. And yet he often presides over this battle to the death with the leering malevolence of a Bond villain. He goes about either by black limo or black chopper, and he usually emerges from these war chariots with an ominous cuing of the strings. He materializes at the beginning of each episode to issue his entrepreneurial labor of Hercules. Then he often disappears until the very end, when he receives the contestants in a dark boardroom crossed with menacing shadows. And at the end of each episode, he administers the famous Blofeldian order of execution: "You're fired!" ... Donald Trump is an egomaniacal, germophobic multi-multi-millionaire, and yet television viewers, and the folks who gather outside Trump Tower hoping for a glimpse, can't get enough of him.
>
> *(Traub 2004)*

Trump in other words, created a brand that was the opposite of the roll-with-the-punches style of many previous presidents, including Barack Obama, Ronald Reagan, and Franklin Delano Roosevelt. Even so, it is an open question whether efforts at inoculation on late-night comedy programs during our particularly combative era of political discourse are worth the trouble, particularly for Republicans. The consistently harsher treatment that conservatives receive from the late-night comics could be a powerful argument for Republican candidates to stay away from their programs. For example, in 2012 Mitt Romney held out against appearing on these shows throughout much of the general election, feeling that he would not get fair treatment from the late-night hosts. His aides finally convinced him to go on *The Tonight Show*, traditionally seen by conservatives as the least hostile option among the late-night talk shows (Farnsworth and Lichter 2020).

In previous years, numerous other Republican candidates appeared on those programs, including Richard Nixon on *Laugh-In* in advance of the

166 Political Consequences of Late-Night Humor

1968 presidential election, and Ronald Reagan, who appeared on Johnny Carson's *The Tonight Show* during his failed 1976 effort to wrest the GOP nomination from incumbent president Gerald Ford. Other Republican presidential nominees who were guests on these shows include George W. Bush in 2000 and John McCain in 2008 (Farnsworth and Lichter 2020).

Cancelling an appearance can have dire consequences, as John McCain discovered in 2008. A late cancellation of his appearance on *The Late Show* brought a profusion of anti-McCain jokes from an angry David Letterman, which ended only when a contrite McCain appeared on the show and delivered an abject apology for his earlier absence (Farnsworth and Lichter 2020).

At its core, these candidate appearances can reshape the narrative relating to the character of the candidate, a key mechanism used by voters as they assess politicians running for office, regardless of political party. If your national reputation starts in a scandal-ridden place, you would want to try to change the narrative as soon as possible. Consider the case of Bill Clinton, whose 1992 presidential campaign was almost derailed by a series of scandals that erupted during the Democratic nomination process that year (Farnsworth and Lichter 2011a). When the scandals hit one after another, maybe the best thing to do is just put on some sunglasses, grab your saxophone, and jam with one of the bands on late-night television. Clinton did just that, in fact, to try to change the narrative. As a Clinton 1992 campaign media adviser Mandy Grunwald put it: Once the late-night comics "are making jokes about you, you have a serious problem. Whatever they have on you is likely to stick much more solidly than what is in the political ads in papers like the *Washington Post*" (quoted in Lichter et al. 2015: 4).

While Clinton's approach may not strike today's jaded college students as the best way to demonstrate that you are cool, his appearance on *Arsenio* that year helped change the subject away from his scandals, particularly for those who had not been following news of the Clinton campaign all that closely. His late-night turn had the effect of presenting the candidate as someone other than a political version of a grinning cartoon character of dubious conduct.

Even Donald Trump, who has been by far the president most hostile to late-night comics, at first engaged in similar efforts to try to tame or at least temper the hosts while he was contemplating his political future. Before the 2016 election, Trump appeared on *The Tonight Show* and *Saturday Night Live*, and it probably did not hurt that both shows aired on NBC, the same network that aired Trump's own reality show offerings. While all successful presidential candidates must be schooled in the arts of looking appealing before the public, Trump had decades of experience in the media spotlight, and that made him as sensitive to maximizing the utility of his public relations efforts as any recent candidate for president.

> Trump knew instinctively that he could enhance his own stature by being seen with celebrities, and he also knew he could do it by breaking the rules and bashing some of those same famous people. No other president has come to the White House as deeply schooled in the methods and madness of the American craft of celebrity. And no other president has used celebrities in quite the same way – both as inspiration to mold policies and as foils to entertain and satisfy his political base.
>
> *(Fisher 2018)*

For Trump, that involved knowing when to appear on late night – and when not to appear. While Trump may have benefitted from his appearance on *The Tonight Show* in 2016 – home to that famous hair-tousling moment with Jimmy Fallon – it might not have helped the show itself. Many viewers viewed Fallon's treatment of Trump as too fawning, and after that controversial segment, Fallon's ratings fell. Hoping to narrow the audience gap with Stephen Colbert, Fallon became more critical treatment of Trump starting in 2017, but *The Tonight Show* did not ever really catch up – either in the volume of mockery of Trump or in the late-night ratings competition (Farnsworth and Lichter 2020).

During his time as president, and then as a former president, Trump avoided personal appearances on the late-night humor shows. Of course, the shows' hosts had plenty to say about him whether he appears onstage or not, or even whether he was in office or not (Farnsworth et al. 2022). But by failing to appear, he loses whatever opportunity he might have to inoculate himself and potentially reduce the severity of mockery on late-night humor shows.

Trump's own use of political humor in recent years, again employed away from the late-night programs, tends toward "sarcastic and exaggerated comments," far from the self-deprecating humor that Reagan used to charm the country in the 1980s (Stewart et al. 2018). During the 2016 candidate debates, both Trump and Clinton used the opposite of the Reagan humor strategy. Both employed aggressive humor to "diminish the stature of the opposition" rather than using self-deprecation to make oneself look more appealing (Stewart et al. 2018: 128).

Inoculation may involve more than a politician's use of humor, whether on a late-night comedy program or not. Fame, for example, may be a particularly effective prophylactic against mockery that generates changes in public opinion. There is some evidence in support of the idea that better-known political figures have more stable public evaluations. In 2004, for

168 Political Consequences of Late-Night Humor

example, critical comments of President George W. Bush on *The Daily Show* did not have as much of an impact on his public evaluations as did similar comments directed at Democratic nominee John Kerry, who was less well-known than the incumbent president (Baumgartner and Morris 2006). Voters who were less informed regarding candidates Al Gore and George W. Bush in 2000 were more persuadable via new information than were more informed voters, who tended to have more fixed opinions about that year's major party nominees (Baum 2005).

A study examining political humor regarding more known and less well-known candidates during the 2016 primaries revealed that public evaluations regarding well-known front-runners Donald Trump and Hillary Clinton were highly resistant to change, while clips that focused on Bernie Sanders and Ben Carson had greater impacts on public assessments (Baumgartner 2018). The study provides further evidence that comedy's impact is the smallest where public knowledge is the greatest.

> Those who think or hope that Trump's approval ratings (or Trump himself) may be affected by the constant barrage of jokes made at his expense may be disappointed. While there may be a correlation between public opinion, negative news and the number of jokes told at the president's expense, this research suggests the correlation may be weaker when the public holds definite opinions about the president ... It is probably the case that one either loves or hates him, irrespective of what the satirists are saying.
>
> *(Baumgartner 2018: 72)*

Late-Night Humor, Information, and Participation

Late-night political humor has gained in attention and influence as people reduce their consumption of traditional media, such as the daily newspaper and the broadcast television networks' evening news shows. This trend has been particularly pronounced among younger adults, many of whom have been turning to soft news as an alternative source of political information for two decades now (Baumgartner and Morris 2011; Feldman and Young 2005; Hoffman and Thomson 2009; Mitchell et al. 2014).

Following the audience declines plaguing traditional news outlets, particularly among young adults, some scholars believe that the late-night television talk shows, particularly *The Daily Show*, deserve to be considered as an alternative news source (Baym 2005). As we noted earlier, during his heyday as host of the Comedy Central program, survey respondents identified Jon Stewart as one of the most trusted journalists in America, comparable to Tom Brokaw or Anderson Cooper (Baumgartner and Morris 2011). As a result of their popularity, presidential candidates have increasingly treated these talk shows as a means of reaching potential voters who have little interest in traditional political news but do not mind receiving campaign information on infotainment programming. For a candidate's appearance on late-night talk shows to be valuable, or for a joke offered by a host to make sense, the viewer must possess some political knowledge. But the fact that many viewers of late-night comedy are not political junkies also makes them an appealing audience for a politician. The late-night audience may include a significant number of viewers without a fixed opinion or perhaps even all that much awareness of a given candidate. Talking to such potential voters creates more opportunities for persuasion than would a comparable appearance on *Meet the Press*, where one is addressing a highly political sophisticated audience.

Growing cynicism regarding traditional news outlets also has enhanced the status of these late-night comedy programs, a response to the so-called "trust deficit" that legacy media have endured in recent years (Feldman and Young 2005; Pew Research Center 2016b, 2017). As a result, presidential candidates and presidents seek to reach voters who have moved away from traditional news outlets and make use of the late-night comedy programs as supplemental vehicles to promote their policies and themselves (Brewer and Cao 2006; Farnsworth 2018). During the wide-open 2008 campaign, when the late-night programs were less one-sided in their treatment of the two main political parties, presidential candidates and family members responded to the importance of these programs by making 80 appearances on late-night shows (Lichter et al. 2015).

In addition to an individual's previous political knowledge, selective news exposure by consumers also may limit the impact of the late-night comic takedowns on the public's estimation of established political figures. Because the first and/or most significant exposure some news consumers receive about political figures is provided by partisan media sources, the impact of late-night skewering may be quite modest (Iyengar and Hahn 2009; Pew Research Center 2014; Stroud 2008; Taber and Lodge 2006). A 2014 Pew Research Center survey, for example, found that liberals were more likely to trust and conservatives more likely to distrust *The Colbert Report* and *The Daily Show*, two of the late-night comedy programs included in its survey (Mitchell et al. 2014). In addition, some critics of talk shows believe the hosts have gone too soft on interviews with political figures (Kinsley 1992).

Despite the disagreements over the potential impact of political humor on citizens, there is a consensus regarding the learning opportunity these programs offer their audiences. Researchers have found these humor programs to be informative, providing current events information to

170 Political Consequences of Late-Night Humor

viewers (Young 2013). They also make use of the information to shape their understanding of politics. Viewing political comedy can encourage citizens to "connect the dots between the comedy they view and what they already know from traditional news sources" (Becker 2018: 80). Indeed, research into the content of such programs has found that they do a better job of talking about substantive issues during presidential campaigns than do journalists on television, who place greater emphasis on the campaign horserace and the candidates' strategies and tactics as well as candidate soundbites and gaffes (Farnsworth and Lichter 2011a, 2020; Lichter et al. 2015).

On balance, research has found that viewing late-night political humor is associated with higher levels of political knowledge (Brewer and Cao 2006). A study that compared learning from interviews with political figures on a late-night comedy program compared with a traditional news program found higher recall of basic information among the comedy program viewers (Becker 2013). According to another study, the political comedy shows led to information acquisition at the same level as network television news, but network news was a more effective source for learning the relative importance of policy (Becker and Bode 2018).

These late-night political conversations appear to increase political knowledge by providing information in a digestible and interesting manner (Xenos and Becker 2009; Young 2006, 2013). One key component of that learning stems from prior expectations: Viewers who watched *The Daily Show* and *The Colbert Report* as news programs or news/entertainment hybrid programs were more likely to engage with the program content than those who did not see a journalistic dimension to the shows (Feldman 2013). Those who are motivated to consume the comedy for the political content or those who possess a general affinity for political humor are more inclined to say they draw links between the news and the jokes (Becker 2018). In addition, individuals who have an interest in the political topics being explored by the late-night hosts have an increased appreciation for the jokes involving themes that match their personal interests (Grill 2018).

The comedy programs also shape political participation activities of their viewers in a variety of dimensions (Moy et al. 2005). Perhaps the mockery makes people consider that they can change the political environment for the better. These increased political activities may be a result of increased internal political efficacy, which is associated with viewing late-night political humor (Baumgartner and Morris 2006). There may even be a sense of self-satisfaction derived from the consumption of political humor, which can reinforce boundaries between those who "get" the jokes and those who do not (McClennen 2018). By attacking ideas and behaviors tagged as "stupid, illogical, arrogant or manipulative," the late-night humorists underscore these divisive group identities between those laughing with the comics and those being laughed at by the comics – and their viewers (McClennen 2018: 141). As one would expect, citizens who resent the choice of comedic targets do not appreciate the political humor itself, further increasing the divisions between viewers and non-viewers of late-night comedy (Grill 2018).

> Not all satire has the same bite. Colbert's satirical comedy, for example, has far more of a playful edge than the searing mockery of Bill Maher or the righteous rage of Samantha Bee. But in the end, regardless of its edge, satire is about criticizing attitudes, beliefs, worldviews, and behaviors that the satirist wants to target.
>
> *(McClennen 2018: 141)*

Along these same lines, one somewhat under-considered aspect of political humor's impacts concerns people who are allied with the joke target (McClennen 2018). Might these people be more inclined to defend their ally, that joke's target, as the mockery increases? After all, jokes aimed at Donald Trump are at least indirectly aimed at the people who support Donald Trump and those who agree with him on many policy issues. (Some jokes are directed at the former president's supporters, to be sure, particularly now that Trump is a former president.) The anger many Trump supporters direct at elites and the status quo seems unlikely to be quelled by late-night mockery. In fact, the elite media voices in New York and Los Angeles mocking the man standing before a sea of "Make America Great Again" red caps probably intensify the anger and harden the support of those who start out in Trump's corner. Research into hostile audience counterreactions might well explain why Trump and other controversial political figures seem to face little consequences to their reputations when they are vigorously attacked on late-night comedy (Baumgartner 2018).

The Survey and Hypotheses

To examine what political humor teaches viewers about real-world politics, we turn now to a 2021 survey of Virginia adults conducted by the nonpartisan firm Research America Inc. (2021). RAI routinely conducts public opinion polling regarding national and state-level politics and policy. This Virginia representative survey was in the field during September 2021. Part of the sample (600) was contacted by phone (80 percent cell and 20 percent landline), and part of the sample (400) was contacted online. All interviews were in English and statistical results were weighted to correct known demographic discrepancies in Virginia, including age, gender, and race/ethnicity. The margin of error on the total sample is +/− 3.1 percent. Further information on the survey, and the questions used here, is found in the Appendix.

The survey asked a variety of questions about acquiring information, asking respondents whether they learned something about the presidential campaign from several possible news sources, including cable television news, local television, and network television news as well as several other online formats, including late-night comedy.

Hypotheses

Based on the research discussed earlier, we would expect to find support for the following hypotheses relating to political humor in the Pew Research Center (2016a) survey:

H1: People who identify as Democrats were more likely to report learning something from late-night comedy than Republicans were.

H2: The more liberal the respondent, the more likely one would report learning something from late-night comedy.

These two hypotheses are consistent with the growing use of partisan and ideologically congenial media sources, which are likely to discourage Republicans and conservatives from using late-night humor given the discrepancy between their preferences and the comedic targets of late night (Gill 2018; Pew 2014; Stroud 2008; Taber and Lodge 2006).

H3: The lower one's level of trust in government, the more likely one was to report learning from late-night comedy.

This hypothesis is consistent with the idea that consuming political humor lowers assessments of the political system and political figures (Baumgartner 2013; McClennen 2018; Young 2004).

Results

Table 6.1 examines self-reported public learning from a range of media sources. Among the eight media sources examined in the study, respondents were most likely to say that they learned something about the 2020 presidential campaign from news websites/apps and cable television news. Traditional media sources, like newspapers, radio, and the nightly network television newscasts were considered somewhat less useful than those top two sources. Late-night comedy brings up the rear, with one-quarter of those responding to the survey saying they learned something about the 2020 campaign from the comedy shows. (One should note that *Gutfeld!*, the commercially successful conservative political humor program discussed in Chapter 5, did not air nightly until April 2021, well after the 2020 election).

The 25 percent figure may seem a relatively small number compared to cable, online, and broadcast sources, until we remember that these other outlets offered here for comparison view their central task – unlike late-night comedy shows – as providing news and information. Given that sharp difference in mission, it is striking that late-night comedy, which exists to entertain mass audiences, is a source of information about politics for about half as many viewers as those who turn to network television news. (We might also note that this Virginia figure is the same as that of an earlier national survey (Pew Research Center 2016a) that asked about political learning from late-night comedy during the 2016 presidential campaign.)

Table 6.1 also reveals that the value of information sources can vary greatly by the age of the respondent. For young adults, those between the ages of 18 and 29, 40 percent of those surveyed said late-night comedy was a source of learning for them – more than those in that age group who attributed learning to radio or national and local daily newspapers. This considerable reported utility of late-night comedy for this age group represents a sharp contrast from older adults: only 25 percent of people in the age group of 30 to 49 said they learned something from the late-night comics. The percentages were even lower for those at least 50 years old.

TABLE 6.1 Sources of Learning about the 2020 Presidential Election by Age

Percentage of Virginia Adults Learning Something about the Election from ...

	18–29	30–49	50–64	65+	Total Average (for All Age Groups)
News websites or apps	59	66	68	56	63
Cable TV news	56	58	67	70	62
Local TV News	63	49	59	66	56
Nightly network TV news	47	44	57	66	52
Radio	38	48	47	41	46
Candidate/campaign websites or apps	49	42	39	38	42
National/local daily newspapers	36	36	44	49	40
Late-night comedy shows	**40**	**25**	**20**	**14**	**25**

Note: RAI 2021 Virginia survey conducted during September 7–13, 2021. N = 1,000.

174 Political Consequences of Late-Night Humor

Table 6.2 examines whether there are partisan differences among those who said they learned something about the 2020 election from the late-night comedy programs and those who did not. This table, and the ones that follow, employ the question about learning from late-night comedy used in Table 6.1. These cross-tabulation reports use that question to mark the columns. The rows will relate to the other variables in the two-variable comparisons; for example, the top half of Table 6.2 relates to partisanship and the bottom half of Table 6.2 relates to presidential candidate vote choice in the 2020 election). The percentages reported in Table 6.2 and in the cross-tabulation results that follow are row percentages. People who refused to answer specific questions are dropped from the relevant cross-tabulations, so the total number of respondents examined in the individual analyses will vary from question to question.

With respect to partisanship, this analysis divided respondents into three groups: Republicans, Democrats, and independents. Those classified as Republicans said they identified with that party (strongly or somewhat) or were independents leaning in that party's direction. Those counted as Democrats identified with (strongly or somewhat) or leaned toward that party. Independents include only those respondents who did not identify with or lean toward either major party, or only those in the middle no-leaners independent category of the traditional seven-point Party Identification scale. Table 6.2 shows that 13 percent of Republicans said they learned something from the comedy programs, as compared to 23 percent of independents. By contrast, 40 percent of Democrats said they learned something about the presidential contest from those programs. Thus, Democrats were more than twice as likely as Republicans to say they learned about politics from late-night humorists.

TABLE 6.2 Partisanship, Candidate Preference, and Learning from Comedy Programs

Partisanship	Learned	Did Not	Total
Democratic (includes leaners)	155	236	391
% within party	40%	60%	100%
Independent	26	87	113
% within party	23%	77%	100%
Republican (includes leaners)	48	331	379
% within party	13%	87%	100%
Total	229	654	883

Table 6.2 also examines political learning on late night as it relates to 2020 presidential vote choice. As expected, Biden voters were more likely to report they learned something about the election from late-night comedy than were Trump voters. The margins once again were substantial: 39 percent of Biden voters reported political learning via late-night content versus 11 percent of Trump voters.

The overall response patterns for the two variables and political learning relating to late-night comedy are examined systematically via chi-square tests, which identified the statistical results as highly significant. The Tau-c test likewise confirms that there is a statistically significant relationship between party identification and whether one learned something from late-night comedy. The Tau-b test confirms a statistically significant relationship between presidential vote choice and learning something from late-night comedy. These findings all provide empirical support for H1.

Table 6.3 looks at the role of political learning from these programs in the context of ideology rather than party preference and vote choice. It considers the intersection of ideology and political learning from late comedy using the traditional five-point ideology scale. As hypothesized, the more liberal one considers oneself to be, the more likely one is to have learned something about the election via the discussions on late-night comedy programs. The question asked respondents to place themselves on a five-point scale ranging from very liberal (1) to very conservative

TABLE 6.3 Ideology and Learning from Comedy Programs

Ideology	Learned	Did Not	Total
Very liberal	38	43	81
% within ideology	47%	53%	100%
Liberal	65	77	142
% within ideology	46%	54%	100%
Moderate	80	257	337
% within ideology	24%	76%	100%
Conservative	29	184	213
% within ideology	14%	86%	100%
Very conservative	13	85	98
% within ideology	13%	87%	100%
Total	225	646	871

176 Political Consequences of Late-Night Humor

(5). Each point along the scale involved a lower percentage of people who said they learned something about the presidential election from Fallon, Colbert et al. For those who said they were very conservative, 13 percent said they learned something from late-night comedy. For self-described moderates, the comparable figure was 24 percent. For the very liberal, it rose to 47 percent. Thus, the most liberal viewers were more than three times as likely as the most conservative viewers to learn about the election from late-night jokes. These findings, including the chi-square and Tau-c tests, provide empirical support for H2.

With Table 6.4, we turn possible connections between political trust and reports of learning from late-night comedy television. As noted earlier, many researchers looking at these potential linkages in previous years found decreased support for political institutions and figures from those watching late-night comedy.

Our results show a very different respondent pattern in the wake of the 2020 election and the political tumult that followed the election of Joe Biden as president. Rather than suggesting a linkage between late-night comedy content and decreased support for political institutions, our data analysis finds the opposite. Those people who say they trust the national government "just about always" are far more likely to say they learned something about the presidential election from late-night comedy than were those respondents with lower levels of political trust. Among those with the highest levels of trust for the national government, 51 percent said they learned something about the presidential election from late-night comedy. In contrast, 39 percent of those who said they trusted the national

TABLE 6.4 Trust in the U.S. Government and Learning from Comedy Programs

Trust in the U.S. Government	Learned	Did Not	Total
Just about always	23	22	45
% within trust	51%	49%	100%
Most of the time	97	149	246
% within trust	39%	61%	100%
Some of the time	87	334	421
% within trust	21%	79%	100%
Never (volunteered)	30	158	188
% within trust	16%	84%	100%
Total	237	663	900

government most of the time said they learned something from late-night comedy. Among the more cynical, 21 percent who said they trusted the government "some of the time" learned something about the presidential election from late-night comedy and 16 percent of those who said they never trusted the national government found political humor informative.

These findings, including the chi-square and Tau-c tests, provide empirical support for the *opposite* of H3.

This unexpected finding is difficult to square with the past research in this area as well as the iconoclastic foundation of political humor itself. Might an iconoclastic treatment of a disruptive and potentially antidemocratic political figure who urged a violent assault on the U.S. Capitol rather than admit defeat in the 2020 presidential election create something along the lines of a civically supportive dynamic for political learning about the political system via the content of late-night comedy? Before reaching such a conclusion, we should examine this possibility more extensively.

In Table 6.5 we present the results of a multivariate examination of the factors connected to whether a person reports he or she learned something about the presidential election from late-night comedy. Since the political learning dependent variable is dichotomous (a person did learn versus a person did not learn), traditional OLS regression is an inadequate statistical tool. We instead employ logistic regression, which is designed for statistical analyses involving dichotomous dependent variables. The logistic regression approach has the advantage of providing coefficients and significant tests comparable to that of OLS regression, including r-squared results to assess the overall utility of the model. This approach also allows for a comparison of the cases correctly classified versus those cases misclassified.

Overall, the model works quite well. The two r-square summary measures used here offer solid results: the Nagelkerke R Square statistic stands at 0.273, while the Cox & Snell R Square measure stands at 0.185. In addition, the seven independent variables used here allow for the correct classification of 77.8 percent of the cases of learning or not learning about the 2020 presidential campaign vial late-night comedy, well above the 50 percent success rate that would come from a random distribution of the sample on a dichotomous dependent variable. The model, it turns out, was far better at correctly classifying people who did not learn anything about the presidential campaign than classifying those who did (by a margin of 39 percent correct for the learners and 91 percent correct for those who said they did not learn anything).

The Table 6.5 model includes seven independent variables, and three of them reach statistical significance: Age Group, Political Trust, and Vote Choice. Four variables did not, Education, Party ID, Ideology, and Sex.

178 Political Consequences of Late-Night Humor

TABLE 6.5 Logistic Regression: Learning from Late-Night Comedy

Variables	B	S.E.	Wald	df	Sig.	Exp(B)
Education	0.008	0.059	0.017	1	0.897	1.008
Presidential vote	1.228	0.370	10.991	1	0.001	3.415
Trust U.S				1		
Ideology				1		
Party ID				1		
Age group				1		
Sex				1		
Constant	–4.377	0.799	29.986	1	0.000	0.013

Using the Wald statistic, we can see that Age Group is the most important measure of the three statistically significant variables, followed by Political Trust and then Vote Choice.

The results in Table 6.5, like those of Table 6.4 support the *opposite* of H3, which followed the previously identified pattern linking political cynicism to learning about politics via the late-night humorists.

Discussion

Before proceeding further, three caveats are in order. First, the survey employed here was conducted nearly a year after the 2020 election, and asking people about what they learned a year earlier is not an optimal approach, to be sure. While the original plan was to put these questions into the field during or shortly after the 2020 presidential campaign, COVID complications, including budgetary challenges, forced a research delay. Funding for this survey was not available until mid-2021.

One other potential concern about the findings here involves the fact that this study examines public opinion in one state, Virginia, and not nationally. Unfortunately, national surveys do not frequently ask questions about political humor, particularly given the greater information role played by other communication vehicles, like news websites, cable news, and social media. (In addition, the funding authorized a Virginia survey, not a national one). But one can note that the Virginia results found in this survey are generally in line with the national results found in Pew Research Center (2016a), one of the most thorough national surveys over the past decade that examined the connection between political learning and late-night political humor.

As for the third caveat, there are often limitations regarding a specific area of scholarly interest in any survey, in this case public opinion regarding political humor. This survey does not ask how much political humor a survey participant consumed, nor did it ask which late-night host was favored by individual respondents. Given the range of topics contained in the survey, understandably there was no opportunity to delve more deeply into the precise questions of information channel use for late-night political humor and other information outlets considered in the survey.

With those three potential caveats in mind, the findings here suggest, as did those in Pew Research Center (2016a), that several key components of one's background are linked to learning about politics from comedy (Farnsworth and Lichter 2020). The analysis here shows that late-night comedy in 2020 remained a key component of presidential election discourse, especially for younger viewers.

Based on this survey, the comics had an impact on political learning that was comparable, if not greater than, that of some media outlets, including local and national newspapers, particularly for younger adults. Not that many years ago, print newspapers represented one of the top two sources of campaign news (Farnsworth and Lichter 2011a). That more young people are learning about politics from watching Jimmy Kimmel and Stephen Colbert than from reading the print editions of their local paper or the *New York Times* and *Washington Post* is a sign of how rapidly both politics and the media are changing.

News consumers of a certain age might wish to see a greater influence commanded by print newspapers, which (as content analyses have consistently shown) do a more substantive job of providing information about political developments than television's briefer and less substantive focus (Farnsworth and Lichter 2006, 2011a). But the stories produced by journalists working for legacy publications do obtain a second life, in outlets ranging from their employers' social media accounts. They even may serve as inspirations for the joke writers on these late-night talk shows, giving the content of those stories an even wider audience.

The results here also suggest the utility of Trump's attacks, both as a president and as a former president, on late-night political hosts. Vote choice, after all, was among the factors that predicted political learning from late-night comedy. In these highly partisan times, a president's criticism of his critics helps solidify partisan loyalties and even intensify them. The former president's combative approach toward the late-night comics, in other words, is another example of the political strategy that is at the core of Trump's approach: appealing to his political base at nearly every opportunity (Busch and Pitney 2021; Ceaser et al. 2017; Cohen et al. 2016). This may inoculate Trump from the criticisms that his supporters might hear if they learn about the content of these late-night shows.

180 Political Consequences of Late-Night Humor

The data here also suggest further support for the idea that political jokes and political information acquisition are linked. The survey results here are consistent with past research that finds people consuming news in a variety of outlets can "connect the dots" between the humor and the news, thereby enabling them to appreciate the humor (Becker 2018; Farnsworth and Lichter 2020; Young 2013). This process of making use of a variety of media outlets that one respects can create a sense of self-satisfaction regarding one's own political learning (Baumgartner and Morris 2006; McClennen 2018).

This chapter also revealed that late-night viewers were not replacing traditional political news with political humor. They were more – rather than less – likely to find interest and value in political news. Their interest in late-night humor was an expression of general interest in political information, just as those who discussed the news more frequently were drawn to other nontraditional sources of political information.

The most important and most novel finding here, of course, is the idea that learning about politics via the late-night comedy shows does not appear, in the wake of the contentious 2020 election and of the attack on the U.S. Capitol that followed, to generate the kind of cynicism and negativity seen in past studies of the impacts of political humor. Perhaps the extraordinary circumstances of the Trump era, and the intense, overwhelming focus of these comics on Trump during his presidency, during the assault on the U.S. Capitol by his supporters, and even on the former president during the first year of the Joe Biden presidency, upset traditional patterns of iconoclastic political humor (Farnsworth and Lichter 2020; Farnsworth et al. 2022). After all, Biden has received relatively genteel treatment from late-night comedy, which continues to focus much of the mockery at the former president. These system-supporting results might have been reversed if late-night comics had treated Biden as they had treated previous incumbent presidents.

Rather than undermining support for the political system or helping create negative assessments about political system, there now seems to be a connection between learning about the 2020 presidential campaign via late-night comedy and having higher levels of trust in government (a government, one should note, being run by Democrats). At this early stage of discovery, this research only offers an opportunity for speculation regarding these linkages. There is an old saying that "the enemy of my enemy is my friend." Perhaps the system-weakening norms of the former president, culminating in his unwillingness to accept the results of the 2020 election at the time and even years later, created an environment where the late-night attacks on Trump came to represent system-strengthening activities rather than the more traditional system-challenging (if not

Political Consequences of Late-Night Humor **181**

undermining) nature of political humor during other times. Attacking Trump can make Biden look better, after all.

Clearly, we need to have further study involving this important and highly unexpected finding before we can say too much about this newly identified relationship between Political Trust and learning from late-night comedy. But the results here suggest that some of the conventional wisdom about this relationship may need to be reconsidered in the wake of the significant adjustments of political humor and political discourse generally seen in recent years.

We now turn to this work's final chapter, Chapter 7, which considers possible future trends in political humor in the wake of the findings of recent elections and public opinion results discussed so far in this book.

Chapter 6 Appendix: Survey Questions

Survey details: The Virginia Survey Fall 2021 was conducted by Research America Inc. during September 7–13, 2021. The total sample included 1,000 Virginia residents, including 885 registered voters and 528 likely voters. Part of the sample (600) was contacted by phone (80 percent cell and 20 percent landline), and part of the sample (400) was contacted online. All interviews were in English. Statistical results are weighted to correct known demographic discrepancies, including age, gender, and race/ethnicity. The margin of error on the total sample is +/– 3.1 percent.

Media Sources: Now thinking back to the 2020 presidential campaign ... During the campaign, did you learn something about the presidential campaign or candidates from each of the following sources? [RANDOMIZE]

Cable television news (such as CNN, the Fox News cable channel, or MSNBC)

Local TV news

National nightly network television news

News websites or apps

National newspapers or your local daily newspaper in print

News on the radio

Late-night comedy shows

Candidate or campaign websites, apps, or emails

Age Groups: 18–29, 30–49, 50–64, 65+

Party ID: Traditional seven-point scale

Partisanship: Democrats (strong, weak, leaners), Independents, Republicans (strong, weak, leaners)

Ideology: Very Liberal, Liberal, Moderate, Conservative, Very Conservative

Trust U.S.: "How much of the time do you think you can trust the FEDERAL government to do what is right – just about always, most of the time, or only some of the time?" (Never was volunteered)

Vote20. "Did you vote for Trump, Biden or someone else?"

Education: "What is the highest level of school you have completed or the highest degree you have received? Less than high school (Grades 1–8 or no formal schooling); high school incomplete (Grades 9–11 or Grade 12 with no diploma); high school graduate (Grade 12 with diploma or GED certificate); some college, no degree (includes some community college); two-year associate degree from a college or university; four-year college or university degree/bachelor's degree (e.g., BS, BA, AB); some postgraduate or professional schooling, no postgraduate degree; postgraduate or professional degree, including master's, doctorate, medical, or law degree (e.g., MA, MS, PhD, MD, JD).

Chi-square significance	0.000
Tau-c	0.266***

Candidate Preference	*Learned*	*Did Not*	*Total*
Biden	160	246	406
% within candidate	39%	61%	100%
Trump	39	305	344
% within candidate	11%	89%	100%
Total	199	551	750

Chi-square significance	0.000
Tau-b	0.317***

Statistical significance: *p < 0.05 **p < 0.01 ***p < 0. 001.
Note: RAI 2021 Virginia survey conducted during September 7–13, 2021. N = 1,000

Chi-square significance	0.000
Tau-c	0.266***

Statistical significance: *p < 0.05 **p < 0.01 ***p < 0. 001.
Note: RAI 2021 Virginia survey conducted during September 7–13, 2021. N = 1,000.

| Chi-square significance | 0.000 |
| Tau-c | 0.218*** |

Statistical significance: *p < 0.05 **p < 0.01 ***p < 0. 001.
Note: RAI 2021 Virginia survey conducted during September 7–13, 2021. N = 1,000.

Classification Table

	Predicted Learned	Predicted Did Not	Percentage Correct
Observed learned	61	95	39.1
Observed did not	40	411	91.2

Overall percentage correct		77.8

Model Summary

–2 Log likelihood	Cox & Snell R Square	Nagelkerke R Square
566.630	0.185	0.273

Note: RAI 2021 Virginia survey conducted during September 7–13, 2021. N = 1,000.

7

THE (NEAR) FUTURE OF POLITICAL HUMOR

For years, survey results and academic analyses have found that the late-night comedy programs promote political learning. The effect is greatest on young adults, but it is not confined to them. Recent research into adolescents' consumption of political humor likewise has found a great affinity for this form of comedy, as they follow the lead of their parents, peers, and somewhat older family members (Edgerly 2018).

These trends also increase the likelihood that the late-night television comedy programs will remain commercially successful for at least another generation (Edgerly 2018). As with adults, political humor is not generally the dominant form of news exposure for adolescents, but it is an important component of political learning even for those too young to vote (Edgerly 2018).

Thus, as late-night comedy seems to be picking up another generation of future viewers, we will consider the trajectory of humor now that Trump is no longer president (but is running for president in the 2024 election). To what extent have the norms of late-night comedy changed permanently in response to a president who represented – and as ex-president still represents – an unusually target-rich environment?

The Coarsening of Political Humor

Throughout this book, we have talked about how political comedy during the Trump and Biden presidencies has been qualitatively and quantitatively different from what came before it. While it once seemed impossible that any president would generate more white-hot "burns"

DOI: 10.4324/9781003283041-7

on late night than the aging Lothario Bill Clinton, Trump set a new standard for the volume of comedic attacks both as a president and as a former president. Trump has been (and is) mocked as a sexual libertine like Clinton, to be sure, but the former president also routinely has been referred to as a liar, a fraud, and sometimes even a criminal. Given the extent to which these attacks have increased the attention paid to late night – and they have – one can hardly imagine a return to the jovial banter of the Carson years and Chevy Chase's good-natured ribbing of Gerald Ford's alleged clumsiness.

Late-night comedy can't quit Trump, even three years into his ex-presidency, because he is trying so hard to remain politically relevant in the 2024 presidential campaign. Trump, one must never forget, is good for the communication business. As we have discussed throughout this book, Trump generated a financial windfall for media companies of all sorts – the highs and lows of this operatic presidency helped media businesses that had fallen on hard times survive, and in the case of the late-night comics, to thrive. So, for business reasons at least, late-night comedy and others in the media may be very glad that Trump remains visible, despite any comments from the comics that they would be glad to be rid of him. One other way that Trump has been good for business has been the willingness of scandal-plagued individuals, like Rep. George Santos (R-NY), to enter public life and give these humorists more to work with. It is hard to imagine that Rep. Santos, who fabricated nearly every major aspect of his biography, would have been endorsed by Republicans and elected to Congress in a pre-Trump age given all the lies Santos told along the way (Fandos 2023a, 2023b, 2023c). The rise of Trump-like political figures are yet another indication that the comics must thank their lucky stars to have such a bountiful feast of comedic targets.

Unlike previous former presidents, who largely retired and mostly would keep themselves busy by writing books, painting, or going on "those were the days" lecture tours, Trump's ex-presidency has focused on continuing to express the false claims that the 2020 election was stolen and on defending those who assaulted the U.S. Capitol on his behalf. Trump even was the first major figure to declare he was running for president in 2024 (Hounshell 2022). In addition, Trump and the current crop of late-night comedians, excluding Gutfeld, are perfect foils for each other. Business has been good for the comedic hosts, particularly when they attack Trump, so they will likely offer more of the same mockery during his remaining time in public life. Trump's attacks on the late-night comics who are attacking him also pay off in terms of retaining the loyalty of his political base and distracting them from trickier topics of his time in office, including Russia, the costs to consumers of tariffs and trade wars, and above all the various

186 The (Near) Future of Political Humor

scandals and indictments emerging from his behavior as well as that of his campaign team and his administration. For those truly dissatisfied with the Trump-focused critical content offered by Colbert et al., there is always Fox News and Gutfeld.

In one of his many attacks on late-night humor, Trump complained that the comics offered "one-sided hatred." In response, Jimmy Kimmel replied that Trump and his allies have been such extraordinary figures of misconduct that he and his fellow hosts had no alternative but to emphasize what they emphasize and make the jokes that they do.

> I don't want to talk about Donald Trump every night. None of us do. But he gives us no choice. If he sat in the White House all day quietly working on things, I would almost never mention him, because it's not interesting … But today – not even today, before 10 a.m. today, before 10 o'clock this morning, his former campaign chairman was sentenced to prison for the second time in a week, he called himself the most successful president in history and he tweeted to let people know his wife hasn't been replaced with a body double. I'm not supposed to mention that?
>
> *(Kimmel, quoted in Russonello 2019a)*

Stephen Colbert also believes that Trump brings all the negative comedy content upon himself with all the lies he tells the country. Colbert has presented his role as, at least in part, that of a watchdog and fact-checker.

> Trump consumes the news cycle, and our mandate, as we've established for ourselves, is that I want to inform the audience of my opinion about what they've been thinking about all day … I'm going to do my best to stand in the teeth of that particular [expletive] hurricane and make jokes about how we're all being lied to. For my own heart's ease, I'm not going to pretend that Trump is not lying to me. The alternative is to stick your head in the sand.
>
> *(Colbert, quoted in Marchese 2019)*

Thus, Colbert's and Kimmel's justifications for their political material sound similar to the way journalists define their roles, as watchdogs who serve the public by holding the powerful to account. This may seem presumptuous to some, but it recalls a joke by Will Rogers:

> Everything is changing. People are taking their comedians seriously and their politicians as a joke.
>
> *(Rogers, quoted in Schwartz 2011)*

The (Near) Future of Political Humor **187**

So, expect the volume of political humor directed at Trump to remain high for the near future, at least if he remains a candidate into 2024. If all or even most of the potential criminal charges against the former president are filed, such a step could extend the time he remains an appealing target for mockery well beyond the 2024 campaign, even if Trump does not become president again.

The coarsening of political humor, which has intensified during Trump's presidency, also seems unlikely to revert to more modest past norms during the remainder of his time in public life or during the tenure of future chief executives. Even if the personal life of Biden or the president who comes after him does not encourage comedic crassness, other political figures and their personal missteps will offer alternative targets for late-night mockery. When George W. Bush replaced Bill Clinton and Bush's quiet personal life offered comparatively little material, the comics simply continued to talk about Clinton's foibles. During 2001, Bush's first year in office, there were more jokes about Bill Clinton, the outgoing president, than there were about his successor (Lichter et al. 2015: 49). Since the late-night humorists like to play a winning hand for as long as it works, it should not be surprising that former president Trump faced so much mockery after his time in office concluded. Of course, how can the comics miss Trump when he never leaves the public arena?

That being said, the late-night comics have suggested that Trump might benefit from a thicker skin, or at least become a more responsible figure. As Jimmy Kimmel said of Trump, "Obama wore mom jeans one time, and we made jokes about it for six straight years. How about this: You stop being terrible, we'll stop pointing it out, O.K.?" (quoted in Russonello 2019a).

For all of Trump's bluster about Alec Baldwin's imitation, critics have suggested that the impersonation is not as harsh as it could be. In fact, many of Baldwin's treatments of Trump portray him more overwhelmed and befuddled than sinister. Trump also comes across in Baldwin's portrayal as relatively introspective and wistful (Canellos 2019).

> By giving Trump qualities he's shown little evidence of in public – conscience, introspection, even regret – *SNL* does him an enormous favor. It offers a glimmer of sympathy about his motives, inviting the generous assumption that there's a better and more self-aware man lurking behind the Twitter feed. In portraying the president as a beleaguered figure, it even allows the conclusion that the real threat to democracy isn't Trump's venomous rhetoric or disregard for constitutional norms, but the ruthlessness of the Washington system that confronts this blustering, fumbling uncle.
>
> *(Canellos 2019)*

188 The (Near) Future of Political Humor

In other words, despite Trump's many complaints about Baldwin's impersonation, it could have been far worse. Even so, this portrayal of Trump as befuddled may be problematic to Trump, who bristled at news reports suggesting he was not in full command of his administration – or his temper (Miller and Riechmann 2019; Parker and Rucker 2019). His visible anger leads to frequent insults directed at the late-night comics, treating them almost as if they were rival presidential candidates. This then draws even more attention and higher ratings to the hosts of late night, arguably his most persistent and most visible critics (Marchese 2019).

Trump's public speaking style, with his apparently off-the-cuff insults and many false statements that he apparently wishes were true, helped him win the White House in 2016 (Ceaser et al. 2017). Given his political success in 2016 and his near miss in 2020, one should not expect a rhetorical retool from the former president heading into 2024. As he once told a Conservative Political Action Committee (CPAC) meeting, Trump said he sticks with what worked for him, regardless of the consequences.

> "This is how I got elected, by being off script," the president said, briefly walking a half circle away from the podium, as if to physically illustrate just how far he had veered from his teleprompter remarks. "And if we don't go off script, our country is in big trouble, folks." Little of what Trump said was factual – he made 102 false or misleading claims in the speech, according to an analysis by *The Washington Post*'s Fact Checker – yet to this crowd and millions of supporters around the country, his broader points rang true and carried the imprimatur of authority because he delivered them.
>
> *(Parker and Rucker 2019)*

Trump's own combative and misleading rhetoric, and his expressed lack of interest in doing things differently in the future, is part of the reason why the coarsening of the political debate on late-night comedy and elsewhere is not going away anytime soon, neither on those programs nor in more general political discourse. Without the former president's lies, there is much less opportunity to offer Trump humor, according to Stephen Colbert. The nature of Trump's deceits, he argues, shapes the nature of the jokes.

> When you make jokes about politicians, there's what they say and what they do. It's hard to make jokes about someone who says something and then kind of does it. But with a guy who points east with his words and west with his action, that's where all the jokes live. Now, what

The (Near) Future of Political Humor **189**

are the things he's lying about? If the things he's lying about have a moral component, then your jokes will have a moral component. In other words, you don't choose the flavor. The flavor is chosen by politics itself.

(Colbert, quoted in Marchese 2019)

Trump's use of humor during the 2016 presidential debates focused attention where Trump wanted it focused, on the shortcomings of his rivals rather than his own character. While his jokes might have been sharper about his opponents than jokes by some of the late-night critics were, Trump's humor was effective in rallying supporters and disarming critics. Trump, in other words, used harsh comments to build a rapport with the audience watching his rallies and debates in ways that were somewhat similar to the ways the hosts of late-night comedy build connections with the audience watching their programs. As scholars noted in an analysis of Trump's humor during a 2016 debate with Hillary Clinton:

Trump's sarcastic and hostile humor, when combined with his multiple interruptions used to discombobulate, may be seen as a successful strategy to focus scrutiny on Clinton with audience collaboration through their laughter, while avoiding examination of his substantive shortcomings. While Clinton's humor responded in kind, she was not able to respond in volume; this may have had greater and more strategically debilitating results on the election by focusing on style, not policy substance. Whereas entering into the debate, the stage appeared to be Clinton's domain, stylistically Trump made it his own through the studio audiences' support.

(Stewart et al. 2018: 129)

Whatever the future brings for Trump, he has already shown how to diminish rivals and opponents via brief and pointed verbal dismissals reminiscent of comedy that focuses on personal insults. This builds him up and keeps his supporters enthusiastic about him and fearful of or dismissive about his adversaries. Though sometimes brutal, Trump's own brand of mockery is effective because it responds to core dynamics of human nature. Trump and his supporters were energized by the "Crooked Hillary" rhetoric and "lock her up" chants, and even years later one-time Republican rivals for the 2016 presidential nomination struggle to shake off the insults Trump hurled at them several years ago (Allsop 2019). Above all, these personal insults feed deep human desires for a world that is simple, where there is good on the one side and evil on the other – with few shades of gray found in between. Trump, a reality show star before he was a president,

190 The (Near) Future of Political Humor

demonstrated that he could be a first-rate insult comic, landing rhetorical blows of considerable power throughout his years on the political stage.

Like tabloid journalists, the screeching voices of cable television and talk radio as well as the late-night comics, Trump appreciates that entertainers need to avoid complexity to maximize the size of their audience, and their influence (Postman 1985). As a result, Trump offers his audience what one critic calls the modern equivalent of traditional children's' stories, tales that contain sharply drawn elements that are comforting and fear-inducing at the same time (Allsop 2017).

> Donald Trump has always spoken in fairy tale language. With a rhetorical swish, he turns complicated figures into witches, bogeymen, and, often, pumpkins, and reduces opponents – including politicians, the media, and other national leaders – to their most simplistic. At its darkest, it is a language that cleaves the world into opposing spheres of good and evil, pulling up the drawbridge to keep the hordes at bay. His dragon-like threat to rain "fire and fury" on North Korea is just one recent example. But it is also chauvinistic, trading in strength, moral failure, and cartoonishly rendered virtue.
>
> *(Allsop 2017)*

The personal insults connect effectively with emotional rather than intellectual dimensions of the brain. "Name-calling has always been a raw, primal assertion of power," writes Allsop (2017) in the *Columbia Journalism Review*. Given Trump's successes with employing personal insults to degrade and demonize rivals throughout his decades in business and politics, one should not expect him to change course. Trump's insults and harsh jokes are hardly the primary cause of the coarsening of politics in this country, but his behavior exacerbates a trend underway long before he became a presidential candidate and a president.

As he sought reelection in 2020, the Democratic nomination contest offered Trump a new round of political rivals to mock, including "Pocahontas" Elizabeth Warren and "Crazy Bernie" Sanders. Media critics increasingly encouraged those talking about politics to move beyond the repetition of Trump's personal attacks. "Journalists may not be able to ignore these nicknames altogether, but they should stop doing Trump's dirty work for him: amplifying their power through prominent placement and frequent, unquestioning repetition," according to Margaret Sullivan (2019), then the media columnist for the *Washington Post*.

The success of that appeal to reporters was destined to be modest at best. For reporters, that proposal would be like asking them to walk away from a front-page byline. For comedians, it would be like asking them

The (Near) Future of Political Humor **191**

to give up paid public appearances. Given those professional dynamics, it seems unlikely that reporters or the late-night comics will ever follow Sullivan's advice to go easy on the reporting of insults and ridicule offered by such a prominent public figure. Further, Trump's aggressive use of social media platforms allows him to demonstrate daily that sarcasm counts for a lot in politics (and in the news). Before he was banned from Twitter over his comments that encouraged the January 6, 2021 insurrection, Trump's tweets functioned as the equivalent of the assignment desk for Washington reporters and the topical agenda for the late-night comics. Day after day, White House reporters chased the president's early morning tweets, and as they do, reporters and editors learn anew the marketing behemoth that is Trump. The president's tweets and the resulting stories bring news consumers to their portals, be they intense fans of Trump or intense foes of him (Farnsworth 2018). Trump's own social media platform, Truth Social, may not have the reach of Twitter, but reporters have often reposted commentary from the former president, allowing his Truth Social commentary to reach a far larger audience (Thompson and Goldstein 2022). In the evening, the comics take their turn, as they too have learned a vital lesson: When Trump talks, media companies hear a ringing cash register and reporters and comics dream of larger audiences.

Above all, the 2020 campaign revealed a return to form for Trump, starting the moment Democratic hopefuls began announcing their candidacies. For little known candidates, Trump's barbs may have represented the first thing many voters have heard about them. From there on, it's an uphill battle to change initial public impressions. For example, after Trump compared Democratic candidate Pete Buttigieg (then the mayor of South Bend, Indiana) with "Alfred E. Neuman," the fictional cover boy of *Mad* magazine, in the spring of 2019, the characterization dominated the news cycle for days (Allsop 2019). One can understand why: what a president says is news. That the remark is somewhat odd only makes it more newsworthy. In this case, Trump made the connection between comedy and news even closer, using one of America's best-known cartoon characters (at least to people of a certain age) to insult and mock a political rival who had barely stepped onstage.

Insult narrative reports that draw on the norms of comedy – and sometimes even employ clips or quotations from the late-night shows to illustrate the stories – are easy for journalists to write and produce. The ease of story construction is an important aspect of contemporary journalism, as the news business has been shrinking in size for decades. A quip from a late-night comic in a news report only increases the appeal of the story in today's crowded, short-attention-span media marketplace. Trump knows better than any recent president or former president how

192 The (Near) Future of Political Humor

to make himself the story of the day all day long – in the morning paper, during the afternoon cable shows, on the evening news, on late-night television and on social media 24/7.

Thus, Trump is both the subject of such personally oriented attacks and one of the star performers at using that approach. The similarities between the reality TV star dispatching contestants on *The Apprentice* and the social media maven dispatching political opponents with some regularity are there for all to see.

Further, Trump's political insults have largely been consequence-free (for him, that is). His supporters love the attacks and those who objected were not likely to support him anyway. What's more, these adjectival slurs are not likely to receive the sustained factual scrutiny that accompanies policy pronouncements (Allsop 2017). How can they? Buttigieg is obviously not the gap-toothed grinning dolt that is the personification of a youth-oriented humor magazine, so Trump's comment here hardly deserves the attention of the already overworked media fact-checkers. Nevertheless, making the link between the fictional character who personifies *Mad* magazine and the mayor clearly helps both Trump and the media business that reports on the comparison that Trump made (Allsop 2019). Of course, Buttigieg may not have been the best target for Trump to attack. At the time, he was well back in the Democratic primary field. But he was getting positive press as the first openly gay major party presidential candidate, and he was doing better than some of the other presidential candidates in the early polls. And his background as a red state Democrat who served in the military might have made him a threat if his poll numbers had improved (Grynbaum 2019).

A larger question is whether future Democratic candidates will respond to or perhaps mirror Trump's version of humor in their own campaigns. So far, the party's candidates have hesitated to follow that lead. In the 2020 campaign, Democratic-on-Democratic insults were rare indeed. Candidates said they did not think a race to the bottom of personal insults served their purposes, even if they repaid Trump in kind. Joe Biden, a former vice president and the eventual victor in the 2020 election, said that he did not want to get into a mudslinging contest with Trump, but he couldn't resist calling the president a "clown" from time to time (Allsop 2019). Of course, maybe Biden did not seem as bothered by the insults as some previous targets. After all, Trump's mocking description of the former vice president as "sleepy" and "creepy" did not represent one of Trump's better name-calling efforts (Allsop 2019).

It would be depressing indeed if a significant part of winning over the public in a presidential campaign involved a comedic insult face-off. While such an approach clearly does not correspond to the founders' dreams of elections being decided through serious political debate, Trump's 2016 electoral victory stemmed in large measure from his ability to attack opponents in ways a significant number of voters found relatable (Ceaser et al. 2017).

In 2016, First Lady Michelle Obama encouraged Democrats to "go high" when people like Trump "go low." The results of the 2016 election cast doubts on whether that is a successful strategy for candidates facing Trump and his barrage of sarcasm and combative humor. But maybe that case study was the exception, not the rule. In 2020, Biden tried a strategy similar to that one advocated by Michelle Obama four years earlier, and he became president after doing so (Busch and Pitney 2021).

While the future seems quite likely to resemble the past where political humor is concerned, one should not entirely rule out the possibility of change. Scholars have debated one potential factor that might change the nature of political humor: the possibility that comedians lose their sense of optimism, the idea that tomorrow could be better than today. At the very core of mocking the present is the sense that the future might be better than the present (even though one might rationally expect that the future may be less different than one might hope). The jokes about Trump were funny in part because he might be followed by another president soon. Given the extremely critical treatment of Trump by the late-night comics, one might wonder if they or their generally liberal audiences would fall victim to despair if their target-in-chief were to prevail in the upcoming presidential election. The "sense of play" that animated comedy for comics and audiences could possibly disappear or at least go into remission for some if Trump wins in 2024. One might suppose that humor would not be as funny to those for whom the present seemed bleak, and the future seemed even more so.

If history tells us anything, though, bleak times, even very bleak times, do not kill political humor. Humor is a perennial, which thrives in the sunlight of optimism and in the shadows of extremely hard times. Political humor flourishes in wartime, in peace, in famines, and in times of plenty. Human beings laughed during the Irish famine, during the U.S. Civil War, as Stalin starved and tortured his people, and shortly after 9/11. Concerns that the comedians of late night might never laugh again – or that half the country would be too bitter to laugh along with them – if Trump were elected in 2024 seem misplaced. Things are never too bleak for a joke. The experience of history tells us to expect that the political humor of another Trump term would likely look a lot like the political humor of his first term. If he were to win in 2024, the Constitution's two-term presidential limit would keep Trump from running again in 2028, once again creating an environment where Trump's comedic critics could imagine better days ahead.

194 The (Near) Future of Political Humor

Comedic Insulation?

Given the size of the late-night audiences and the commercial stability of their platforms, Trump's insults never did all that much to harm the late-night comics who attacked him so frequently. Does that insulation from Trump's rage make them the ideal choices to challenge Trump and otherwise cut him down to size? Some might argue that Trump has met his match with the late-night comics, some of whom have shown themselves to be every bit as willing as Trump to engage in the politics of personal insults and character assassination. They certainly do seem to get under Trump's skin. What's more, these late-night humorists are no more tied to journalism's strict standards of accuracy than is Trump himself. So far, they have faced little in the way of a backlash because many of their viewers view Trump negatively and enjoy their attacks on him. (The success of *Gutfeld!* after all seems tied to people unlikely to be persuaded to watch Colbert et al. under any circumstances). In some ways, the loyalty of late-night viewers is a mirror image of the way that Trump's supporters insulate him from a political backlash for his nasty commentaries and inaccurate statements. Both those who watch Trump's rallies and those who tune in for the sarcasm of Colbert, Noah, and others enjoy the attacks on the other side a great deal. In this "battle of the insult titans," it should not surprise anyone that the nation's senators and governors, who have built careers in public policy rather than as nightclub headliners, cable jokesters, and reality TV stars, find it difficult to compete in a humor discourse that mixes laughter with personal character attacks.

On the other hand, the nonstop late-night attacks on the former president may encourage his supporters to double-down in their defenses of Trump. These jesters personify those coastal elites that serve as effective foils of Middle America. There is a sense in parts of the Midwest and elsewhere, that the educated urbanites in the Northeast and the West view residents between the coasts with contempt (Walsh 2012). Certainly, some of the jokes discussed in this book contain some disdain for the unsophisticated. It's an old saying that good comedy punches up and bad comedy punches down (McClennen 2018). But who decides the point from which to determine what is up and what is down? Might the humor directed at Trump feel to his supporters like the elite voices on the coasts are punching down at working-class whites like themselves?

Indeed, that perspective may very well explain the rise of *Gutfeld!*, the Fox News answer to the Trump-bashing comics of late night. For television viewers more supportive of Trump, or perhaps those television viewers put off by the sometimes strident, earnest political commentary by the former president's late-night critics, the self-deprecating, conservative-friendly comedic host of Fox News' late-night offering could be a welcome respite. Indeed, the high ratings enjoyed by this upstart comedic offering demonstrates a ready audience for people who want their late-night humor aimed more at Democratic figures and delivered by a comic who presents himself as a person who is not taking current events all that seriously.

Since the days of court jesters, one of the advantages comedians have possessed is their sense of relative powerlessness (Gilbert 2004). That sense of separation allowed them to exercise their craft more freely, and it protected them from the wrath they could face if they were no longer seen as outsiders. Jon Stewart sometimes fended off criticism of his political views or *The Daily Show*'s public impact by insisting on his own insignificance. In an argument with a host of CNN's *Crossfire*, he protested, "You're on CNN! The show that leads into me is *puppets* making crank phone calls" (Stewart, quoted in Stanley 2004).

When comedians try to shape policy outcomes, as Jimmy Kimmel did with his personal stories about his child's health care crisis and its relevance to federal health care policy, we can see how far we have come from those arguments of comedic powerlessness (France 2017). That is certainly not how some of these hosts appear to see themselves today. If comedians start to appear part of a partisan power structure, that sense of powerlessness that Stewart spoke of may disappear. If that happens, that will complicate the ability of those comics to withstand attacks from their critics by claiming their commentary is all harmless fun.

Comedians as Politicians?

In the first part of this chapter, we talked about the many links between Trump and the late-night comics. The former president cannot stop talking about late-night comedy, and the late-night hosts cannot stop talking about him. Both parties apply insulting monikers and acidic humor to their targets, which these days are often each other. Trump's rise to national prominence involved a large number of media appearances, including more than a few on late-night venues, and even through his reality television shows. He was born to compete in the media arena, and it is striking to see how much he dominates the late-night political discourse even though he is no longer the president. Biden has been the president for more than two years, as of this writing, but you would hardly know it by watching the late-night comics.

Trump's political success, more than any other political figure in recent U.S. history, represents the convergence of media and politics. Even Ronald Reagan, who worked as a film actor and television pitchman for General Electric before entering politics, built up experience in elective

196 The (Near) Future of Political Humor

office before entering the White House. Reagan's eight years as governor of California provided him with considerable governmental experience, and he knew much more about governing than his critics sometimes recognized (Cannon 1991). Trump's successes, in contrast, were entirely in the private sector domains of business and media; his first day in elective office was the day of his presidential inauguration on January 20, 2017.

Whether Donald Trump's 2024 campaign succeeds or not, one might still ask whether Trump is a model for future presidential candidates. Probably not. While candidates have long had to cultivate the mass media to be successful in politics, Trump's ability to draw so much public and media attention to himself makes him a reality show president superstar, really a one-of-a-kind melding of marketing, media, and politics. Finding another figure with such abilities would be a challenge. Preliminary discussions about finding a Democratic media star to compete with Donald Trump in 2020 – Oprah Winfrey, perhaps? – fizzled almost immediately (Kruse and Zelizer 2019). In other words, while one might be able to beat LeBron James with the next LeBron James, finding someone that good at basketball is a tall order.

Joe Biden, when it comes to late-night comedy as well as many other matters, does not seem to have a great deal in common with Donald Trump. Biden's election is the latest example of a long-running pattern in U.S. politics where voters select a president who has qualities that the current White House occupant lacks (Farnsworth 2018). When George H.W. Bush did not seem to appreciate the problems that ordinary citizens faced in the 1991–1992 recession, Bill Clinton promised he would feel their pain. After Clinton's sexual dalliances nearly derailed his presidency, George W. Bush noted that he had long ago sown his wild oats and was a happily married family man. After Bush's multiple second-term policy stumbles (the bloody resistance to the occupation of Iraq, the bungled Katrina recovery, and the burst housing bubble), Barack Obama offered an image of a more competent and cerebral chief executive. When Obama seemed too aloof to many Americans, Donald Trump was the populist cure. Biden offered a competence, and maybe a quiet professionalism, that Trump lacked. Given this oscillating pattern of presidential preferences, it always seemed unlikely that voters would replace a reality television star turned president with another politically inexperienced celebrity.

How about a comedian turned politician? The closest U.S. match so far would be Al Franken (D-MN), a *Saturday Night Live* alumnus turned U.S. Senator from Minnesota, until he resigned under a cloud of personal misconduct allegations. But he was never viewed as an aspirant or likely candidate for national office. As to the current crop of humorists, regular viewers of the late-night comedy shows will note that these programs have been sharpening their policy discussions. It is happening across the program genres: John Oliver regularly produces deep dives into policy details on a variety of topics for *Last Week Tonight* on HBO, not unlike a sort of *60 Minutes* of political humor. Samantha Bee likewise dropped a great deal of policy content into her critiques of the Trump presidency during her years on the air.

As we discussed at various times throughout the book, late-night host Jimmy Kimmel also has engaged aggressively in policy debates, bringing his infant son's health care troubles into the discussion of why Trump and Republican members of Congress should not kill the Affordable Care Act, also known as Obamacare (France 2017). During the legislative debate over the health care, Sen. Bill Cassidy (R-LA) even proposed considering health care bills in light of what the senator called "the Kimmel test," which would provide insurance coverage to all infants, regardless of the family's ability to pay (Russonello 2017). Kimmel charged that the bill that Cassidy was promoting failed to meet that test, and he spent several minutes on air talking about how the senator had broken his word (Russonello 2017).

> We want quality, affordable health care. Dozens of other countries figured it out. So instead of jamming this horrible bill down our throats, go pitch in and be a part of that. I'm sure they could use a guy with your medical background. And if not, stop using my name, O.K.? Because I don't want my name on it. There's a new Jimmy Kimmel test for you. It's called the lie detector test. You're welcome to stop by the studio and take it anytime.
>
> *(Kimmel, quoted in Russonello 2017)*

The sharpest of Kimmel's attacks demonstrated just how political – and how aggressive – the late-night shows can be in today's era of white-hot politics. Though the Obamacare repeal measure eventually failed, Kimmel has not consistently weighed in on subsequent policy debates with the aggressiveness he employed when talking about health care. Of course, he does sometimes engage in comparable fashion on a few topics, including challenging the Trump administration's anti-immigration policies (Russonello 2019b).

Candidate Colbert?

Then, of course, there is Stephen Colbert, who has worked at the intersection of politics and comedy for quite some time. Throughout this book, we have focused on how this top-ranked late-night host has challenged Trump as both candidate and president, just as he attacked conservative punditry with his parody portrayal on *The Colbert Report*. Among the comics actively working on television today, he has one of the longest careers focusing on the convergence of politics, media, and comedy. As such, Colbert seems a particularly interesting example of how a comedian might turn to elective politics – should he wish to do so. After all, if America can elect a reality TV star as president, who is to say that electing a late-night comic is a bridge too far?

In this regard, Colbert has a particularly interesting history. More than a dozen years ago, when he worked at Comedy Central, Colbert teamed up with *The Daily Show* host Jon Stewart to host a large demonstration on the Washington mall, which they dubbed "The Rally to Restore Sanity and/or Fear." The 2010 event drew large cable audiences and far more attendees in person than a rally earlier that year by Glenn Beck, a prominent conservative radio and television commentator (Stelter 2010). The Stewart/Colbert rally offered satirical content, including mock media awards for promoting public fear via media content (Carr 2010). Crowd size estimates exceeded 200,000 attendees, and the Washington Metropolitan Area Transit Authority, which oversees the Washington subway system, said Metrorail set a Saturday record that day for ridership, with 825,437 trips, compared to the average Saturday Metrorail ridership of about 350,000 (Stelter 2010).

That same year, Colbert also testified, largely in his Comedy Central character of a blow-hard conservative talk show host, about the plight of migrant farm workers (Compton 2019; Parker 2010). The media packed the congressional hearing on the issue, thanks largely to Colbert's star power.

> "When the comedian was challenged by one disgruntled lawmaker about his expertise, which was based on a single day spent hamming it up in a bean field for his show on Comedy Central, Mr. Colbert, keeping completely in character, said that was enough time to make him an expert on anything," the *New York Times* reported.
>
> *(Parker 2010)*

Colbert did drop his character briefly during the hearing to address why he wished to focus on the plight of migrant workers. "I like talking about people who don't have any power, and it seems like one of the least powerful people in the United States are migrant workers who come and do our work but don't have any rights themselves," he said. "Migrant workers suffer and have no rights" (Colbert, quoted in Parker 2010).

Colbert has in fact toyed with the idea, with uncertain seriousness, of running for president. In 2007, he filed papers to enter both the 2008 Democratic and Republican presidential primaries in his home state of South Carolina. But he was put off by the Republican Party's $35,000 filing fee, and the Democratic Party rejected his application (Parker 2010). With tongue apparently in cheek, Colbert created a Super PAC, "Americans for a Better Tomorrow, Tomorrow," to further his political ambitions – or perhaps his comedic ones (Stelter 2012). When Colbert learned that he could not run for president and run a Super PAC at the same time, he handed over control of the Super PAC to *The Daily Show* host Jon Stewart, whose program preceded *The Colbert Report* on the Comedy Central late-night lineup (Stelter 2012).

When he announced the decision to transfer the Super PAC to Stewart, Colbert made the discussion a teachable moment about how difficult it is to enforce laws that require separation from Super PACs and the candidates they support.

> "You cannot be a candidate and run a super PAC. That would be coordinating with yourself," Trevor Potter, Mr. Colbert's lawyer and a former chairman of the Federal Election Commission, told him on Thursday's show. But "you could have it run by somebody else," even a friend or business partner, Mr. Potter said – illuminating what critics say is an inappropriate loophole in the law. So Mr. Colbert brought out Mr. Stewart of "The Daily Show," who played along with the joke, saying, "I'd be honored to" help.
>
> Sarcastically emphasizing that they would not coordinate Mr. Colbert's real or imagined presidential race with Mr. Stewart's ad spending, Mr. Colbert said "From now on, I will have to talk about my plans on my TV show." Mr. Stewart, whose show immediately precedes Mr. Colbert's at 11 p.m., shot back, "I don't even know when it's on."
>
> *(Stelter 2012)*

While Colbert did not choose to run for president, the educational effort had an impact. A study found that citizens said they learned more about campaign finance from Colbert's discussion of Super PACs and his creation of one for his own campaign than from traditional news segments (Hardy et al. 2014).

While he might be a compelling candidate to some Americans, Colbert insists he really does not want to be one. Nor does he want to have that influential a role in selecting candidates. Colbert, who says that he has read *The Lord of the Rings* dozens of times, uses an example from that story to place his role on the outside, not seeking power.

200 The (Near) Future of Political Humor

Question: What's been the most interesting or weirdest idea you've noticed people projecting onto you?

Answer. That I want to be a political force. That's the weirdest thing. I said to Jon [Stewart], back in the day: "You and I are like Frodo and Samwise. We're trying to throw the damn ring in the volcano. It doesn't occur to them that we don't want to use it." Our way of throwing the ring in the volcano is to make fun of political behavior. But people got mad at me. "Oh, now he's fashioning himself as a player." And I'm like, you could not be more wrong. If you think I want that, you know nothing about me. I just want to make jokes. I care about what happens in the news. I have an audience that seems to care, too. We mesh on the jokes. It's not complicated.

(Marchese 2019)

The idea of electing comedians to government does not seem so odd, when one considers that as recently as 2016 America's voters selected a reality television star with no governing experience for the presidency. Other nations have explicitly turned to comedians in their elections. The political and economic pressures on the nations of Europe, clearly greater than those facing the U.S., have been fueling the rise of both extreme and unconventional politicians for years. Italy's Five Star Movement, led by a former comedian, first demonstrated several years ago that it was a force to contend within that nation's politics (Unger 2013), though the renegade party has been facing hard times since it became part of a governing coalition (Povoledo 2019). Despite the party's uneven performance in government, the party continues to generate considerable public support (Horowitz 2022).

The Zelensky Example

In April 2019, Ukraine elected a comedian as president in a landslide. This meant turning aside an incumbent president in the midst of a highly unstable military situation with Russia, which at the time was occupying much of Ukraine's Donbass region in the country's east and the Crimea region in the nation's south (Higgins and Mendel 2019). The election of Volodymyr Zelensky turned out to be an example of life imitating art.

This ability to convince and connect with people made Mr. Zelensky a natural for the stage, television and now politics, said Alina Fialka-Smal, a friend from university days. "He was always a whole pile of different characters," she said.

But the character that stuck – and the one that many Ukrainians now look to to clean up their graft-addled country – is that of Vasyl Holoborodko, Mr. Zelensky's role in a hit television series, "Servant of the People," about an unwaveringly honest high school history teacher who is elected president after a viral video shows him ranting against corruption.

(Higgins 2019)

When Russia tested the celebrity president next door by expanding its invasion of Ukraine in early 2022, it began with what international military observers expected would be a lightning-fast assault by hardened military forces on Kyiv. In those chaotic first few days, the situation became so dire for Ukraine that U.S. military officials urged Zelensky to evacuate ahead of the expected Russian takeover of the capital. A defiant Zelensky refused and offered the perfect sound bite: "I need ammunition, not a ride" (quoted in Braithwaite 2022). The heroic, potentially fatal, last stand in Kyiv helped turn the tide of the war. The courageous rebuff demonstrated how a leader with command of the media could seize the moment. Zelensky's well-publicized resolve during the winter of 2022 strengthened the resistance of Ukrainians to the Russian invaders. It also prompted international leaders to ramp up assistance to the beleaguered nation (Cohen 2022). Indeed, the president's forceful commitment to stay as Russians drew ever closer, broadcast via traditional news outlets and via personal social media messages, encouraged many in the west to start comparing the television star turned president to some of the bravest western leaders of the past. Zelensky was compared, in those dark days, to Shakespeare's Henry V at Agincourt or U.K. Prime Minister Winston Churchill, who led Britain as it held back Nazi Germany during the darkest days of World War II (Cohen 2022; Dawber et al. 2022). By the end of 2022, the media-savvy president had succeeded not only pushing back Russian forces and in shaping the narrative of the war to Ukraine's advantage but also in getting NATO nations to ramp up assistance repeatedly to help the nation fight back against its much-larger neighbor (Kramer 2022).

As goes Ukraine, so goes the U.S.? Probably not, particularly if Colbert, arguably the most prominent of the current generation of political humorists, retains his belief that he should not seek elected office. But the choices by the current generation of comedians are hardly the last word on the matter. Perhaps a more politically ambitious comedian in the years to come someday will have his or her chance to steer the ship of state in the U.S. After all, Zelensky has provided a much more compelling case than one could have imaged a few years ago for the capacity of people who made their living as entertainers to become national heroes.

202 The (Near) Future of Political Humor

The Possible Futures of Political Humor

One of the key roles the late-night comics have played in recent election cycles has been helping shape public assessments of the unusually large number of potential candidates. Indeed, the immense Democratic field that emerged in advance of the 2020 election increased the pressure for roughly two dozen presidential wannabes to appear on the late-night programs (Parkin 2018). In one month-long period, a full year before the 2020 Iowa Caucus, Stephen Colbert hosted a wide range of potential presidential candidates. The list included Sen. Bernie Sanders of Vermont, who finished second to Hillary Clinton in the 2016 Democratic nomination process, Sen. Kamala Harris of California, former Housing and Urban Development Secretary Julian Castro, and Sen. Kirsten Gillibrand of New York (Stelter 2019). The range of political guests, and the topics for humor, grew as the 2020 presidential field continued to expand.

> Of course, the comedy route works better for some politicians than for others. A politician's comfort and charm in a late-night setting is considered when the show's bookers work with communications directors to schedule a guest. But the list of Colbert guests since last summer tells the story. [Former Attorney General] Eric Holder visited last July. [New Jersey Senator] Cory Booker in August. [Former Secretary of State] John Kerry, [Former Congressman and then-Senate candidate] Beto O'Rourke and [2016 Democratic presidential nominee] Hillary Clinton in September. [Then-House Minority Leader] Nancy Pelosi in October. [Minnesota Senator] Amy Klobuchar in November.
> *(Stelter 2019)*

Kamala Harris, who made Colbert's program one of the first stops on a pre-campaign book tour, was rewarded prime comedic real estate: She was the first guest on the program, appearing right after the monologue segment. She even received the high honor of a second segment with the host, a rare privilege usually bestowed only to the most important and compelling guests (Stelter 2019).

Vanity Fair's Chris Smith, who was backstage at the theater that day, wrote that Harris "smiled and exhaled" afterward. "The senator seemed most proud of having gotten a laugh out of Colbert, a moment that happened after the TV cameras shut down," he wrote (Stelter 2019).

Indeed, the prominence of late-night comedy appearances, CNN and Fox News town halls and other television and online forums may be eclipsing the traditional clout of Iowa and New Hampshire, the first caucus and primary state, respectively, in the presidential nomination process (Martin

2019). When Democratic candidates have to establish a minimum number of donors and a minimum level of public support to qualify for the televised debates, it is hard to argue that a day spent greeting voters in Iowa is better than a day spent preparing for an appearance on *The Late Show*. As Ted Devine, a veteran Democratic campaign strategist, noted, "You don't have to be in Des Moines or Manchester to have a viral moment, and if that happens, you're in front of millions of people and can raise potentially millions of dollars" (quoted in Martin 2019).

In keeping with that expending importance of late night, Colbert has evolved over his years in comedy. The 2020 Democratic contest, taking place in a shadow of a possible Trump reelection, created a challenging environment: Colbert was trying to balance making his viewers laugh with giving them the opportunity to learn about the candidates for the Democratic nomination.

> Colbert is said to be keenly aware of his power broker status with the Democratic electorate. He pays close attention to the Democratic field of candidates, sizing them up like so many others in the media business. But Colbert also knows he is hosting a late-night talk show, not an MSNBC broadcast. He straddles both worlds – joking with Rep. Adam Schiff one minute, asking about Russian espionage the next.
>
> *(Stelter 2019)*

As more and more of these 2020 Democratic hopefuls made their way to the sets of the late-night programs, critics started to wonder whether these shows run the risk of becoming too partisan in tone. This could limit their audiences as well as making them less-than-appealing venues for would-be presidents who are not Democratic candidates (Parkin 2018).

> As candidates gear up for the 2020 race, they face an increasingly partisan political communications environment in which comedy programs are deciding between maintaining their impartiality or offering a satirical critique that emulates wider partisan divisions. Democratic and Republican candidates may come to believe that certain shows are "friendlier" than the others, and if interviews become increasingly partisan, viewers may see them as less legitimate in terms of their ability to offer a fresh perspective rather than just another venue for partisan acrimony.
>
> *(Parkin 2018: 287)*

Colbert, who sometimes has indicated that he would like to talk less about Trump, said that he welcomed the start of the 2020 presidential election

204 The (Near) Future of Political Humor

campaign, which provides him more material to offer jokes about a wide range of political figures beyond Trump – even though he admitted the president remained a far more interesting target for political humor.

> [Now] there are Democrats to talk about. When Joe Biden got heat for sniffing women's heads, we did an act that he was doing A.S.M.R. We make jokes about Beto O'Rourke. We make jokes about Elizabeth Warren. We make jokes about Andrew Yang. We make jokes about Pete Buttigieg. What I'm happy about is that my audience is laughing at all of them, which is good. But not everybody is as mockable as everybody else, and some mockability doesn't have consequences. Now, maybe Andrew Yang will be president – I don't know [expletive] about politics; I only know about human behavior – but his running on no circumcision, free money and legalized pot – is of no consequence compared with Donald Trump. So in terms of balance, I don't really care. I care about being honest about what people talked about today.
>
> *(Colbert, quoted in Marchese 2019)*

The large number of Democratic presidential candidates running for the 2020 nomination became a punch line on its own. As Jimmy Kimmel noted in the spring of 2019: "At this point, announcing you're running for president is like announcing you're running a 5K: Good for you. No one cares. Don't post pictures" (quoted in Russonello 2019b). Kimmel even made up a song to the tune of a number from the 1964 film *Mary Poppins*, "Supercalifragilisticexpialidocious," to help recall the 23 names in the Democratic contest as of late May 2019 (Epstein 2019).

Of course, Colbert is not the only show where presidential candidates can find a mass audience. The success of late-night comedy in recent years has created many opportunities for candidates. Even those who may not get a lengthy opportunity – or any opportunity – to chat with Colbert on CBS can promote their campaign elsewhere (Parkin 2018).

As the 2024 presidential campaign begins to take shape, it appears that President Biden will run for reelection, which will limit, if not eliminate, the emergence of a serious challenger with the party. So the free-for-all among the candidates competing for time with the late-night comedy hosts on the Democratic side may not reemerge until 2028 at the earliest.

For Republicans, late-night comedy's intense attacks on Donald Trump over all these years have made these shows less than appealing places for Republican candidates to appear (Parkin 2018) Gutfeld, of course, would be a Republican-friendlier host than the other late-night comedians, but it remains unclear if that iconoclastic and idiosyncratic program could be retooled for 2024 or 2028 to create a Republican counterpart of the

The (Near) Future of Political Humor **205**

Colbert primary for the Democrats seen in 2020. Nor is it clear that the host would want to go in that direction – one can note from our previous discussion of *Gutfeld!* that the show is not primarily a promotional vehicle for Republicans. Rather the program focuses on attacking key Democratic political and cultural figures.

Conclusion

Until the 1990s, politicians had to compete with increasingly critical, if not adversarial journalists to get their messages out to the public, but they were largely ignored by the entertainment media. Then an expansion of the news agenda, together with a kind of political awakening among the hosts of television talk shows, permanently altered the landscape, bringing a new source of negativity into political discourse. Social media would then go on to amplify those trends. Today the journalists knock the politicians off their stride, and then the humorists kick them while they are down.

In this narrow sense, Donald Trump was quite right to view journalists and the bulk of the late-night comics part of what he termed the "the opposition party." Any other administration might have made the same claim, but in the case of Trump the evidence is particularly strong. In addition, previous presidential administrations likely would have been more reticent than Trump has been about expressing publicly this objection to the growing one-sided nature of late-night humor.

In their effort to get their messages to the public in the form and content they prefer, all presidents and presidential candidates necessarily come into conflict with information sources of all types, including the mainstream media, whose professional norms dictate that they strip the propaganda out of politicians' messages (Farnsworth and Lichter 2006). But in this endless battle between the reporters and politicians, late-night talk shows have emerged as a second front. As a result, the culture of personal ridicule in public discourse is stronger than ever.

In fact, the format of late-night comedy creates a huge advantage for the hosts when compared to traditional news reporters, who have less of an opportunity to present themselves as individuals and also face much higher standards of content accuracy. The exaggerations and objectively untrue comments that permit effective punch lines on late-night talk shows make general character criticisms of political figures more accessible and more appealing to casual news consumers. ABC News, for example, could never exaggerate the way Jimmy Kimmel et al. do regarding the personal foibles of political leaders – nor could news reporters present themselves as people as intimately as does a late-night host engaging in friendly banter with celebrity figures night after night. The best a network news division

206 The (Near) Future of Political Humor

can do to narrow the entertainment gap with late night is to quote the comics as part of its own news programs (as is now done with increasingly regularity to maximize "clicks" from online news consumers). Even the august *New York Times* features a "Best of Late Night" online column that provides a rundown of the best political jokes from the previous night's talk shows.

The personal connections that these late-night comics cultivate with their audiences allow them to present themselves as policy experts and more. The most notable example we discussed occurred when Jimmy Kimmel set his jokes aside and used his infant son's health care troubles to advocate for universal health care (Yahr 2017a, 2017b). For the moment, Kimmel's aggressive, personal policy engagement on health care remains the exception, even on his own program. Given the public's low esteem for reporters and politicians and their positive evaluations of the stars of late night, perhaps Kimmel's foray into policy advocacy, along with Oliver's policy deep dives, will embolden other comics to do more of the same in the years ahead. Engaging more with policy matters seems to be an option as well for former late-night hosts, like David Letterman, who recently interviewed Ukrainian President Zelensky for a Netflix special, and Jon Stewart, who has long advocated on behalf of the health concerns of 9/11 first responders (Edgers 2022; Gold 2019).

To be sure, laughing at political leaders is a healthy expression of public skepticism about the powers that be in a democratic society, as well as a safety valve for public disaffection with its leaders (and would-be leaders). The current talk show hosts are following in a tradition that stretches back well over a century and includes the likes of Will Rogers and Mark Twain. And there is no doubt that the failings and antics of the political class frequently deserve a good horselaugh. But in an era of heightened negativity in political discourse, the hollowing out of public support in recent years for both political and media institutions raises questions of proportionality.

Thus, in and of themselves, the nightly monologues of comedians may be all in good fun. As part of the larger universe of political communication, though, they may accentuate trends in political discourse that bode ill for a healthy polity. In the words of Neil Postman (1985), someday we may look back on these days and conclude that we were "amusing ourselves to death."

BIBLIOGRAPHY

Abramowitz, Alan I. 2017. "It Wasn't the Economy Stupid: Racial Polarization, White Racial Resentment and the Rise of Trump." In *Trumped: The 2016 Election That Broke All the Rules*, eds. Larry J. Sabato, Kyle Kondik, and Geoffrey Skelly. Lanham, MD: Rowman & Littlefield. 202-210.

Adorno, Theodor, Else Frankel-Brunswick, Daniel J. Levinson, and Nevitt R. Sanford. 1950. *The Authoritarian Personality*. New York, NY: Harper and Row.

Aikins, Matthieu, Sharif Hassan, Thomas Gibbons-Neff, Eric Schmitt, and Richard Pérez-Peña. 2021. "Suicide Bombers in Kabul Kill Dozens, Including 13 U.S. Troops." *New York Times*, August 26. www.nytimes.com/2021/08/26/world/asia/kabul-airport-bombing.html?searchResultPosition=15

Allsop, Jon. 2017. "Inside the Fairy Tale Mind of Trump." *Columbia Journalism Review*, September 27. www.cjr.org/special_report/trump-fairy-tale.php

Allsop, Jon. 2019. "The Dangerous Power of Trump's 'Fairy Tale' Nicknames." *Columbia Journalism Review*, May 13. www.cjr.org/the_media_today/trump_buttigieg_neuman_nickname.php

Anderson, Dave. 1987. "Boxing by the Boardwalk." *New York Times*, October 16. www.nytimes.com/1987/10/16/sports/sports-of-the-times-boxing-by-the-boardwalk.html?searchResultPosition=10

Andrews-Dyer, Helena. 2020. "*SNL* Introduces a New Joe Biden after Jim Carrey Announced the End of his Stint." *Washington Post*, December 20. www.washingtonpost.com/arts-entertainment/2020/12/20/snl-new-joe-biden-cold-open/

Andrews, Travis M. 2017. "Jimmy Fallon Says People 'Have a Right to Be Mad' at His Friendly Hair-Tousling of Trump." *Washington Post*, May 18. www.washingtonpost.com/news/morning-mix/wp/2017/05/18/jimmy-fallon-says-people-have-a-right-to-be-mad-at-his-friendly-hair-tousling-of-trump/?utm_term=.8cf5bb9fe9bb

Associated Press. 2017. "Trump Hits Back at Late Night Shows Critical of Republicans." *Boston Globe*, October 7. www.boston.com/news/politics/2017/10/07/trump-hits-back-at-late-night-shows-critical-of-republicans

208 Bibliography

Baker, Peter. 2020. "Investigation of His Son Is Likely to Hang Over Biden as He Takes Office." *New York Times*, December 10. www.nytimes.com/2020/12/10/us/politics/hunter-biden-investigation.html?searchResultPosition=9

Baum, Matthew A. 2005. "Talking the Vote: Why Presidential Candidates Hit the Talk Show Circuit." *American Journal of Political Science* 49(2): 213–234.

Baumgartner, Jody C. 2013. "No Laughing Matter? Young Adults and the 'Spillover Effect' of Candidate-Centered Political Humor." *Humor* 26(1): 23–43.

Baumgartner, Jody C. 2018. "The Limits of Attitude Change: Political Humor during the 2016 Campaign." In *Political Humor in a Changing Media Landscape*, eds. Jody C. Baumgartner and Amy B. Becker. Lanham, MD: Lexington. 61–78.

Baumgartner, Jody C., and Amy B. Becker. 2018. ' "Still Good for a Laugh?' Political Humor in a changing Media Landscape." In *Political Humor in a Changing Media Landscape*, eds. Jody C. Baumgartner and Amy B. Becker. Lanham, MD: Lexington. 1–8.

Baumgartner, Jody C., and Jonathan S. Morris. 2006. "The *Daily Show* Effect: Candidate Evaluations, Efficacy and American Youth." *American Politics Research* 36: 341–367.

Baumgartner, Jody C., and Jonathan S. Morris. 2011. "Stoned Slackers or Super Citizens? *Daily Show* Viewing and Political Engagement of Young Adults." In *The Stewart/Colbert Effect: Essays on the Real Impacts of Fake News*, ed. Amarnath Amarasingam. Jefferson, NC: McFarland, pp. 63–78.

Baumgartner, Jody C., Jonathan S. Morris, and Natasha L. Walth. 2012. "The Fey Effect: Young Adults, Political Humor and Perceptions of Sarah Palin in the 2008 Presidential Election Campaign." *Public Opinion Quarterly* 76(1): 95–104.

Baym, Geoffrey. 2005. "*The Daily Show*: Discursive Integration and the Reinvention of Political Journalism." *Political Communication* 22: 259–276.

Baym, Geoffrey. 2012. "Rush Limbaugh with a Laugh-Track: The (Thankfully) Short Life of the '1/2 Hour News Hour.' " *Cinema Journal* 51(4): 172–178.

Becker, Amy B. 2013. "What about Those Interviews? The Impact of Exposure to Political Comedy and Cable News on Factual Recall and Anticipated Political Expression." *International Journal of Public Opinion Research* 25(3): 344–356.

Becker, Amy B. 2018. "Interviews and Voting Motivations: Exploring Connections between Political Satire, Perceived Learning and Elaborative Processing." In *Political Humor in a Changing Media Landscape*, eds. Jody C. Baumgartner and Amy B. Becker. Lanham, MD: Lexington. 79–94.

Becker, Amy B., and Jody C. Baumgartner. 2018. "Looking Ahead to the Future: Why Laughing and Political Humor Will Matter Even More in the Decade to Come." In *Political Humor in a Changing Media Landscape*, eds. Jody C. Baumgartner and Amy B. Becker. Lanham, MD: Lexington. 309–318.

Becker, Amy B., and Leticia Bode. 2018. "Satire as a Source for Learning? The Differential Impact of News versus Satire Exposure on Net Neutrality Knowledge Gain." *Information, Communication & Society* 21(4): 612–625.

Bender, Marylin. 1983. "The Empire and Ego of Donald Trump." *New York Times*, August 7. www.nytimes.com/1983/08/07/business/the-empire-and-ego-of-donald-trump.html?searchResultPosition=49

Benkler, Yochai, Robert Faris, Hal Roberts, and Ethan Zuckerman. 2017. "Study: Breitbart-Led Right-Wing Media Ecosystem Altered Broader Media Agenda." *Columbia Journalism Review*, March 3. www.cjr.org/analysis/breitbart-media-trump-harvard-study.php

Berger, Arthur Asa. 1997. *The Art of Comedy Writing*. Piscataway, NJ: Transaction Publishers.

Berger, Arthur Asa. 2011. "Coda: Humor, Pedagogy and Cultural Studies." In *A Decade of Dark Humor: How Comedy, Irony, and Satire Shaped Post-9/11 America*, eds. Viveca Greene and Ted Gournelos. Jackson, MS: University of Mississippi Press. 233–242.

Blake, Aaron. 2019. "Trump Tries to Re-write His Own History on Charlottesville and 'Both Sides.'" *Washington Post*, April 26. www.washingtonpost.com/politics/2019/04/25/meet-trump-charlottesville-truthers/?utm_term=.788e1687ff39

Bodroghkozy, Aniko. 1997. '"The Smothers Brothers Comedy Hour' and the Youth Rebellion." In *The Revolution Wasn't Televised: Sixties Television and Social Conflict*, eds. Lynn Spigel and Michael Curtin. New York, NY: Routledge. 201–220.

Bohlen, Celestine. 2001. "In New War on Terrorism, Words Are Weapons, Too." *New York Times*, September 29. www.nytimes.com/2001/09/29/arts/think-tank-in-new-war-on-terrorism-words-are-weapons-too.html

Bond, Jon R., and Richard Fleisher. 2000. *Polarized Politics: Congress and the President in a Partisan Era*. Washington, DC: CQ Press.

Boot, Max. 2018. "Trump Is a Grifter, Same as Ever." *Washington Post*, May 2. www.washingtonpost.com/opinions/global-opinions/trump-is-a-grifter-same-as-ever/2018/05/02/5afa43d2-4e2f-11e8-84a0-458a1aa9ac0a_story.html?utm_term=.67502b804744

Borchers, Callum. 2016. "The Amazing Story of Donald Trump's Old Spokesman, John Barron – Who Was Actually Donald Trump Himself." *Washington Post*, May 13. www.washingtonpost.com/news/the-fix/wp/2016/03/21/the-amazing-story-of-donald-trumps-old-spokesman-john-barron-who-was-actually-donald-trump-himself/?utm_term=.0d0fbf6099df

Borchers, Callum. 2017a. "A *Saturday Night Live* Spinoff Would Complete NBC's Turnaround on Trump." *Washington Post*, February 7. www.washingtonpost.com/news/the-fix/wp/2017/02/07/a-saturday-night-live-spinoff-would-complete-nbcs-turnaround-on-trump/?utm_term=.58b6710bbafb

Borchers, Callum. 2017b. "*Saturday Night Live* Is the Newest, Hottest Place to Punk – and Persuade – President Trump." *Washington Post*, February 11. www.washingtonpost.com/news/the-fix/wp/2017/02/11/saturday-night-live-is-the-place-to-punk-and-persuade-president-trump/?utm_term=.7b8df65c66b5

Borchers, Callum. 2018. "The Forbes 400 and How Trump's Shameless Self-Promotion Helped Make Him President." *Washington Post*, April 20. www.washingtonpost.com/news/the-fix/wp/2018/04/20/the-forbes-400-and-how-trumps-shameless-self-promotion-helped-make-him-president/?utm_term=.6bee614b8596

Braithwaite, Sharon. 2022. "Zelensky Refuses U.S. Offer to Evacuate, Saying 'I Need Ammunition, Not a Ride.'" *CNN*, February 26. www.cnn.com/2022/02/26/europe/ukraine-zelensky-evacuation-intl/index.html

Brewer, Paul, and Xiaoxia Cao. 2006. "Candidate Appearances on Soft News Shows and Public Knowledge about Primary Candidates." *Journal of Broadcasting and Electronic Media* 50: 18–30.

210 Bibliography

Brice-Sadler, Michael. 2018. "*SNL* Imagined a World without Trump as President. Trump Was Not Amused." *Washington Post*, December 16. www.washingtonpost.com/politics/2018/12/16/snl-imagined-world-without-trump-president-trump-was-not-amused/?utm_term=.5161f443e647

Brooks, David. 2011. "Why Trump Soars." *New York Times*, April 18. www.nytimes.com/2011/04/19/opinion/19brooks.html?searchResultPosition=54

Brozan, Nadine. 1992. "Chronicle." *New York Times*, August 3. www.nytimes.com/1992/08/03/style/chronicle-456992.html?searchResultPosition=35

Bump, Philip. 2019. "His Fox News Gig Was the Perfect Transition from 'Apprentice' Trump to Politician Trump." *Washington Post*, April 17. www.washingtonpost.com/politics/2019/04/17/his-fox-news-gig-was-perfect-transition-apprentice-trump-politician-trump/?utm_term=.81f57052a9b3

Burns, James MacGregor, and Susan Dunn. 2001. *The Three Roosevelts: Patrician Leaders Who Transformed America*. New York, NY: Atlantic Monthly Press.

Busch, Andrew E., and John J. Pitney, Jr. 2021. *Divided We Stand: The 2020 Election and American Politics*. Lanham, MD: Rowman & Littlefield.

Butler, Bethonie. 2016. "The Nightly Show Ends with Heartfelt Messages from Larry Wilmore and Jon Stewart." *Washington Post*, August 19. www.washingtonpost.com/news/arts-and-entertainment/wp/2016/08/19/the-nightly-show-ends-with-heartfelt-messages-from-larry-wilmore-and-jon-stewart/?utm_term=.5b0fdd636c36

Campbell, Colin. 2000. "Demotion? Has Clinton Turned the Bully Pulpit into a Lectern?" In *The Clinton Legacy*, eds. Colin Campbell and Bert Rockman. New York, NY: Seven Bridges Press, pp. 48–70.

Campbell, James E. 2016. *Polarized: Making Sense of a Divided America*. Princeton, NJ: Princeton University Press.

Canellos, Peter. 2019. "Why Trump Should Be Thanking Alec Baldwin: Once, *Saturday Night Live* Could Take Down a President. Now It's Doing Trump a Favor." *Politico*, May 17. www.politico.com/magazine/story/2019/05/17/trump-snl-impression-baldwin-saturday-night-live-226920?nname=playbook&nid=0000014f-1646-d88f-a1cf-5f46b7bd0000&nrid=0000014e-f10b-dd93-ad7f-f90fad5b0001&nlid=630318

Cannon, Lou. 1991. *President Reagan: The Role of a Lifetime*. New York, NY: Simon & Schuster.

Cappella, Joseph. N., and Kathleen Hall Jamieson. 1997. *Spiral of Cynicism: The Press and the Public Good*. New York, NY: Oxford University Press.

Carr, David. 2007. "Carson-Era Humor, Post-Colbert." *New York Times*, April 23. www.nytimes.com/2007/04/23/business/media/23carr.html

Carr, David. 2010. "Rally to Shift the Blame." *New York Times*, October 31. www.nytimes.com/2010/11/01/business/media/01carr.html?searchResultPosition=9

Carter, Bill. 1989. "Another Trump Project: A TV Game Show." *New York Times*, September 7. www.nytimes.com/1989/09/07/arts/another-trump-project-a-tv-game-show.html?searchResultPosition=24

Carter, Bill. 2003. "MSNBC Cancels the Phil Donahue Talk Show." *New York Times*, February 26. www.nytimes.com/2003/02/26/business/msnbc-cancels-the-phil-donahue-talk-show.html

Carter, Bill. 2009. "Leno Takes a Turn towards the Political." *New York Times*, September 20. www.nytimes.com/2009/09/21/business/media/21letterman.html

Ceaser, James, Andrew Busch, and John J. Pitney, Jr. 2009. *Epic Journey: The 2008 Elections and American Politics*. Lanham, MD: Rowman & Littlefield.

Ceaser, James, Andrew Busch, and John J. Pitney, Jr. 2017. *Defying the Odds: The 2016 Elections and American Politics*. Lanham, MD: Rowman & Littlefield.

Chadwick, Andrew. 2013. *The Hybrid Media System*. Oxford: Oxford University Press.

Chaplin, Charles, director. 1936. *Modern Times*. Film, United Artists.

Chaplin, Charles, director. 1940. *The Great Dictator*. Film, United Artists.

Chaplin, Charles. 1964. *My Autobiography*. London: Penguin Classics.

Cillizza, Chris. 2020. "The Coronavirus Clash of Donald Trump vs. Andrew Cuomo." *CNN*, March 17. www.cnn.com/2020/03/17/politics/donald-trump-andrew-cuomo-coronavirus/index.html

Clement, Scott, and David Nakamura. 2018. "Post-ABC Poll: Trump Disapproval Swells as President, Republicans Face Lopsided Blame for Shutdown." *Washington Post*, January 25. www.washingtonpost.com/politics/poll-major ity-of-americans-hold-trump-and-republicans-responsible-for-shutdown/2019/01/25/e7a2e7b8-20b0-11e9-9145-3f74070bbdb9_story.html?utm_term= .28d8297d6193

Cohen, Eliot A. 2022. "The Words about Ukraine That Americans Need to Hear." *The Atlantic*, October 22. www.theatlantic.com/ideas/archive/2022/10/volody myr-zelensky-ukraine-speech-churchill/671836/

Cohen, Marty, David Karol, Hans Noel, and John Zaller. 2016. "Party versus Faction in the Reformed Presidential Nominating System." *PS: Political Science & Politics* 49(4): 701–708.

Cohen, Steven. 2006. *Understanding Environmental Policy*. New York, NY: Columbia University Press.

Combs, James E., and Dan Nimmo. 1996. *The Comedy of Democracy*. Westport, CT: Praeger.

Compton, Josh. 2018. "Inoculation against/with Political Humor." In *Political Humor in a Changing Media Landscape*, eds. Jody C. Baumgartner and Amy B. Becker. Lanham, MD: Lexington.95–114.

Compton, Josh. 2019. "Late Night Television Comedy, Mid-Afternoon Congressional Testimony: Attacks on Stephen Colbert's House Judiciary Committee Appearance." *Comedy Studies*, DOI: 10.1080/2040610X.2019.1623439.

Cooper, Helene. 2011. "Obama Zings Trump at White House Correspondents' Dinner." *New York Times*, April 30. https://thecaucus.blogs.nytimes.com/2011/04/30/obama-zings-trump-at-gala/?searchResultPosition=9

Craig, Stephen C. 1993. *The Malevolent Leaders*. Boulder, CO: Westview.

Craig, Stephen C. 1996. "The Angry Voter: Politics and Popular Discontent in the 1990s." In *Broken Contract? Changing Relationships between Americans and Their Government*, ed. Stephen C. Craig. Boulder, CO: Westview. 46–66.

Crowley, Michael, and Julian E. Barnes. 2021. "Grilled by G.O.P. Senators, Blinken Defends Biden Administration's Afghanistan Exit." *New York Times*, September 14. www.nytimes.com/2021/09/14/us/politics/blinken-senate-afgh anistan.html?searchResultPosition=35

D'Addario, Daniel. 2021. "*Gutfeld!* Is a Concentrated Dose of Fox News." *Variety*, April 8. https://variety.com/2021/tv/columns/gutfeld-fox-news-review-comedy-late-night-1234947223/

212 Bibliography

Dagnes, Alison. 2012. *A Conservative Walks into a Bar: The Politics of Political Humor*. New York, NY: Palgrave MacMillan.

Davis, Murray. 1993. *What's So Funny? The Comic Conception of Culture and Society*. Chicago, IL: University of Chicago Press.

Davis, Richard, and Diana Owen. 1998. *New Media and American Politics*. New York: Oxford.

Dawber, Alistair, Mike Evans, and Marc Bennetts. 2022. "Zelensky Echoes Churchill as He Tells Congress: We Will Never Surrender." *The Times* (U.K), December 22. www.thetimes.co.uk/article/biden-hands-zelensky-a-heros-welc ome-and-patriot-missiles-ngkgxt3gb

Deen, Phillip. 2018. "Senses of Humor as Political Virtues." *Metaphilosophy* 49(3): 371–87.

Diamond, Dan. 2017. "Kimmel Tells Viewers: 'We Have until Sept. 30' to Stop GOP Health Bill." *Politico*, September 21. www.politico.com/story/2017/09/ 21/jimmy-kimmel-obamacare-repeal-bill-cassidy-243002

Doyle, Patrick. 2019. "Conan O'Brien Remembers When Trump Stormed off His Show." *Rolling Stone*, January 22. www.rollingstone.com/tv/tv-news/conan-obr ien-donald-trump-video-782294/

Dullea, Georgia. 1993. "It's a Wedding Blitz for Trump and Maples." *New York Times*, December 21. www.nytimes.com/1993/12/21/nyregion/vows-it-s-a-wedding-blitz-for-trump-and-maples.html?searchResultPosition=17

Edgerly, Stephanie A. 2018. "A New Generation of Satire Consumers? A Socialization Approach to Youth Exposure to News Satire." In *Political Humor in a Changing Media Landscape*, eds. Jody C. Baumgartner and Amy B. Becker. Lanham, MD: Lexington. 253–272.

Edgers, Geoff. 2022. "David Letterman on His Surprise Ukraine Trip and Zelensky Interview." *Washington Post*, December 9. www.washingtonpost.com/tv/2022/ 12/09/david-letterman-interview-zelensky/

Eggerton, John. 2005. "No CBS News for Stewart." *BroadcastingCable.com*, April 21. www.broadcastingcable.com/news/no-cbs-news-stewart-71445

Elliott, Floyd. 2014. "Satire Is What Closes on Saturday Night: The Outrage of #CancelColbert." *Huffington Post*, May 28. www.huffingtonpost.com/floyd-ell iot/satire-is-what-closes-on-_b_5052046.html

Epstein, Kayla. 2019. "Jimmy Kimmel Made up a Song to Help You Remember All the 2020 Candidates." *Washington Post*, May 29. www.washingtonpost.com/ arts-entertainment/2019/05/29/jimmy-kimmel-made-up-song-help-you-remem ber-all-candidates/?utm_term=.134ee918d602

Eskenazi, Gerald. 1984. "USFL Votes to Switch to Playing Fall Schedule." *New York Times*, August 23. www.nytimes.com/1984/08/23/sports/usfl-votes-to-switch-to-playing-fall-schedule.html?searchResultPosition=3

Fandos, Nicholas. 2023a. "The Lying Congressman: George Santos Is Stretching the Tolerance for Lies in U.S. Politics." *New York Times*, January 6. www.nyti mes.com/2023/01/06/world/congress-george-santos-falsehoods-politics.html

Fandos, Nicholas. 2023b. "George Santos's Secret Résumé: A Wall Street Star with a 3.9 G.P.A." *New York Times*, January 11. www.nytimes.com/2023/01/11/ nyregion/george-santos-resume.html

Fandos, Nicholas. 2023c. "Santos's Lies Were Known to Some Well-Connected Republicans." *New York Times*, January 13. www.nytimes.com/2023/01/13/nyregion/george-santos-republicans-lies.html

Farnsworth, Stephen J. 2001. "Patterns of Political Support: Examining Congress and the Presidency." *Congress & the Presidency* 28(1): 45–60.

Farnsworth, Stephen J. 2003a. *Political Support in a Frustrated America*. Westport, CT: Praeger.

Farnsworth, Stephen J. 2003b. "Congress and Citizen Discontent: Public Evaluations of the Membership and One's Own Representative." *American Politics Research* 31(1): 66–80.

Farnsworth, Stephen J. 2009. *Spinner in Chief: How Presidents Sell Their Policies and Themselves*. Boulder, CO: Paradigm.

Farnsworth, Stephen J. 2018. *Presidential Communication and Character: White House News Management from Clinton and Cable to Twitter and Trump*. New York, NY: Routledge.

Farnsworth, Stephen J., and S. Robert Lichter. 2006. *The Mediated Presidency: Television News and Presidential Governance*. Lanham, MD: Rowman & Littlefield.

Farnsworth, Stephen J., and S. Robert Lichter. 2011a. *The Nightly News Nightmare: Media Coverage of US Presidential Elections, 1988–2008*. Lanham, MD: Rowman & Littlefield. Third Edition.

Farnsworth, Stephen J., and S. Robert Lichter. 2011b. "The Return of the Honeymoon: Television News Coverage of New Presidents, 1981–2009." *Presidential Studies Quarterly* 41: 590–603.

Farnsworth, Stephen J., and S. Robert Lichter. 2012a. "News Coverage of New Presidents in the *New York Times*, 1981–2009." *Politics & Policy* 40(1): 69–91.

Farnsworth, Stephen J., and S. Robert Lichter. 2012b. "Authors' Response: Improving News Coverage in the 2012 Presidential Campaign and Beyond." *Politics & Policy* 40(4): 547–556.

Farnsworth, Stephen J., and S. Robert Lichter. 2016. "News Coverage of US Presidential Campaigns: Reporting on Primaries and General Elections, 1988–2012." *The Praeger Handbook of Political Campaigning in the United States*, ed. William Benoit. Santa Barbara, CA: Praeger, pp. 233–53 (Volume 1).

Farnsworth, Stephen J., and S. Robert Lichter. 2018. "Dominating Late Night: Political Humor and the Donald Trump Presidency." Paper Presented at the American Political Science Association Pre-Conference in Political Communication. Boston, MA. August.

Farnsworth, Stephen J., and S. Robert Lichter. 2020. *Late Night with Trump: Political Humor and the American Presidency*. New York, NY: Routledge.

Farnsworth, Stephen J., S. Robert Lichter, and Deanne Canieso. 2017. "Donald Trump Will Probably Be the Most Ridiculed President Ever." *Washington Post*, January 21. www.washingtonpost.com/news/monkey-cage/wp/2017/01/21/donald-trump-will-probably-be-the-most-ridiculed-president-ever/?utm_term=.98d31b3485e9

Farnsworth, Stephen J., S. Robert Lichter, and Deanne Canieso. 2018. "Donald Trump and the Late-Night Political Humor of Campaign 2016: All the Donald

All the Time." In *The Presidency and Social Media: Discourse, Disruption and Digital Democracy in the 2016 Presidential Election,* eds. Dan Schill and John Allen Hendricks. New York, NY: Routledge, pp. 330–345.

Farnsworth, Stephen J., S. Robert Lichter, Farah Latif, Kate Seltzer, and Sally Burkley. 2021. "Winning (and Losing) on Late Night: Political Humor and the 2020 Presidential Campaign." Paper Presented Online at the 2021 American Political Science Association Pre-conference in Political Communication. (September).

Farnsworth, Stephen J., S. Robert Lichter, Farah Latif, and Sally Burkley. 2022. "Late-Night Political Humor and the Two Presidents of 2021." Paper Presented at the Annual Meeting of the American Political Science Association. Montreal, Canada. September.

Feldman, Lauren. 2013. "Learning about Politics from the *Daily Show*: The Role of Viewer Orientations and Processing Mechanisms." *Mass Communication and Society* 16(4): 586–607.

Feldman, Lauren, and Dannagal G. Young. 2005. "Late-Night Comedy as a Gateway to Traditional News." *Political Communication* 25: 401–422.

Ferré-Sadurní, Luis. 2021. "Cuomo Has Lost Popularity, but Half of N.Y. Voters Say He Shouldn't Resign." *New York Times*, March 15. www.nytimes.com/2021/03/15/nyregion/cuomo-resign-sexual-harrassment-poll.html?searchResultPosition=8

Fisher, Marc. 2018. "Master of Celebrity: How Trump Uses – and Bashes – the Famous to Boost Himself." *Washington Post*, June 21. www.washingtonpost.com/lifestyle/style/master-of-celebrity-how-trump-uses--and-bashes--the-famous-to-boost-himself/2018/06/20/fef51c98-6b33-11e8-bf8c-f9ed2e672adf_story.html?utm_term=.6139373ec115

Fisher, Marc, John Woodrow Cox, and Peter Hermann. 2016. "Pizzagate: From Rumor, to Hashtag, to Gunfire in D.C." *Washington Post*, December 6. www.washingtonpost.com/local/pizzagate-from-rumor-to-hashtag-to-gunfire-in-dc/2016/12/06/4c7def50-bbd4-11e6-94ac-3d324840106c_story.html?utm_term=.f26c611c40e1

Folley, Aris. 2019. "'SNL' Mocks Tulsi Gabbard after 'Present' Vote on Impeachment: 'Democrats, I'll Get You, My Party, and Your Little Mayor Too.'" *The Hill*, December 22. https://thehill.com/blogs/in-the-know/in-the-know/475640-snl-mocks-tulsi-gabbard-after-present-vote-democrats-ill-get

Fox, Julia R. 2018. "Journalist or Jokester: An Analysis of *Last Week Tonight with John Oliver*." In *Still Good for a Laugh? Political Humor in a Changing Media Landscape*, eds. Jody Baumgartner and Amy Becker. Lanham, MD: Lexington Books, pp. 29–44.

France, Lisa Respers. 2017. "Jimmy Kimmel Tearfully Reveals Son's Health Crisis." *CNN*, May 3. www.cnn.com/2017/05/02/entertainment/jimmy-kimmel-baby-surgery/index.html

Franzen, Carl. 2009. "Which Way Does Leno Lean?" *The Atlantic*, September 27. www.theatlantic.com/entertainment/archive/2009/09/which-way-does-leno-lean/348011/

Freedman, Samuel G. 1987. "Trump Feud: Barbs Show Deeper Split." *New York Times*, July 6. www.nytimes.com/1987/07/06/nyregion/trump-feud-barbs-show-deeper-split.html?searchResultPosition=114

Freud, Sigmund. 2003. *The Joke and Its Relation to the Unconscious*. Translated by J. Carey. New York, NY: Penguin Books. (Originally published in 1905).

Full Frontal with Samantha Bee. 2016a. "Nativist Son." YouTube Video, 6:11. June 20. www.youtube.com/watch?v=A98QTdzyZA8

Full Frontal with Samantha Bee. 2016b. "GÖP-erdämmerung." YouTube Video, 7:40. July 25. www.youtube.com/watch?v=zQuFPxCb-_o

Full Frontal with Samantha Bee. 2016c. "This Week in WTF: Latinos for Trump." YouTube Video, 6:02. September 12. www.youtube.com/watch?v=cYgo4gsD-38

Full Frontal with Samantha Bee. 2016d. "A Totally Real, 100% Valid Theory." YouTube Video, 8:35. October 31. www.youtube.com/watch?v=7LFkN7QGp2c

Full Frontal with Samantha Bee. 2016e. "The Morning After." YouTube Video, 7:41. November 9. www.youtube.com/watch?v=s1SaD-gSZO4

Full Frontal with Samantha Bee. 2016f. "Something That Actually "Existed": Trump Policy Shop." YouTube Video, 6:01. November 9. www.youtube.com/watch?v=sxf4dFINMTY

Full Frontal with Samantha Bee. 2016g. "Steve Bannon: Trump's Alt-Right Hand Man." YouTube Video, 4:17. November 14. www.youtube.com/watch?v=dbKT22idntg

Full Frontal with Samantha Bee. 2016h. "Trump's New Cabinet Installation." YouTube Video, 4:48. November 14. www.youtube.com/watch?v=yve_oz-D5nI

Full Frontal with Samantha Bee. 2016i. "Sore Winners." YouTube Video, 4:43. November 14. www.youtube.com/watch?v=XpDjqbPyqRM

Full Frontal with Samantha Bee. 2016j. "The Big Lie." YouTube Video, 6:47. December 5. www.youtube.com/watch?v=Z4jz4mLvsWY

Full Frontal with Samantha Bee. 2017a. "Coronation Street." YouTube Video, 7:30. January 25. www.youtube.com/watch?v=k1AvNnJRMts

Full Frontal with Samantha Bee. 2017b. "Who March the World? Girls." YouTube Video, 8:10. January 25. www.youtube.com/watch?v=kY6aUo2PkaM

Full Frontal with Samantha Bee. 2017c. "The Not-a-Muslim-Ban Muslim Ban." YouTube Video, 7:12. February 1. www.youtube.com/watch?v=4RM2HtvLSLs

Full Frontal with Samantha Bee. 2017d. "Donald and the Terrible, Horrible, No Good, Very Bad Sanctuary Cities." YouTube Video, 8:12. February 8. www.youtube.com/watch?v=vypzrtAHyXk

Full Frontal with Samantha Bee. 2017e. "Heir to the White House Throne." YouTube Video, 7:05. April 5. www.youtube.com/watch?v=AzeL_8bdrQA

Full Frontal with Samantha Bee. 2017f. "We Told You So: Russian Hacking." YouTube Video, 6:47. April 5. www.youtube.com/watch?v=L6tVjqfIXFY

Full Frontal with Samantha Bee. 2017g. "Dr. Sebastian L. v. Gorka, Trump Whisperer." YouTube Video, 7:26. April 12. www.youtube.com/watch?v=398HJb0_PFg

Full Frontal with Samantha Bee. 2017h. "AHCA: Winners & Die-ers." YouTube Video, 6:14. May 10. www.youtube.com/watch?v=DeAziTKb7vQ

Full Frontal with Samantha Bee. 2017i. "Our Weekly Constitutional Crisis: Comey Edition." YouTube Video, 6:48. May 10. www.youtube.com/watch?v=3NxenCGfxEk

Full Frontal with Samantha Bee. 2017j. "The War on Drugs Reboot." YouTube Video, 7:19. June 7. www.youtube.com/watch?v=Ex-hyHZulNY

216 Bibliography

Full Frontal with Samantha Bee. 2017k. "The Mooch Will Set Trump Free." YouTube Video, 7:12, July 26. www.youtube.com/watch?v=kY6aUo2PkaM

Full Frontal with Samantha Bee. 2017l. "John Kelly Is NOT the Adult." YouTube Video, 5:44. November 1. www.youtube.com/watch?v=F8-pY3n3MAs

Full Frontal with Samantha Bee. 2019a. "A Message to Democratic Presidential Candidates: Run for Senate, God damn it!" YouTube video, 8:24. June 19. www.youtube.com/watch?v=VhwL1UvqzWg&ab_channel=FullFrontalwith SamanthaBee

Full Frontal with Samantha Bee. 2019b. "Democratic Candidates, Please Drop Out on Our Show!" YouTube video, 0:59. June 28. www.youtube.com/watch?v= 8WQJeUhaZ_4&ab_channel=FullFrontalwithSamanthaBee

Full Frontal with Samantha Bee. 2020a. "Democratic Debate: Drama in Iowa." YouTube video, 8:29. January 15. www.youtube.com/watch?v=wz44I3mx jQc&ab_channel=FullFrontalwithSamanthaBee

Full Frontal with Samantha Bee. 2020b. "Have Yourself a Merry Super Tuesday." YouTube video, 7:18. March 4. www.youtube.com/watch?v=KuNJYo5r meM&ab_channel=FullFrontalwithSamanthaBee

Full Frontal with Samantha Bee. 2020c. "Sam Responds to the First (and God, Not the Last??) 2020 Presidential 'Debate.' " YouTube Video, 7:20. September 30. www.YouTube.com/watch?v=qRNOAdXL99U

Full Frontal with Samantha Bee. 2020d. "Predicting the Republican's 2020 October Surprise." YouTube Video, 6:02. September 24. www.YouTube.com/watch?v= 6bMZhfY0swU&t=6s

Full Frontal with Samantha Bee. 2020e. "The Last Free and Fair Election?" YouTube Video, 7:32. October 28. www.YouTube.com/watch?v=KXW7 6pXy1FM

Full Frontal with Samantha Bee. 2020f. "A Very COVID Thanksgiving Pt. 1." YouTube Video, 5:30. November 18. www.YouTube.com/watch?v=dlC8 EEeqI58

Full Frontal with Samantha Bee. 2020g. "A Very COVID Thanksgiving Pt. 2." YouTube Video, 4:25. November 18. www.YouTube.com/watch?v=YHMk wo9IHdg

Full Frontal with Samantha Bee. 2021a. "It's a Little too Late for Republicans to Denounce Trump, Part 1." YouTube Video, 5:41. January 13. www.youtube. com/watch?v=tRZ6Wix_SAM

Full Frontal with Samantha Bee. 2021b. "It's a Little too Late for Republicans to Denounce Trump, Part 2." YouTube Video, 4:15. January 13. www.youtube. com/watch?v=WmZfrDVIs7c

Full Frontal with Samantha Bee. 2021c. "We Made It to Biden/Harris Inauguration Day!" YouTube Video, 1:18. January 20. www.youtube.com/watch?v=-okJ EsR7K9I

Full Frontal with Samantha Bee. 2021d. "The Fight for A $15 Minimum Wage." YouTube Video, 5:38. February 10. www.youtube.com/watch?v=Y19Q Y9y7BhU

Full Frontal with Samantha Bee. 2021e. "The Racist Past (and Present!) of Greek Life." YouTube Video, 7:06. February 11. www.youtube.com/watch?v=UNGp fap2em0

Full Frontal with Samantha Bee. 2021f. "Meet the White Women Empowering QAnon, Part 1." YouTube Video, 6:27. March 10. www.youtube.com/watch?v= a9YRQaIUNHY

Full Frontal with Samantha Bee. 2021g. "Meet the White Women Empowering QAnon, Part 2." YouTube Video, 3:10. March 10. www.youtube.com/watch?v= OvPrhQ_0GfM

Full Frontal with Samantha Bee. 2021h. "Sam Addresses the Murder of Daunte Wright." YouTube Video, 4:17. April 14. www.youtube.com/watch?v=RkVu ZBAxvdc

Full Frontal with Samantha Bee. 2021i. "Attacks on the Asian American Community, Part 2." YouTube Video, 4:13. April 14. www.youtube.com/ watch?v=21qsTOI1T4k

Full Frontal with Samantha Bee. 2021j. "Republican Attacks on Trans Athletes Are Escalating – Extended Cut." YouTube Video, 9:13. May 6. www.youtube. com/watch?v=raDTn2TBCkc

Full Frontal with Samantha Bee. 2021k. "Why No Progressive Agenda Can Survive the Senate Filibuster." YouTube Video, 6:13. June 2. www.youtube. com/watch?v=d1XPCrGYQX0

Full Frontal with Samantha Bee. 2021l. "It's Time to Take Responsibility for What We've Done in Afghanistan." YouTube Video, 6:57. September 1. www.yout ube.com/watch?v=Bf8wG7T2TEE

Full Frontal with Samantha Bee. 2021m. "Passing the Infrastructure Bill Was a Huge Win. Let's Celebrate!" YouTube Video, 5:49. November 10. https://youtu. be/uNF6oocjFm0

Garber, Megan. 2009. "Shocker of the Day: Stewart (Still) Most Trusted Newscaster in America." *Columbia Journalism Review*, July 23. http://archives.cjr.org/the_ kicker/shocker_of_the_day_stewart_sti.php

Garber, Megan. 2018. "Forgiving Jimmy Kimmel: It's a Thoroughly Modern Irony: The Host Who Will Set the Tone for the #MeToo Oscars Got His Start on a Show That Gleefully Ogled Women." *The Atlantic*, March 2. www.thea tlantic.com/entertainment/archive/2018/03/forgiving-jimmy-kimmel/554675/

Geist, William E. 1984. "The Expanding Empire of Donald Trump." *New York Times*, April 8. www.nytimes.com/1984/04/08/magazine/the-expanding-emp ire-of-donald-trump.html?searchResultPosition=57

Geist, William E. 1986. "Pssst, Here's a Secret: Trump Rebuilds Ice Rink." *New York Times*, November 15. www.nytimes.com/1986/11/15/nyregion/ about-new-york-pssst-here-s-a-secret-trump-rebuilds-ice-rink.html?searchRes ultPosition=6

Geer, John G. 2006. *In Defense of Negativity: Attack Ads in Presidential Campaigns.* Chicago, IL: University of Chicago Press.

Gergen, David. 2000. *Eyewitness to Power: The Essence of Leadership.* New York, NY: Simon & Schuster.

Gilbert, Joanne R. 2004. *Performing Marginality: Humor, Gender, and Cultural Critique.* Detroit, MI: Wayne State University Press.

Gold, Michael. 2019. "How Jon Stewart Became a Fierce Advocate for 9/11 Responders." *New York Times*, June 12. www.nytimes.com/2019/06/12/nyreg ion/jon-stewart-9-11-congress.html?searchResultPosition=2

218 Bibliography

Goldberg, Emma. 2020. "What 'The Babylon Bee' Thinks Is So Funny about Liberals." *New York Times*, October 11. www.nytimes.com/2020/10/11/us/politics/babylon-bee-conservative-satire.html

Goldman, Adam. 2020. "What We Know and Don't about Hunter Biden and a Laptop." *New York Times*, October 22. www.nytimes.com/2020/10/22/us/politics/hunter-biden-laptop.html?searchResultPosition=1

Goldman, Adam, Katie Benner, and Ben Protess. 2020. "Material from Giuliani Spurred a Separate Justice Dept. Pursuit of Hunter Biden." *New York Times*, December 11. www.nytimes.com/2020/12/11/us/politics/hunter-biden-justice-department-pittsburgh.html?searchResultPosition=4

Goodwin, Doris Kearns. 1994. *No Ordinary Time*. New York, NY: Simon & Schuster.

Gould, Jack. 1968. "Laugh-in Team Back with a Nixon Line." *New York Times*, September 17, p. 95.

Grady, Constance. 2022. "Is the Right Winning the Comedy Wars?" *Vox*, December 20. www.vox.com/the-highlight/23440579/comedy-wars-greg-gutfeld-jon-stewart-stephen-colbert-liberal-conservative

Grayer, Annie, and Clare Foran. 2021. "House Votes to Censure and Remove Gosar from Committees over Violent Video Targeting AOC and Biden." *CNN*, November 17. www.cnn.com/2021/11/17/politics/house-vote-censure-gosar-aoc-video/index.html

Green, Joshua. 2017. *Devil's Bargain: Steve Bannon, Donald Trump and the Storming of the Presidency*. New York, NY: Penguin.

Greenberg, Jonathan. 2018. "Trump Lied to Me about His Wealth to Get onto the Forbes 400. Here Are the Tapes." *Washington Post*, April 20. www.washingtonpost.com/outlook/trump-lied-to-me-about-his-wealth-to-get-onto-the-forbes-400-here-are-the-tapes/2018/04/20/ac762b08-4287-11e8-8569-26fda6b404c7_story.html?utm_term=.44a2d0cd1026

Greene, Viceca. 2011. "Critique, Counternarratives, and Ironic Intervention in 'South Park' and Stephen Colbert." In *A Decade of Dark Humor: How Comedy, Irony, and Satire Shaped Post-9/11 America*, eds. Viveca Greene and Ted Gournelos. Jackson, MS: University of Mississippi Press. 119–136.

Greene, Viceca, and Ted Gournelos. 2011. "Popular Culture and Post-9/11 Politics." In *A Decade of Dark Humor: How Comedy, Irony, and Satire Shaped Post-9/11 America*, eds. Viveca Greene and Ted Gournelos. Jackson, MS: University of Mississippi Press. Xi–xxv.

Grill, Christiane. 2018. "What Is Funny to Whom? Applying an Integrative Theoretical Framework to the Study of Political Humor Appreciation." In *Political Humor in a Changing Media Landscape*, eds. Jody C. Baumgartner and Amy B. Becker. Lanham, MD: Lexington. 157-182.

Grynbaum, Michael M. 2019. "Fox News Welcomes Pete Buttigieg. Trump and 'Fox & Friends' Aren't Pleased." *New York Times*, May 20. www.nytimes.com/2019/05/20/business/media/fox-news-pete-buttigieg-chris-wallace.html?searchResultPosition=3

Gurney, David. 2011. "Everything Changes Forever (Temporarily): Late Night Television Comedy after 9/11." In *A Decade of Dark Humor: How Comedy, Irony, and Satire Shaped Post-9/11 America*, eds. Viveca Greene and Ted Gournelos. Jackson, MS: University of Mississippi Press. 3–19.

Habermas, Jurgen. 1973. *Legitimation Crisis*. Translated by Thomas McCarthy. Boston, MA: Beacon Press.

Halbfinger, David M. 1997. "Death Penalty Will Stand, Court Rules." *New York Times*, December 23. www.nytimes.com/1997/12/23/nyregion/death-penalty-will-stand-court-rules.html?searchResultPosition=9

Hardy, Bruce W., Jeffrey A. Gottfried, Kenneth M. Winneg, and Kathleen Hall Jamieson. 2014. "Stephen Colbert's Civics Lesson: How the Colbert SuperPAC Taught Viewers about Campaign Finance." *Mass Communication and Society* 17(3): 329–353.

Hartung, Adam. 2017. "Colbert Beat Fallon by Following Trends, Which Will Make CBS More Money." *Forbes*, September 28. www.forbes.com/sites/adam hartung/2017/09/28/colbert-beat-fallon-by-following-trends-which-will-make-cbs-more-money/#3a1464b926ef

Hayes, Britt. 2020. "Jim Carrey Shares the Extremely Dark Origin Story of Fire Marshall Bill." *AV Club*, July 20. www.avclub.com/jim-carrey-shares-the-extremely-dark-origin-story-of-fi-1844442398

Hesse, Josiah. 2013. "Why Does Every 'Conservative *Daily Show*' Fail?" *Vulture*, December 2. www.vulture.com/2013/12/why-does-every-conservative-daily-show-fail.html

Hetherington, Marc J., and Jonathan D. Weiler. 2009. *Authoritarianism and Polarization in American Politics*. Cambridge: Cambridge University Press.

Hibbing, John R., and Elizabeth Theiss-Morse. 1995. *Congress as Public Enemy: Public Attitudes towards American Political Institutions*. Cambridge: Cambridge University Press.

Higgins, Andrew. 2019. "Ukraine Election: Comedian Dismissed by President Is Favored to Get Last Laugh." *New York Times*, April 20. www.nytimes.com/2019/04/20/world/europe/ukraine-election.html?searchResultPosition=1

Higgins, Andrew, and Iuliia Mendel. 2019. "Ukraine Election: Volodymyr Zelensky, TV Comedian, Trounces President." *New York Times*, April 21. www.nytimes.com/2019/04/21/world/europe/Volodymyr-Zelensky-ukraine-elections.html?searchResultPosition=2

Hoffman, Lindsay, and Tiffany Thomson. 2009. "The Effect of Television Viewing on Adolescents' Civic Participation: Political Efficacy as a Mediating Mechanism." *Journal of Broadcasting & Electronic Media* 53: 3–21.

Hopper, Jennifer R. 2017. *Presidential Framing in 21st Century News Media: The Politics of the Affordable Care Act*. New York, NY: Routledge.

Hopper, Tristin. 2018. "The CIA Has Declassified a Bunch of Jokes. Here Are the Best Ones." *National Post*, September 20. https://nationalpost.com/news/the-cia-has-declassified-a-bunch-of-jokes-here-are-the-best-ones

Horowitz, Jason. 2022. "Giorgia Meloni Wins Voting in Italy, in Breakthrough for Europe's Hard Right." *New York Times*, September 25. www.nytimes.com/2022/09/25/world/europe/italy-meloni-prime-minister.html?searchResultPosition=6

Hounshell, Blake. 2022. "Where Trump Stands in Early (Very Early) 2024 Polls." *New York Times*, December 7. www.nytimes.com/2022/12/07/us/politics/trump-2024-republicans-desantis.html?searchResultPosition=12

Hulse, Carl. 2020. "Daines Holds Off Bullock in Montana, Keeping Key Senate Seat in G.O.P. Hands." *New York Times*, November 4. www.nytimes.com/2020/11/04/us/politics/montana-daines.html?searchResultPosition=2

220 Bibliography

Hurt, Harry III. 1993. *Lost Tycoon: The Many Lives of Donald J. Trump*. New York, NY: Norton.

Inglehart, Ronald. 1977. *The Silent Revolution*. Princeton, NJ: Princeton University Press.

Inglehart, Ronald. 1981. "Post-Materialism in an Environment of Insecurity." *American Political Science Review* 75: 880–900.

Inglehart, Ronald. 1988. "The Renaissance of Political Culture." *American Political Science Review* 82: 1203–1230.

Inglehart, Ronald. 1990. *Culture Shift in Advanced Industrial Society*. Princeton, NJ: Princeton University Press.

Inside Edition. 2015. "Watch the Donald Trump Sketch That Was Mysteriously Deleted from 2004 SNL Episode." *Inside Edition*, October 15. www.insideedit ion.com/headlines/12399-watch-the-donald-trump-sketch-that-was-mysteriou sly-deleted-from-2004-snl-episode\

Isikoff, Michael. 2000. *Uncovering Clinton: A Reporter's Story*. New York, NY: Three Rivers Press.

Itzkoff, Dave. 2017. Jimmy Fallon Was on Top of the World. Then Came Trump." *New York Times*, May 17. www.nytimes.com/2017/05/17/arts/television/jimmy-fallon-tonight-show-interview-trump.html

Itzkoff, Dave. 2018. "Trump Slings Twitter Insults with Alec Baldwin, His 'S.N.L.' Impersonator." *New York Times*, March 2. www.nytimes.com/2018/03/02/arts/television/trump-alec-baldwin-snl.html

Iyengar, Shanto, and Kyu S. Hahn. 2009. "Red Media, Blue Media: Evidence of Ideological Selectivity in Media Use." *Journal of Communication* 59: 19–39.

Jones, Jeffrey P. 2010. *Entertaining Politics: Satiric Television and Political Engagement*. Lanham, MD: Rowman & Littlefield.

Kaczynski, Andrew, and Nathan McDermott. 2016. "Donald Trump Said a Lot of Gross Things about Women on 'Howard Stern.'" *Buzzfeed*, February 24. www.buzzfeednews.com/article/andrewkaczynski/donald-trump-said-a-lot-of-gross-things-about-women-on-howar

Kerr, Peter. 1984. "TV Notes: 2 New Cable Networks Being Planned." *New York Times*, January 30. www.nytimes.com/1984/01/30/movies/tv-notes-2-new-cable-networks-being-planned.html?searchResultPosition=2

Kerr, Sarah, and Maya Blackstone. 2021. "Cuomo Resigns amid Pressure over Sexual Harassment Allegations." *New York Times*, August 10. www.nytimes.com/video/nyregion/100000007915331/cuomo-resigns-amid-pressure-over-sex ual-harassment-allegations.html?searchResultPosition=1

Kinsley, Michael. 1992. "Ask a Silly Question." *New Republic*, July 6.

Klemesrud, Judy. 1976. "Donald Trump, Real Estate Promoter, Builds Image as He Buys Buildings." *New York Times*, November 1. www.nytimes.com/1976/11/01/archives/donald-trump-real-estate-promoter-builds-image-as-he-buys-buildi ngs.html?searchResultPosition=14

Kolbert, Elizabeth. 1992. "The 1992 Campaign: Media; Whistle-Stops a la 1992: Arsenio, Larry and Phil." *New York Times*, June 5. www.nytimes.com/1992/06/05/us/the-1992-campaign-media-whistle-stops-a-la-1992-arsenio-larry-and-phil.html

Kolbin, John. 2017. "A Sharp Decline for Jimmy Fallon's *Tonight Show*." *New York Times*, November 28. www.nytimes.com/2017/11/28/business/media/jimmy-fal lon-tonight-show-ratings-colbert-kimmel-decline.html

Kramer, Andrew E. 2022. "With Speeches to Ukraine, and the World, Zelensky Shapes Narrative of the War." *New York Times*, December 31. www.nyti mes.com/2022/12/31/world/europe/zelensky-ukraine-war.html?searchResultP osition=1

Kruse, Kevin M., and Julian Zelizer. 2019. "Why Billionaires with Big Egos Now Dream of Being President." *Washington Post*, January 29. www.washingtonp ost.com/outlook/2019/01/29/why-billionaires-with-big-egos-now-dream-being-president/?utm_term=.ff402cf20d87

Last Week Tonight with John Oliver. 2016a. "Donald Trump." YouTube Video, 21:53. February 28. www.youtube.com/watch?v=DnpO_RTSNmQ

Last Week Tonight with John Oliver. 2016b. "Border Wall." YouTube Video, 18:32. March 20. www.youtube.com/watch?v=vU8dCYocuyI

Last Week Tonight with John Oliver. 2016c. "Republican National Convention." YouTube Video, 11:31. July 24. www.youtube.com/watch?v=zNdkrtfZP8I

Last Week Tonight with John Oliver. 2016d. "Campaign Songs." YouTube Video, 7:25. July 24. www.youtube.com/watch?v=32n4h0kn-88

Last Week Tonight with John Oliver. 2016e. "Democratic National Convention." YouTube Video, 18:09. July 31. www.youtube.com/watch?v=BUCnjlTfXDw

Last Week Tonight with John Oliver. 2016f. "Scandals." YouTube Video, 21:15. September 25. www.youtube.com/watch?v=h1Lfd1aB9YI

Last Week Tonight with John Oliver. 2016g. "President-Elect Trump." YouTube Video, 29:00. November 13. www.youtube.com/watch?v=-rSDUsMwakI

Last Week Tonight with John Oliver. 2016h. "Trump University." YouTube Video, 12:37. November 29. www.youtube.com/watch?v=cBUeipXFisQ

Last Week Tonight with John Oliver. 2017a. "Trump vs. Truth." YouTube Video, 23:49. February 12. www.youtube.com/watch?v=xecEV4dSAXE

Last Week Tonight with John Oliver. 2017b. "American Health Care Act." YouTube Video, 18:30. March 12. www.youtube.com/watch?v=Ifi9M7DRazI

Last Week Tonight with John Oliver. 2017c. "Federal Budget." YouTube Video, 12:04. March 19. www.youtube.com/watch?v=ySTQk6updjQ

Last Week Tonight with John Oliver. 2017d. "Stupid Watergate." YouTube Video, 24:05. May 21. www.youtube.com/watch?v=FVFdsl29s_Q

Last Week Tonight with John Oliver. 2017e. "Paris Agreement." YouTube Video, 20:57. June 4. www.youtube.com/watch?v=5scez5dqtAc

Last Week Tonight with John Oliver. 2017f. "Coal." YouTube Video, 24:20. June 18. www.youtube.com/watch?v=aw6RsUhw1Q8

Last Week Tonight with John Oliver. 2017g. "Alex Jones." July 30. https://play. hbonow.com/episode/urn:hbo:episode:GWTeRBgjxyiuZwwEAAAA-

Last Week Tonight with John Oliver. 2017h. "North Korea." YouTube Video, 26:59. August 13. www.youtube.com/watch?v=TrS0uNBuG9c

Last Week Tonight with John Oliver. 2017i. "The Trump Presidency." YouTube Video, 23:50. November 12. www.youtube.com/watch?v=1ZAPwfrtAFY

Last Week Tonight with John Oliver. 2020a. "Medicare for All." YouTube video, 19:53. February 16. www.youtube.com/watch?v=7Z2XRg3dy9k&ab_chan nel=LastWeekTonight

Last Week Tonight with John Oliver. 2020b. "Season 7, Episode 2." HBO. February 23. https://play.hbomax.com/episode/urn:hbo:episode:GXidhM AdAw6jCwgEAAAUz

222 Bibliography

Last Week Tonight with John Oliver. 2020c. "Election 2020." YouTube Video, 20:30. October 5. www.youtube.com/watch?v=AytDzZ2ecCc

Last Week Tonight with John Oliver. 2020d. "Election Results 2020." YouTube Video, 27:05. November 9. www.youtube.com/watch?v=LyC855KdBKo&t=1127s

Last Week Tonight with John Oliver. 2020e. "Trump & Election Results." YouTube Video, 17:57. November 16. www.youtube.com/watch?v=cMz_sTgoydQ

Last Week Tonight with John Oliver. 2021a. "Season 8 Official Trailer." YouTube Video, 1:46. January 15. www.youtube.com/watch?v=S5_4wPW6jJQ

Last Week Tonight with John Oliver. 2021b. "The Next Pandemic." YouTube Video, 20:28. February 15. www.youtube.com/watch?v=_v-U3K1sw9U

Last Week Tonight with John Oliver. 2021c. "Trump's Second Impeachment." YouTube Video, 4:57. February 15. www.youtube.com/watch?v=uD4_x2s7wQo

Last Week Tonight with John Oliver. 2021d. "Tucker Carlson." YouTube Video, 24:52. March 15. www.youtube.com/watch?v=XMGxxRRtmHc

Last Week Tonight with John Oliver. 2021e. "Immigration and Refugees." YouTube Video, 4:56. April 12. www.youtube.com/watch?v=u73ZG66_tDI

Last Week Tonight with John Oliver. 2021f. "Afghanistan." YouTube Video, 23:39. August 23. www.youtube.com/watch?v=dykZyuWci3g

Last Week Tonight with John Oliver. 2021g. "Voting Rights." YouTube Video, 19:47. September 27. www.youtube.com/watch?v=EN9OdruH_qM

Last Week Tonight with John Oliver. 2021h. "Biden's Spending Plan." HBO Max, 4:08. November 6.

Lee, Jasmine, C., and Kevin Quealy. 2019. "The 567 People, Places and Things Donald Trump Has Insulted on Twitter: A Complete List." *New York Times*, February 20. www.nytimes.com/interactive/2016/01/28/upshot/donald-trump-twitter-insults.html

Leonnig, Carole, D. Adam Entous, Devlin Barrett, and Matt Zapotosky. 2017. "Michael Flynn Pleads Guilty to Lying to FBI on Contacts with Russian Ambassador." *Washington Post*, December 1. www.washingtonpost.com/polit ics/michael-flynn-charged-with-making-false-statement-to-the-fbi/2017/12/01/e03a6c48-d6a2-11e7-9461-ba77d604373d_story.html?utm_term=.4e8a1 1b25dce

Lerer, Lisa. 2021. "In Virginia Governor's Race, Biden Barely Rates a Mention." *New York Times*, October 26. www.nytimes.com/2021/10/26/us/politics/terry-mcauliffe-biden.html?searchResultPosition=7

Lewis, Hilary. 2020. "Samantha Bee Says Leading Political Candidates Are Reluctant to Appear on 'Full Frontal.'" *Hollywood Reporter*, March 4. www.hollywoodreporter.com/live-feed/samantha-bee-interviewing-2020-election-can didates-full-frontal-1282641

Lichter, S. Robert, Jody C. Baumgartner, and Jonathan S. Morris. 2015. *Politics Is a Joke! How TV Comedians Are Remaking Political Life.* Boulder, CO: Westview.

Lichter, S. Robert, Stephen J. Farnsworth, and Deanne Canieso. 2016. "Late Night Tells 3 Times as Many Jokes about 2016 Republicans as Democrats." *Washington Post*, March 8. www.washingtonpost.com/news/the-fix/wp/2016/03/08/late-night-tells-3-times-as-many-jokes-about-2016-republicans-as-democrats/

Liebovich, Louis W. 2001. *The Press and the Modern Presidency: Myths and Mindsets from Kennedy to Election 2000.* Westport, CT: Praeger.

Bibliography   **223**

MacWilliams, Matthew. C. 2016. "Who Decides When the Party Doesn't? Authoritarian Voters and the Rise of Donald Trump." *PS: Political Science & Politics* 49: 716–721.

Manjoo, Farhad. 2017. "Can Facebook Fix Its Own Worst Bug?" *New York Times*, April 25. www.nytimes.com/2017/04/25/magazine/can-facebook-fix-its-own-worst-bug.html

Mann, Thomas E., and Norman J. Ornstein. 2012. *It's Even Worse than It Looks: How the American Constitutional System Collided with the New Politics of Extremism*. New York, NY: Basic Books.

Marchese, David. 2019. "Stephen Colbert on the Political Targets of Satire." *New York Times Magazine*, June 2. www.nytimes.com/interactive/2019/06/03/magazine/stephen-colbert-politics-religion.html?searchResultPosition=1

Markowicz, Karol. 2022. "Nobody Watched Trevor Noah – and No One Will Watch His Unfunny Liberal Replacement Either." *New York Post*, October 2. https://nypost.com/2022/10/02/nobody-watched-trevor-noah-and-no-one-will-watch-his-unfunny-liberal-replacement-either/

Martin, Jonathan. 2019. "'You Don't Have to Be in Des Moines.' Democrats Expand Primary Map, Spurred by Social Media." *New York Times*, June 1. www.nytimes.com/2019/06/01/us/politics/2020-democratic-primaries.html?searchResultPosition=1

Martin, Rod A. 2007. *The Psychology of Humor: An Integrative Approach*. Burlington, MA: Elsevier Academic Press.

Martinelli, Marissa. 2016. "Obama Burns Trump, Sings Rihanna as He Slow Jams the News with Jimmy Fallon." *Slate*, June 10. www.slate.com/blogs/browbeat/2016/06/10/barack_obama_slow_jams_the_news_with_jimmy_fallon_slams_trump_video.html

Marx, Nick, and Matt Sienkiewicz. 2022. "A Fox News Host's Strange Backstory Shows How Liberals Lost Comedy." *Slate*, June 13. https://slate.com/culture/2022/06/greg-gutfeld-fox-news-show-conservative-comedy.html

Mayer, Kenneth R., and David T. Canon. 1999. *The Dysfunctional Congress? The Individual Roots of an Institutional Dilemma*. Boulder, CO: Westview.

McClennen, Sophia A. 2018. "The Joke Is on You: Satire and Blowback." In *Political Humor in a Changing Media Landscape*, eds. Jody C. Baumgartner and Amy B. Becker. Lanham, MD: Lexington. 137–156.

McKain, Aaron. 2005. "Not Necessarily the News: Gatekeeping, Remediation and The Daily Show." *Journal of American Culture* 28(4): 415–430.

Media Monitor. 1991. Washington, WA: Center for Media and Public Affairs, November.

Merry, Stephanie. 2016. "No One Should Have Expected Jimmy Fallon to Go Tough on Trump. That Was Letterman's Job." *Washington Post*, September 16. www.washingtonpost.com/news/arts-and-entertainment/wp/2016/09/16/no-one-should-have-expected-jimmy-fallon-to-go-tough-on-trump-that-was-lettermans-job/?utm_term=.ed2ca76e6e81

Miller, Zeke, and Deb Riechmann. 2019. "Seeking Affirmation: Trump Has Aides Vouch He's 'Very Calm.'" *Associated Press*, May 24. www.washingtonpost.com/politics/congress/iso-affirmation-trump-has-aides-vouch-that-hes-very-calm/2019/05/23/2d47af30-7dc5-11e9-b1f3-b233fe5811ef_story.html?utm_term=.b3baaeeadd07

224 Bibliography

Mitchell, Amy, Jeffrey Gottfried, Jocelyn Kiley, and Katerina Eva Matsa. 2014. "Political Polarization and Media Habits." *Pew Research Center*. www.journal ism.org/2014/10/21/political-polarization-media-habits/

Moran, Lee. 2020. "Sam Bee Shreds CNN's Stoking of Tensions between Warren, Sanders." *HuffPost*, January 16. www.huffpost.com/entry/samantha-bee-cnn-debate-coverage_n_5e2034c5c5b674e44b93049a

Morris, Jonathan S. 2009. "*The Daily Show* and Audience Attitude Change during the 2004 Party Conventions." *Political Behavior* 31: 79–102.

Morris, Jonathan S., and Jody C. Baumgartner. 2008. "*The Daily Show* and Attitudes toward the News Media." In *Laughing Matters: Humor and American Politics in the Media Age*, eds., Jody C. Baumgartner and Jonathan S. Morris. New York, NY: Routledge. 315–332.

Morrison, Oliver. 2015. "Waiting for the Conservative Jon Stewart: A Unified Theory of Why Political Satire Is Biased toward, and Talk Radio Is Biased against, Liberals in America." *The Atlantic*, February 14. www.theatlantic. com/entertainment/archive/2015/02/why-theres-no-conservative-jon-stewart/ 385480/

Moy, Patricia, Michael Xenos, and Verena Hess. 2005. "Communication and Citizenship: Mapping the Political Effects of Infotainment." *Mass Communication & Society* 8: 111–131.

Nagourney, Adam. 1999. "A Question Trails Trump: Is He Really a Candidate?" *New York Times*, December 10. www.nytimes.com/1999/12/10/us/a-question-trails-trump-is-he-really-a-candidate.html?searchResultPosition=4

Nagourney, Adam. 2000. "Reform Bid Said to Be a No-Go for Trump." *New York Times*, February 14. www.nytimes.com/2000/02/14/us/reform-bid-said-to-be-a-no-go-for-trump.html?searchResultPosition=1

Nazaryan, Alexander. 2017. "Jimmy Kimmel Is Killing the Health Care Bill, and Delighting His Viewers in the Process." *Newsweek*, September 22. www.newsw eek.com/jimmy-kimmel-bill-cassidy-obamacare-republicans-repeal-replace-669309

Newport, Frank. 2016. "As Debate Looms, Voters Still Distrust Clinton and Trump." Gallup, release dated September 23. www.gallup.com/poll/195755/ debate-looms-voters-distrust-clinton-trump.aspx?g_source=Obama+honest+ and+trustworthy&g_medium=search&g_campaign=tiles

Newport, Frank. 2017a. "U.S. Energy Concerns Continue to Diminish; Near Record Lows." Gallup, release dated March 10. https://news.gallup.com/poll/ 205754/energy-concerns-continue-diminish-near-record-low.aspx?utm_sou rce=link_newsv9&utm_campaign=item_206681&utm_medium=copy

Newport, Frank. 2017b. "Trump Disapproval Rooted in Character Concerns." Gallup, release dated July 13. www.gallup.com/poll/214091/trump-disappro val-rooted-character-concerns.aspx

Niven, David, S. Robert Lichter, and Daniel Amundson. 2003. "The Political Content of Late-Night Comedy." *Harvard International Journal of Press/ Politics* 8: 118–133.

O'Brien, David. M. 1988. "The Reagan Judges: His Most Enduring Legacy?" In *The Reagan Legacy: Promise and Performance*, ed. Charles O. Jones. Chatham, NJ: Chatham House, pp. 60–101.

O'Connor, Roisin. 2020. "John Oliver Urges US Not to Vote for Bloomberg: 'Don't Even F***ing Think about It.'" *The Independent*, February 24. www.independent.co.uk/arts-entertainment/tv/news/john-oliver-mike-bloomberg-last-week-tonight-2020-us-election-campaign-a9354321.html

Owen, Diana. 2017. "Twitter Rants, Press Bashing, and Fake News: The Shameful Legacy of Media in the 2016 Election." In *Trumped: The 2016 Election That Broke All the Rules*, eds. Larry J. Sabato, Kyle Kondik, and Geoffrey Skelly. Lanham, MD: Rowman & Littlefield. 167–180.

Pagliary, Jose. 2016. "Donald Trump Was a Nightmare Landlord in the 1980s." *CNN*, March 28. https://money.cnn.com/2016/03/28/news/trump-apartment-tenants/index.html

Palmer, Jerry. 1988. *The Logic of the Absurd: On Film and Television Comedy*. London: British Film Institute.

Parker, Ashley. 2010. "The Whole Truthiness and Nothing But." *New York Times*, September 24. https://thecaucus.blogs.nytimes.com/2010/09/24/the-whole-truthiness-and-nothing-but/?searchResultPosition=2

Parker, Ashley. 2016. "Covering Donald Trump, and Witnessing the Danger up Close." *New York Times*, March 12. www.nytimes.com/2016/03/13/us/politics/covering-donald-trump-and-witnessing-the-danger-up-close.html

Parker, Ashley. 2018. "Real or 'Fake News'? Either Way, Allegations of Lewd Tape Pose Challenge for Trump." *Washington Post*, April 13. www.washingtonpost.com/politics/real-or-fake-news-either-way-lewd-tape-allegations-pose-a-challenge-for-trump/2018/04/13/098cdedc-3f2b-11e8-8d53-eba0ed2371cc_story.html?utm_term=.3f963d0513da

Parker, Ashley, and Philip Rucker. 2019. "The 10 Personas of Donald Trump in a Single Speech." *Washington Post*, March 9. www.washingtonpost.com/news/national/wp/2019/03/09/feature/the-10-personas-of-donald-trump-in-a-single-speech/?utm_term=.874211e813db

Parker, James. 2022. "A Late-Night Show for Red America: Greg Gutfeld Has Owned the Libs All the Way to the Top of the Ratings." *The Atlantic*, May 5. www.theatlantic.com/magazine/archive/2022/06/fox-news-greg-gutfeld-late-night-rise/629634/

Parkin, Michael. 2018. "The Context for Comedy: Presidential Candidates and Comedy Television." In *Still Good for a Laugh? Political Humor in a Changing Media Landscape*, eds. Jody Baumgartner and Amy Becker. Lanham, MD: Lexington Books. 273–292.

Patterson, Thomas. E. 1994. *Out of Order*. New York, NY: Vintage.

Patterson, Thomas. E. 2013. *Informing the News*. New York, NY: Vintage.

Patterson, Thomas E. 2016a. "News Coverage of the 2016 Presidential Primaries: Horse Race Reporting Has Consequences." Shorenstein Center on Media, Politics and Public Policy, Kennedy School of Government, Harvard University, release dated July 11. https://shorensteincenter.org/news-coverage-2016-presidential-primaries/

Patterson, Thomas E. 2016b. "News Coverage of the 2016 General Election: How the Press Failed the Voters." Shorenstein Center on Media, Politics and Public Policy, Kennedy School of Government, Harvard University, December 7. https://shorensteincenter.org/news-coverage-2016-general-election/

226 Bibliography

Petty, Richard E., and John T. Cacioppo. 1986. *Communication and Persuasion: Central and Peripheral Routes to Attitude Change*. New York, NY: Springer-Verlag.

Pew Research Center. 2007. "Today's Journalists Less Prominent." Report dated March 8. www.people-press.org/2007/03/08/todays-journalists-less-prominent/

Pew Research Center. 2014. "Political Polarization and Media Habits." Report dated October 21. www.journalism.org/2014/10/21/political-polarization-media-habits/

Pew Research Center. 2016a. "The 2016 Presidential Campaign – a News Event That's Hard to Miss." Report dated February 4. www.journalism.org/2016/02/04/the-2016-presidential-campaign-a-news-event-thats-hard-to-miss/http://www.journalism.org/2016/02/04/the-2016-presidential-campaign-a-news-event-thats-hard-to-miss/

Pew Research Center. 2016b. "Many Americans Believe Fake News Is Sowing Confusion." Report dated December 15. www.journalism.org/2016/12/15/many-americans-believe-fake-news-is-sowing-confusion/

Pew Research Center. 2017. "Trump, Clinton Voters Divided in Their Main Source for Election News." www.journalism.org/2017/01/18/trump-clinton-voters-divided-in-their-main-source-for-election-news/

Pogrebin, Robin. 1996. "52-Story Comeback Is So Very Trump; Columbus Circle Tower Proclaims That Modesty Is an Overrated Virtue." *New York Times*, April 25. www.nytimes.com/1996/04/25/nyregion/52-story-comeback-so-very-trump-columbus-circle-tower-proclaims-that-modesty.html?searchResultPosition=35

Poniewozik, James. 2017. "Colbert Rides a Trump Wave, While Fallon Treads Water." *New York Times*, February 22. www.nytimes.com/2017/02/22/arts/television/colbert-fallon-trump-late-night.html

Porter, Ethan, and Thomas J. Wood. 2019. "Did Jon Stewart Elect Donald Trump? Evidence from Television Ratings Data." *Electoral Studies* [in production]. https://doi.org/10.1016/j.electstud.2019.03.007

Postman, Neil. 1985. *Amusing Ourselves to Death*. New York, NY: Penguin.

Povoledo, Elisabetta. 2019. "Italy's Fading Five Star Movement Puts Its Leader on the Block." *New York Times*, May 30. www.nytimes.com/2019/05/30/world/europe/italy-five-star-di-maio-confidence-vote.html?searchResultPosition=1

Prior, Markus. 2003. "Any Good News in Soft News? The Impact of Soft News Preferences on Political Knowledge." *Political Communication* 20: 149–171.

Prior, Markus. 2005. "News vs. Entertainment: How Increasing Media Choices Widen Gaps in Political Knowledge and Turnout." *American Journal of Political Science* 20: 149–171.

Purdum, Todd S. 1993. "Trump Pledge: In This Plaza, I Thee Wed." *New York Times*, December 18. www.nytimes.com/1993/12/18/nyregion/trump-pledge-in-this-plaza-i-thee-wed.html?searchResultPosition=16

Putnam, Robert D. 2000. *Bowling Alone: The Collapse and Revival of American Community*. New York, NY: Simon & Schuster.

Research America Inc. 2021. The RAI Virginia Survey Was Conducted by Research America Inc. during September 7–13, 2021. The Total Sample Included 1,000 Adult Virginia Residents.

Robinson, David. 1986. *Chaplin: His Life and Art*. London: Paladin.
Roig-Franzia, Manuel. 2022. "Greg Gutfeld Has Risen to the Top at Fox News – and That's No Joke." *Washington Post*, January 10. www.washingtonpost.com/lifestyle/media/greg-gutfeld-fox-news/2022/01/09/5318c528-5874-11ec-a808-3197a22b19fa_story.html
Rosenwald, Michael S. 2018. "'Wouldn't be Prudent': George H.W. Bush's Unlikely Friendship with Dana Carvey." *Washington Post*, December 2. www.washingtonpost.com/news/retropolis/wp/2018/12/01/wouldnt-be-prudent-george-h-w-bushs-unlikely-friendship-with-dana-carvey/?utm_term=.52f754e7e80b
Russonello, Giovanni. 2017. "Jimmy Kimmel Accuses Bill Cassidy, G.O.P. Senator behind Health Bill, of Lying." *New York Times*, September 20. www.nytimes.com/2017/09/20/arts/television/jimmy-kimmel-test-bill-cassidy-health-care.html?searchResultPosition=2
Russonello, Giovanni. 2019a. "Jimmy Kimmel Fires Back after Trump Attacks Late-Night Shows." *New York Times*, March 14. www.nytimes.com/2019/03/14/arts/television/jimmy-kimmel-trump-jay-leno.html?searchResultPosition=8
Russonello, Giovanni. 2019b. "Jimmy Kimmel Slams Trump's Immigration Proposal." *New York Times*, May 17. www.nytimes.com/2019/05/17/arts/television/jimmy-kimmel-trump-immigration-proposal.html?searchResultPosition=2
Rutenberg, Jim. 2017. "Colbert, Kimmel and the Politics of Late Night." *New York Times*, September 24. www.nytimes.com/2017/09/24/business/colbert-kimmel-and-the-politics-of-late-night.html
Ryan, Michael, and Douglas Kellner. 1988. *Camera Politica*. Bloomington, IN: Indiana University Press.
Sabato, Larry. J. 1993. *Feeding Frenzy: How Attack Journalism Has Transformed American Politics*. New York, NY: Free Press.
Sabato, Larry J. 2017. "The 2016 Election That Broke All, or at Least Most, of the Rules." In *Trumped: The 2016 Election That Broke All the Rules*, eds. Larry J. Sabato, Kyle Kondik, and Geoffrey Skelly. Lanham, MD: Rowman & Littlefield. 1–29.
Sabato, Larry. J., Mark Stencel, and S. Robert Lichter. 2000. *Peepshow: Media and Politics in an Age of Scandal*. Lanham, MD: Rowman & Littlefield.
Sanford, Bruce. 1999. *Don't Shoot the Messenger: How Our Growing Hatred of the Media Threatens Free Speech for All of Us*. New York, NY: Free Press.
Saturday Night Live. 2016a. "Palin Endorsement Cold Open." YouTube Video, 5:09. January 24. www.youtube.com/watch?v=0pinZNYxQeo
Saturday Night Live. 2016b. "Voters for Trump Ad." YouTube Video, 1:25. March 6. www.youtube.com/watch?v=Qg0pO9VG1J8
Saturday Night Live. 2016c. "At This Hour Cold Open." YouTube Video, 5:13. April 3. www.youtube.com/watch?v=r4q1L_JtMiI
Saturday Night Live. 2016d. "Trumpémon GO." YouTube Video, 2:13. July 20. www.youtube.com/watch?v=y_7uw0LoZqs
Saturday Night Live. 2016e. "Donald Trump vs. Hillary Clinton Debate Cold Open." YouTube Video, 9:45. October 1. www.youtube.com/watch?v=-nQGBZQrtT0

228 Bibliography

Saturday Night Live. 2016f. "Donald Trump vs. Hillary Clinton Town Hall Debate Cold Open." Youtube Video, 8:26. October 16. www.youtube.com/watch?v=qVMW_1aZXRk

Saturday Night Live. 2016g. "Donald Trump Prepares Cold Open." YouTube Video, 6:08. November 20. www.youtube.com/watch?v=JUWSLlz0Fdo

Saturday Night Live. 2016h. "Donald Trump Christmas Cold Open." YouTube Video, 5:55. December 18. www.youtube.com/watch?v=3Ar80sFzViw

Saturday Night Live. 2017a. "Vladimir Putin Cold Open." YouTube Video, 4:05. January 22. www.youtube.com/watch?v=LNK430YOiT4

Saturday Night Live. 2017b. "Sean Spicer Press Conference (Melissa McCarthy)." YouTube Video, 8:06. February 5. www.youtube.com/watch?v=UWuc18xISwI

Saturday Night Live. 2017c. "Weekend Update on Donald Trump's Executive Orders." YouTube Video, 5:12. February 5. www.youtube.com/watch?v=RD9hzW3_xE8

Saturday Night Live. 2017d. "Trump People's Court." YouTube Video, 4:53. February 12. www.youtube.com/watch?v=dLYfwprjtog

Saturday Night Live. 2017e. "Weekend Update on the Ninth Circuit Court's Ruling." YouTube Video, 7:38. February 12. www.youtube.com/watch?v=Q-iX_G-nosc

Saturday Night Live. 2017f. "Through Donald's Eyes." YouTube Video, 2:13. February 25. www.youtube.com/watch?v=rJ6WuWeBoY8

Saturday Night Live. "2017g. "Weekend Update on Trumpcare." YouTube Video, 4:26. March 12. www.youtube.com/watch?v=gGtOWYAjZWY

Saturday Night Live. 2017h. "Weekend Update on Donald Trump's Syria Missile Strike." YouTube Video, 4:55. April 9. www.youtube.com/watch?v=ttAbFhnIVog

Saturday Night Live. 2017i. "Weekend Update on Failed North Korean Missile Launch." YouTube Video, 5:49. April 15. www.youtube.com/watch?v=2MFIRoHHg3g

Saturday Night Live. 2017j. "Weekend Update on Comey's Investigation into Trump." YouTube Video, 5:47. May 20. www.youtube.com/watch?v=Rdskdey9uns

Saturday Night Live. 2017k. "Kellywise." YouTube Video, 3:59. October 14. www.youtube.com/watch?v=Hlt3rA-oDao

Saturday Night Live. 2017l. "Paul Manafort's House Cold Open." YouTube Video, 5:19. November 4. www.youtube.com/watch?v=spkfIpPmPgs

Saturday Night Live. 2019. "PBS Democratic Debate Cold Open." YouTube video, 9: 48. December 21. www.youtube.com/watch?v=142DfJ4Ch1U&ab_channel=SaturdayNightLive

Saturday Night Live. 2020a. "New Hampshire Democratic Debate Cold Open." YouTube video, 9:31. February 9. www.youtube.com/watch?v=qLz6ydbq3D8&ab_channel=SaturdayNightLive.

Saturday Night Live. 2020b. "Coronavirus Cold Open." YouTube video, 8:33. February 29. www.youtube.com/watch?v=H4qvO0StKto&ab_channel=SaturdayNightLive

Saturday Night Live. 2020c. "First Debate Cold Open." NBC Video, 13:30. October 3. www.nbc.com/saturday-night-live/video/first-debate-cold-open/4242424

Saturday Night Live. 2020d. "VP Fly Debate Cold Open." NBC Video, 12:10. October 10. www.nbc.com/saturday-night-live/video/vp-fly-debate-cold-open/4246186

Saturday Night Live. 2020e. "Dueling Town Halls Cold Open." NBC Video, 12:46. October 17. www.nbc.com/saturday-night-live/video/dueling-town-halls-cold-open/4249848

Saturday Night Live. 2020f. "Final Debate Cold Open." NBC Video, 11:17. October 24. www.nbc.com/saturday-night-live/video/final-debate-cold-open/4254860

Saturday Night Live. 2020g. "Biden Halloween Cold Open." YouTube Video, 7:47. October 31. www.YouTube.com/watch?v=alaen4fno20

Saturday Night Live. 2020h. "Biden Victory Cold Open." NBC Video, 8:02. November 7. www.facebook.com/snl/videos/biden-victory-cold-open/394323408608940/

Saturday Night Live. 2020i. "Michigan Hearings Cold Open." NBC Video, 9:13. December 5. www.nbc.com/saturday-night-live/video/michigan-hearings-cold-open/4277072

Saturday Night Live. 2021a. "What Still Works Cold Open." YouTube Video, 7:50. January 30. www.youtube.com/watch?v=9LqK8GiIMYw

Saturday Night Live. 2021b. "John Krasinski." NBC Video. January 30. www.nbc.com/saturday-night-live/video/january-30-john-krasinski/4300118

Saturday Night Live. 2021c. "Pandemic Game Night." YouTube Video, 3:53. January 30. www.youtube.com/watch?v=rSTu1I5t700

Saturday Night Live. 2021d. "Dan Levy." NBC Video. February 6. www.nbc.com/saturday-night-live/video/february-6-dan-levy/4304301

Saturday Night Live. 2021e. "Nick Jonas." NBC Video. February 27. www.nbc.com/saturday-night-live/video/february-27-nick-jonas/4315864

Saturday Night Live. 2021f. "Maya Rudolph." NBC Video. March 27. www.nbc.com/saturday-night-live/video/march-27-maya-rudolph/4334471

Saturday Night Live. 2021g. "Daniel Kaluuya." NBC Video, 1:08:40. April 3. www.nbc.com/saturday-night-live/video/april-3-daniel-kaluuya/4335197

Saturday Night Live. 2021h. "Keegan-Michael Key." NBC Video, 1:08:13. May 15. www.nbc.com/saturday-night-live/video/may-15-keeganmichael-key/4358937

Saturday Night Live. 2021i. "Owen Wilson." NBC Video, 1:06:13. October 2. www.nbc.com/saturday-night-live/video/october-2-owen-wilson/9000199358

Saturday Night Live. 2021j. "Jason Sudeikis." NBC Video, 1:07:01. October 23. www.nbc.com/saturday-night-live/video/october-23-jason-sudeikis/9000199360

Saturday Night Live. 2021k. "Kieran Culkin." NBC Video, 1:08:00. November 6. www.nbc.com/saturday-night-live/video/november-6-kieran-culkin/9000199362

Saturday Night Live. 2021l. "Simu Liu." NBC Video, 1:08:00. November 20. www.nbc.com/saturday-night-live/video/november-20-simu-liu/9000199365

Scacco, Joshua, and Kevin Coe. 2016. "The Ubiquitous Presidency: Toward a New Paradigm for Studying Presidential Communication." *International Journal of Communication* 10: 2014–2037.

Schier, Steven E., and Todd E. Eberly. 2017. *The Trump Presidency: Outsider in the Oval Office*. Lanham, MD: Rowman & Littlefield.

230 Bibliography

Schwartz, Alex F. 2014. *Housing Policy in the United States*. New York, NY: Routledge. Third Edition.

Schwartz, John. 2011. "Will Rogers, Populist Cowboy." *New York Times*, March 25. www.nytimes.com/2011/03/27/books/review/book-review-will-rogers-a-political-life-by-richard-d-white-jr.html

Segal, David. 2004. "His Casino Business May Be Down, but Donald Trump Is on a Roll." *Washington Post*, September 9. www.washingtonpost.com/polit ics/his-casino-business-may-be-down-but-donald-trump-is-on-a-roll/2016/08/01/522c07ec-5811-11e6-9aee-8075993d73a2_story.html?utm_term=.65a28 053df9f

Shales, Tom. 1987a. "Che-e-e-e-ers Johnny!" *Washington Post*, October 1. www.washingtonpost.com/archive/lifestyle/1987/10/01/che-e-e-e-e-rs-johnny/62a65 81a-244b-4e2c-80ff-c88534ae431e/?utm_term=.e34268697539

Shales, Tom. 1987b. "The Bork Turnoff." *Washington Post*, October 9. www.washingtonpost.com/archive/lifestyle/1987/10/09/the-bork-turnoff/5342ccb1-404c-4540-92af-7f5a4b6b9b82/?utm_term=.3a5373369b73

Sienkiewicz, Matt, and Nick Marx. 2021. "Appropriating Irony: Conservative Comedy, Trump-era Satire and the Politics of Television Humor." *JCMS: Journal of Cinema and Media Studies* 60(4): 85–108.

Sienkiewicz, Matt, and Nick Marx. 2022. *That's Not Funny: How the Right Makes Comedy Work for Them*. Berkeley, CA: University of California Press.

Skocpol, Theda. 1997. *Boomerang: Health Care Reform and the Turn against Government*. New York, NY: Norton.

Skocpol, Theda, and Vanessa Williamson. 2012. *The Tea Party and the Remaking of Republican Conservatism*. Oxford: Oxford University Press.

Sniderman, Paul M. 1981. *A Question of Loyalty*. Berkeley, CA: University of California Press.

Stanley, Alessandra. 2004. "No Jokes or Spin. It's Time (Gasp) to Talk." *New York Times*, October 20. www.nytimes.com/2004/10/20/arts/television/no-jokes-or-spin-its-time-gasp-to-talk.html

Stelter, Brian. 2010. "Final Tallies for 'Sanity' Rally." *New York Times*, November 1. https://thecaucus.blogs.nytimes.com/2010/11/01/final-tallies-for-sanity-rally/?searchResultPosition=6

Stetler, Brian. 2012. "Colbert for President: A Run or a Comedy Riff?" *New York Times*, January 12. www.nytimes.com/2012/01/13/us/politics/stephen-colbert-to-explore-or-pretend-to-run-for-president.html?searchResultPosition=4

Stelter, Brian. 2019. "Welcome to the Stephen Colbert Primary." *CNN*, January 14. www.cnn.com/2019/01/14/media/stephen-colbert-primary/index.html

Stewart, Patrick A., Reagan G. Dye, and Austin D. Eubanks. 2018. "The Political Ethology of Debate Humor and Audience Laughter: Understanding Donald Trump, Hillary Clinton and their Audiences." In *Political Humor in a Changing Media Landscape*, eds. Jody C. Baumgartner and Amy B. Becker. Lanham, MD: Lexington. 117–136.

Stromer-Galley, Jennifer. 2014. *Presidential Campaigning in the Internet Age*. Oxford: Oxford University Press.

Stroud, Natalie J. 2008. "Media Use and Political Predispositions: Revisiting the Concept of Selective Exposure." *Political Behavior* 30(3): pp. 341–366.

Sullivan, Margaret. 2019. "Trump Won't Stop Coining Nasty Nicknames for His Foes – but the Media Must Stop Amplifying Them." *Washington Post*, May 16. www.washingtonpost.com/lifestyle/style/trump-wont-stop-coining-nasty-nicknames-for-his-foes--but-the-media-must-stop-amplifying-them/2019/05/15/fa49cb52-7727-11e9-b3f5-5673edf2d127_story.html?utm_term=.0883ca48f7be

Swanson, Ana. 2016. "The myth and the reality of Donald Trump's business empire." *Washington Post*, February 29. URL: www.washingtonpost.com/news/wonk/wp/2016/02/29/the-myth-and-the-reality-of-donald-trumps-business-empire/?utm_term=.16baf08342dc

Taber, Charles S., and Milton Lodge. 2006. "Motivated Scepticism in the Evaluation of Political Beliefs." *American Journal of Political Science* 50: 755–769.

Thompson, Stuart A., and Matthew Goldstein. 2022. "Truth Social's Influence Grows despite Its Business Problems." *New York Times*, November 1. www.nytimes.com/2022/11/01/technology/truth-social-conservative-social-app.html?searchResultPosition=1

Toto, Christian. 2014. "Goodnight, Jay. Leno last Fair, Balanced Late Night Host." *Breitbart.com*, February 6. www.breitbart.com/big-hollywood/2014/02/06/leno-last-fair-balanced-late-night/

Traub, James. 2004. "Trumpologies." *New York Times*, September 12. www.nytimes.com/2004/09/12/magazine/trumpologies.html?searchResultPosition=40

Tropiano, Stephen. 2013. *Saturday Night Live FAQ: Everything Left to Know about Television's Longest-Running Comedy*. Montclair, NJ: Applause.

Trump, Donald J., and Charles Leerhsen. 1990. *Trump: Surviving at the Top*. New York, NY: Random House.

Trump, Donald J., and Kate Bohner. 1997. *Trump: The Art of the Comeback*. New York, NY: Times Books.

Trump, Donald J., with Tony Schwartz. 2004. [Originally 1987]. *Trump: The Art of the Deal*. New York, NY: Grand Central Publishing.

Tyler, Tom R. 1988. "What Is Procedural Justice?" *Law & Society Review* 22(1): 103–135.

Tyler, Tom R., and Kenneth A. Rasinksi. 1991. "Procedural Justice, Institutional Legitimacy and the Acceptance of Unpopular U.S. Supreme Court Decisions: A Reply to Gibson." *Law & Society Review* 25(3): 621–630.

Tynan, Kenneth. 1978. "Fifteen Years of the Salto Mortale." *The New Yorker*, February 20.

Unger, David. 2013. "Europe's Social Contract, Lying in Pieces." *New York Times*, June 8. www.nytimes.com/2013/06/09/opinion/sunday/europes-social-contract-lying-in-pieces.html?searchResultPosition=9

Van Luling, Todd. 2017. "This Aggressive Ad for Trump's '90s Game Show Seems Just Like His Campaign." *HuffPost*, March 10. www.huffpost.com/entry/trump-card-gameshow_n_58c06960e4b054a0ea67787e

Vogel, Kenneth P., and Michael S. Schmidt. 2022. "For Financial Help and Counsel, Hunter Biden Turns to Hollywood Lawyer." *New York Times*, May 10. www.nytimes.com/2022/05/10/us/politics/hunter-biden-kevin-morris-lawyer.html?searchResultPosition=2

232 Bibliography

Wagtendonk, Anya V. 2020. "Desperate Candidates Toss Out Memes, New Taglines, and #whiteobama in SNL's Democratic Debate." *Vox*, February 9. www.vox.com/culture/2020/2/9/21130192/snl-cold-open-2020-new-hampshire-democratic-primary-debate

Waisanen, Don J. 2018. "The Rise of Advocacy Satire." In *Still Good for a Laugh? Political Humor in a Changing Media Landscape*, eds. Jody Baumgartner and Amy Becker. Lanham, MD: Lexington Books, pp. 11–27.

Walder, Joyce. 1999. "A Model as First Lady? Think Traditional." *New York Times*, December 1. www.nytimes.com/1999/12/01/nyregion/public-lives-a-model-as-first-lady-think-traditional.html?searchResultPosition=32

Walsh, Katherine Cramer. 2012. "Putting Inequality in Its Place: Rural Consciousness and the Power of Perspective." *American Political Science Review* 106(3): 517–532.

Warner, Jamie. 2007. "Political Culture Jamming: The Dissident Humor of *The Daily Show* with Jon Stewart." *Popular Communication* 5: 17–36.

Wayne, Stephen. J. 2000. "Presidential Personality and the Clinton Legacy." In *The Clinton Scandals and the Future of American Government*, eds., Mark J. Rozell and Clyde Wilcox. Washington, WA: Georgetown University Press, pp. 211–224.

Weber, Bruce. 1997. "Donald and Marla Are Headed for Divestiture." *New York Times*, May 3. www.nytimes.com/1997/05/03/nyregion/donald-and-marla-are-headed-for-divestiture.html?searchResultPosition=27

Weinraub, Bernard. 1992. "Fade Out for Johnny Carson, His Dignity and Privacy Intact." *New York Times*, May 23. www.nytimes.com/1992/05/23/arts/fade-out-for-johnny-carson-his-dignity-and-privacy-intact.html

Wilson, Glenn D. 1990. "Ideology and Humor Preferences." *International Political Science Review* 11(4): 461–472.

Wilson, Michael. 2002. "Trump Draws Criticism for Ad He Ran after Jogger Attack." *New York Times*, October 23. www.nytimes.com/2002/10/23/nyregion/trump-draws-criticism-for-ad-he-ran-after-jogger-attack.html?searchResultPosition=13

Winter, Aaron. 2011. "Laughing Doves: U.S. Anti-war Satire from Niagara to Fallujah." In *A Decade of Dark Humor: How Comedy, Irony, and Satire Shaped Post-9/11 America*, eds. Viveca Greene and Ted Gournelos. Jackson, MS: University of Mississippi Press.163–181.

Wootson, Cleve R., Jr. 2017. "Donald Trump Was Proud of his 1990 Playboy Cover. Hugh Hefner, Not So Much." *Washington Post*, September 28. www.washingtonpost.com/news/arts-and-entertainment/wp/2017/09/28/donald-trump-was-proud-of-his-1990-playboy-cover-hugh-hefner-not-so-much/?utm_term=.3670b61f1ebf

Xenos, Michael, and Amy Becker. 2009. "Moments of Zen: Effects of the *Daily Show* on Information Seeking and Political Learning." *Political Communication* 26: 317–332.

Yahr, Emily. 2017a. "Jimmy Kimmel Gets Heated about Health-Care Bill, Says Sen. Bill Cassidy 'Lied Right to My Face." *Washington Post*, September 20. www.washingtonpost.com/news/arts-and-entertainment/wp/2017/09/19/jimmy-kimmel-gets-heated-about-health-care-bill-says-bill-cassidy-lied-right-to-my-face/?utm_term=.d10135d96e9b

Yahr, Emily. 2017b. "Jimmy Kimmel Doubles Down, Slams Sen. Bill Cassidy, Trump and 'Fox & Friends' over Health-Care Bill." *Washington Post*, September 21. www.washingtonpost.com/news/arts-and-entertainment/wp/2017/09/21/jimmy-kimmel-doubles-down-slams-sen-bill-cassidy-trump-and-fox-friends-over-health-care-bill/?utm_term=.03aa8d70b369

Young, Dannagal. 2004. "Late-night Comedy in Election 2000: Its Influence on Candidate Trait Ratings and the Moderating Effects of Political Knowledge and Partisanship." *Journal of Broadcasting & Electronic Media* 48(1): 1–22.

Young, Dannagal. 2006. "Late-night Comedy and the Salience of the Candidates Caricatured Traits in the 2000 Election." *Mass Communication and Society* 9: 339–366.

Young, Dannagal. 2013. "Laughter, Learning or Enlightenment? Viewing and Avoidance Motivations behind *The Daily Show* and *The Colbert Report*." *Journal of Broadcasting & Electronic Media* 57(2): 153–169.

Young, Dannagal. 2020. *Irony and Outrage: The Polarized Landscape of Rage, Fear and Laughter in the United States*. New York, NY: Oxford University Press.

Young, Dannagal, Benjamin Bogozzi, Abigail Goldrin, Shannon Paulsen, and Erin Drouin. 2019. "Psychology, Political Identity, and Humor Appreciation: Why Is Satire So Liberal?" *Psychology of Popular Media Culture* 8(2): 134–147.

Zakrzewski, Cat, Faiz Siddiqui, and Joseph Menn. 2022. "Musk's 'Free Speech' Agenda Dismantles Safety Work at Twitter, Insiders Say." *Washington Post*, November 22. www.washingtonpost.com/technology/2022/11/22/elon-musk-twitter-content-moderations/

INDEX

Note: Page numbers in **bold** refers to figures.

Affordable Care Act (Obamacare) 56, 83, 197
Afghanistan, withdrawal from 126, 127, 129, 142, 154
Allen, Tim 139
Apprentice, The (NBC) 29, 32, 165
arrogance of leaders 4–5; of Trump 39, 191–2
Arsenio 42, 166
Atwater, Lee 16
authoritarianism, humor against 4–5, 132

Babylon Bee 137, 138
Baldwin, Alec 49, 50, 54, 68, 86, 97, 187–8; criticism of Trump 67
Bannon, Stephen 39, 61, 69
"battle of the insult titans" 194
Bee, Samantha 51–2, 69; criticism of cabinet posts 51; and policy content 197; support for Biden 126, 127; on Trump 52, 53, 127; on Trump campaign 51; view of Republicans 126
"Best of Late Night" online 206
Biden, Hunter 110, 140, 142–3, 152
Biden impersonator 84, 87, 98, 124
Biden, Jill 110

Biden, Joe: appearance 123–4; not bothered by insults 192; caricature 123; COVID policies 123; decisions in Afghanistan 123; jokes about 95, 111, 113, 118–119, 123–4, 125, 129, 149–50; lack of action 129; mannerisms 122, 123; mental capacity and capabilities 123, 125, 128, 129; original indifference to 122; support by Bee 126, 127
"Birther" movement 36, 37
Bloomberg, Michael 82, 84, 89, 90–1, 103
Blue Collar Comedy Tour 136
Bork, Judge Robert 11, 12
Bush, George W 6–7, 162, 187, 196; administration criticism 20; impersonator 55
Bush, George H W 121, 196; jokes about 16
Bush, Jeb 42, 84
Buttigieg, Pete 82–3, 84, 87, 103, 191, 192

Cain, Herman 26
campaign ads, spoof 19
candidate joke analysis 44, 80–1, **81**
candidate jokes (2019) 77

Capitol Hill assault 114, 125–6, 148, 177
Carlson, Tucker 128
Carson, Dr Ben 84
Carson Era 15–16
Carson, Johnny 11, 12, 15–17, 133
Cassidy, Senator Bill 197
catharsis humor 8
Celebrity Apprentice, The 29, 38
Central Park jogger assault 28, 31
Center for Media and Public Affairs, The (CMPA) 2, 18, 22, 43, 107
Chaplin, Charlie 131, 132–3
"character cops" 13
Chase, Chevy 14, 55
Clinton, Bill 12, 13, 196; jokes about 24, 27, 114; reaction to jokes 166; and saxophone 42, 166; scandals 24, 114
Clinton, Hillary 13, 39; attacks by Trump 42, 48, 189; characteristics 40; false information about 39; jokes about 74
Colbert Report, The 19, 21, 134
Colbert, Stephen 19–20, 134, 203–4; commentary on George W Bush 6–7; guests (2020) 202; jokes 47–8, 117–18, 119; as politician 197–200; power broker status 203; Russia jokes 62; on Trump 186, 188–9; Trump administration jokes 61; Trump jokes 61, 64–6, 72
"Cold Open" 49, 86, 97, 98, 122
comedians: advantages over news reporters 205; criticism of 57; functions of 19–20; as politicians 196–7; sense of optimism 5–6, 193; sense of powerlessness 6, 195; shaping policy 195; shaping public opinion 19
"comedic insulation" 4, 6, 155, 194–5
comedic latitude 7
Comedy Central 18, 19–20
comedy punching up and down 135, 137, 140, 141, 156, 194
comedy, stand-alone conservative political 134–8
comedy's impact 168, 179
Comey, James 69
Conway, Kellyanne 68
COVID: jokes about 80, 85, 104; policies 143; response to 102; vaccine 93

"Crooked Hillary" 189
Cruz, Ted 42, 44, 61
Cuomo, Andrew 109, 111, 113, 143

Daily Show, The 18–19, 21
death penalty laws 31
Democratic candidate focus (2019) 103; (2020) 104
Democratic candidate jokes (2016) 73
Democratic contenders, large field of 77, 78
Democratic dropouts 86
Devine, Ted 203
Dole, Bob 22, 24–5
Dr Strangelove (film) 6, 8–9

Elaboration Likelihood Model (ELM) of persuasion 162

fake ads 33–4, 49–50
"fake news" 17, 18, 25
Fallon, Jimmy 21, 91; interview with Trump 45, 48, 57, 167; jokes 47, 118; on Obama 93–4; Trump jokes 61, 64, 65, 72
Fey, Tina 10, 161
Flowers, Gennifer 13
Flynn, Michael 66, 146, 147
Ford, President Gerald 14, 55
Fox and Friends 37
Franken, Al 196
free speech, commitment to 160
Full Frontal with Samantha Bee 50–2, 68–70, 88–90, 99–100, 125–7; attacks on Trump 99, 100; on Biden 88, 89, 99–100

Gabbard, Tulsi 82, 86
Galifianakis, Zach 55
Gallup surveys 40, 41
general election (2000) 18–19
general election 2020: challenge to 125; and comedy 91–102; Democratic candidate focus 73; joke analysis 92, **92**; jokes 22, **45**, 74, 76, 93–4, **96**, 105; learning about 173, **173**; Republican candidate focus 73; weekly shows 97–102
Ginsburg, Judge Douglas 12
Giuliani, Rudy 5, 113
Gore, Al 1, 162
Gosar, Paul 144

236 Index

government 160–1; risk of too-powerful 159; trust in 172, 176–8, **176**, 180
Great Dictator, The (film) 133
Greg Gutfeld Show, The 138
gun control, opposition to 18
gun violence 56
Gutfeld! 195, 204–5; Biden jokes 142, 144, 152; on homelessness 141; joke analysis 142–51; Obama jokes 143–4; quoted jokes 152–4; rise of 138–42, 194–5; targets 139, 143, **143**, 144, **144**, 146
Gutfeld, Greg 138–9, 155
Gutierrez, Marco 51

Half-Hour News Hour, The 135
Hall, Arsenio 20
Hammond, Darrell 49, 50
Harris, Kamala 86, 110, 143, 202
Hart, Gary 11–12
Hawley, Senator Josh 148
HBO network 7–8
health care debate 56–7
health care reform bill 69
Hollywood 136
humor: in bleak times 9, 193; as catharsis 3–8, 9; dangerous to comedians and politicians 3; forms of 8; roles of 19–20
Hurricane Katrina 6, 20

impeachment of Trump 85, 104, 125, 126, 128; jokes 104
incongruity humor 8
infidelity 11, 12
inoculation 167, 179
insult narrative reports 191
international politics jokes 47–8
Iowa Caucus 77, 87
Iraq War 6, 7, 20
Italy's Five Star Movement 200

Jimmy Kimmel Live! 21, 56
Joe Rogan Experience, The 138
joke targets 57–60, **58**: (1992–2012) 23, **23**, 25–6; 2015–2016 nomination campaign cycle **43**, 44; 2019–2020 nomination 78–80, **83**; (late 2019) 81–2, **81**; (early 2020) 82–3, **82**; (2020 pre- and

postelection) 92, **92**; (2021) 108, 110–11, **111**, 114–15, **115**
journalists 18

Kennedy, John F 1, 11, 33
Kimmel, Jimmy 21; criticism of health care legislation 56–7, 62, 197; jokes 47, 48, 117, 118, 119; Trump jokes 64, 66, 186
"Kimmel test" 197
Klobuchar, Senator Amy 83, 87–8

Larry King Live 41–2
Last Week Tonight with John Oliver (LWT) 52–4, 70–1, 90–1, 110–2, 127–30; analysis of political issues 90; Biden critique 127; fact checking 100; health care system 90; nomination campaign (2020) 90; Trump commentary 127, 128
Late Night (NBC) 21
Late Show, The (CBS) 17
Leno, Jay 17, 23; interview with Trump 37
Leno-Letterman years 16–19
Letterman, David 7, 17–18, 32, 163; and McCain 17–18, 166
Lewinsky, Monica 13, 25
Limbaugh, Rush 135
Lindell, Mike 109, 111, 112–113
Little, Rich 20
"lock her up" chants" 189
logistic regression approach 177, **178**

Madison, President James 4
Maher, Bill 7, 20–1
Man Show 21
Manchin, Senator Joe 109, 111, 129
Maples, Marla 31
marijuana smoking (Clinton) 13
Markowitz, Karol 141–2
May, Theresa 69–70
McCain, Senator John 22, 48–9, 163; appearance cancellation 17–18
McKinnon, Kate (impersonator) 68, 86, 87
Meyers, Seth 20, 153
migrant farm workers 198
Miller, Dennis 136, 139
Modern Times (film) 132
Mondale, Walter 163
monologues, politicized 17

Mueller, Robert 67; investigation 66
Musk, Elon 138

Nadler, Professor Anthony 137
NATO assistance to Ukraine 201
nervous laughter 134
Neuman, Alfred E 191, 192
newspapers 179
Nightly Show, The 157
Nixon, Richard, appearance on
  "Laugh-In" 41, 165
Noah, Trevor 21; jokes 47, 61, 118,
  119; jokes about Trump 64–5; and
  Republicans 45
nomination campaign (2020) and
  comedy 76–85, **85**; weekly humor
  shows 86–91

Obama, Barack 25, 44, 71; birth
  certificate response 164–5; challenge
  for humorists 71–2; gets even with
  Trump 38; jokes about 25, 61;
  rapport with humorists 55; reasons
  for electing 196; self-deprecating
  humor 164–5; on *The Tonight
  Show* 55
Obama, Michelle 193
Obamacare 56, 83, 197
O'Brien, Conan 20, 33–4
Ocasio-Cortez, Alexandria 143
Oliver, John 70–1, 100, 127–30, 197;
  criticism of reporters 102; employing
  insults 101; on Trump 52–3
Onion, The 137
O'Reilly, Bill 19, 136

Paar, Jack 15
Palin, Sarah 10, 26, 49, 161; Tina Fey
  imitation 10, 161
Pelosi, Nancy 86, 110, 144
Pence, Vice President Mike 59, 80, 86,
  97
Perot, Ross 41–2
Pew Research Center survey 172, 173,
  179
Pirro, Judge Jeanine 124
policy topics by program 62, **63**
policy-oriented jokes 64, 66, **85**
political careers ruined by scandal 11
political humor: and 2016 campaign
  44–9; as anti-authority message 131;
  as cathartic release 131; coarsening

of 184–93; messages in 133; online
  158–9; possible future 202–5;
  saturated market 157; shaping
  public perceptions 162
political learning, comics' impact 179
political trust 176–7
Politically Incorrect show 7, 20–1
politicians: on comedy shows 26, 162;
  damage reduction 162; response to
  attacks 26; self-deprecating 162,
  163; telling jokes 162–8
politics of 1980s and 1990s 10–14
Pompeo, Mike 101
presidential campaign (2024) 204
presidential campaign comedy 41–4;
  quoted jokes (2016) 46–8; weekly
  humor shows 49–50
presidential candidate jokes (2015–
  2016): personal matters 46; topic
  areas 45, 46, **46**; types of jokes 46
presidential candidates (2016):
  characters **40**; number of Democrats
  204
presidential candidates on shows 42,
  166, 169
presidential candidates' response to
  satire 1
presidential nominee jokes
  (1992–2020) 26–7, **27**, 95, **96**
presidential preferences, oscillating
  pattern of 196
presidents and presidential candidate
  jokes (1992–2021) **120**
program jokes (early 2021) **112**, 113;
  Biden 115–17, **116**; Trump 115–17,
  116
public opinion polls 171
Putin, Vladimir 47; connection to
  Trump campaign 47, 48, 50, 68, 69,
  70, 114; impersonator 68; jokes 115

QAnon 126–7
Quayle, Dan 11, 13, 16, 22–4

racism jokes 62
"Rally to Restore Sanity and/or Fear,
  The" 19, 198
Rather, Dan 2
Reagan, Ronald 163–4, 166, 195–6;
  imitations 20
Real Time with Bill Maher (HBO) 7,
  21

238 Index

Red Eye 138
Republican candidate focus: (2019 and 2020) 103
Republican candidate jokes (2016) 73
Research America Inc 171
ridicule as debate 10
Romney, Mitt 22, 165
Roosevelt, Franklin D 164, 165
Russia and Trump campaign 47, 48, 50, 68, 69, 70, 114
Russia, invasion of Ukraine 201
Russia-related jokes 3, 62, 65, 66

Sanders, Bernie 75, 84, 89, 115, 190; impersonator 86–7; jokes about 78–9
Santos, George 185
Saturday Night Live (SNL) 15, 49–50, 67–8, 97–8, 122–5; on Biden 98; "Cold Open" 49, 86, 97, 98, 122; during nomination campaign 86–8; on Trump 31–2, 33–4, 50, 97, 98; Trump as host 29; "Weekend Update" 14, 49, 97, 122
scandals coverage 9–10
Scaramucci, Anthony 59
self-deprecation 33, 140
"sense of play" 155, 169, 193
Shales, Tom 11, 15
show personal jokes (fall 2021) **145–6**, 146, 147–51, **147**, **149**
shows engaging more with policy 206
shows, learning from 169–70, 172–4, **174**, 175–6, **175**, 180; about presidential campaign 180
shows shaping political participation 170
sick humor 9
Smothers Brothers 7
Spicer, Sean 58, 59, 68
Stern, Howard 32, 37, 65
Stewart, Jon 2, 17, 18, 19–20, 195, 199
Stewart/Colbert rally 198
"Stooge of the Night" 18
"stop and frisk" policing 91
"stop-the-steal" 147
superiority humor 8
super PAC 19, 199

target frequency by program (2017) **60**, 61
Taylor Greene, Marjorie 113, 124

terrorist attacks (2001) 5–6, 20–1; emergency responders 19
Tillerson, Rex 64, 66
Tonight Show, The (NBC) 15, 21; Obama on 55
"Town Hall" campaign event 98
traditional news outlets 168, 169
Trump administration: jokes about 61; members of 69
Trump attacks: on comedians 54, 57, 185–6; employing personal insults 189, 190, 192; on New York 143; on opposition 42, 167
Trump backers 146
Trump books 28, 31
Trump campaign and Russia 47, 48, 50, 68, 69, 70, 114
Trump, Donald; affairs 12; alias 28; Americans' view of 37; appearance 68, 69, 71, 115; arrogance 39, 191–2; attacks on Hillary Clinton 42, 48, 189; and ballot legitimacy 100; as businessman 28, 29, 30, 32, 70, 165; caricatures 124; characteristics 40, 41, 165, 187–9; COVID mishandling 99; disrespect to women 32, 98; ego 33; fairy tale language 190; as fraud 85, 185, 187; and immigration 52–3, 67, 68, 69, 128; and the insurrection 109, 147, 125, 128; lawsuits 53; lifestyle 30, 39, 156; narcissism 64, 85; *New York Times* description 29; party registration 36, 37; perceived low intelligence 50, 85; personality 2, 68, 69, 71; popularity 39, 161; problems with truth 2, 47, 85, 99, 185, 188; as racist 99; reaction to attacks 54–5, 159; rudeness 98; self-promotion 29–30, 166–7; setbacks 30; on social media 191; and transgender people 71; use of humor 189; and white supremacy 51; wives 31, 32
Trump jokes 74, 114, 149; appearance 68, 69, 71, 115; as former president 109; lack of knowledge 71, 72; most jokes about 121; quoted 47, 64–6, 117–18
Trump, Donald Junior 59, 61
Trump, Eric 110, 147
Trump family, jokes about 59, 61, 110

Trump impeachment 85, 104, 125, 126, 128; jokes 104
Trump impersonators 49, 124; Alec Baldwin 49, 50, 54, 68, 86, 97, 187–8
Trump, Ivana 31
Trump, Ivanka 69, 110, 143
Trump on late night shows 33; avoiding 167; as host 29; and *Saturday Night Live* 31–2, 33–4, 50, 97, 98
Trump and the media 27–32; interview with Jimmy Fallon 45, 48, 57, 167; interview with Jay Leno 37
Trump, Melania 32, 37, 59–60, 110
Trump supporters 51, 124, 126, 128, 144; anger of 49, 171; criticism of 49; after defeat 101
Trump TV 29
Trump tweets 37, 39, 54, 67, 71, 101
"trust deficit" 169
Truth Social 191
Twitter 1, 87, 138, 191

Ukraine 200–1

Vietnam War 7; avoidance of military service 9, 13
viewers, less informed 162, 168
Virginia survey 171–83; caveats 178–9; hypotheses 172; questions 181–2
vote counting 100
voter suppression 101
voters, reasons for electing 196

Warren, Elizabeth 87, 103, 190
Watters' World 139
"Weekend Update" 14, 49, 97, 122
white nationalist rhetoric 51
Wolfowitz, Paul 6
"working the refs" 42, 162

Youngkin, Glenn 124–5, 142
YouTube channels 158

Zelensky, Volodymyr 200–1

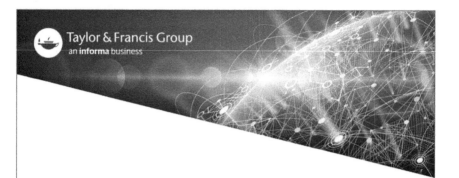

Milton Keynes UK
Ingram Content Group UK Ltd.
UKHW030713231124
451456UK00028B/460